Praise for *Hunting Nature's Fury*

Roger Hill is a true master of storms. This thrilling account of his storm-chasing adventures will leave you almost as breathless as if you were in the path of a deadly twister yourself. There's a reason he's the king!

> —Scott Stabile, TV Producer, Indigo Films–Producer of *Tornado Alley*

Roger Hill… knows how to chase tornadoes with as much success (and safety) as anyone on the planet. Hunting Nature's Fury *is a fun, fast and furious read, taking you not only inside of these powerful and often deadly storms, but also inside the mind and life of a tornado chaser. Roger and co-author Peter Bronski weave the science, the drama and the (often long) drive into a fascinating narrative!*

> —Mike Nelson, Chief Meteorologist, Denver's KMGH-TV 7News

Roger Hill is the kind of story teller that draws you in to a place where you've always been, but never realized. Mother Nature is his actor and the plains of America are his canvas. He has an uncanny sixth sense that pulls him toward the most ominous, powerful, and dangerous weather from which any sensible person would flee. But he does it again and again, with a holler and a smile. He understands and respects weather like an adoring fan who has somehow made his way onto the playing field for a better look.

> —Chris Leavell, Producer/Writer of National Geographic's *Twister Chasers*

HUNTING NATURE'S FURY

*A Storm Chaser's Obsession
with Tornadoes, Hurricanes,
and Other Natural Disasters*

BY ROGER HILL
WITH PETER BRONSKI

 WILDERNESS PRESS · BERKELEY, CA

Hunting Nature's Fury
A Storm Chaser's Obsession with Tornadoes,
Hurricanes, and Other Natural Disasters

1st EDITION October 2009

Copyright © 2009 by Roger Hill and Peter Bronski

Front and back cover photos copyright © by Roger Hill
Interior photos by Roger Hill
Book & cover design: Scott McGrew

Manufactured in Canada

Published by: **Wilderness Press**
1345 8th Street
Berkeley, CA 94710
(800) 443-7227; FAX (510) 558-1696
info@wildernesspress.com
www.wildernesspress.com

Visit our website for a complete listing of our books and for ordering information.

Cover photo: An F4 tornado on June 23, 2002, near Barnard, South Dakota

Library of Congress Cataloging-in-Publication Data:

Hill, Roger, 1957–
Hunting nature's fury : a storm chaser's obsession with tornadoes, hurricanes,
and other natural disasters / by Roger Hill with Peter Bronski.
p. cm.
Includes bibliographical references.
ISBN-13: 978-0-89997-511-5
ISBN-10: 0-89997-511-9
1. Severe storms—Miscellanea. 2. Hill, Roger, 1957– —Anecdotes.
3. Storm chasers—United States—Anecdotes. I. Bronski, Peter. II. Title.
QC941.8.H55 2009
551.55092--dc22

2009009326

For all whose lives have been impacted by
Mother Nature's wrath

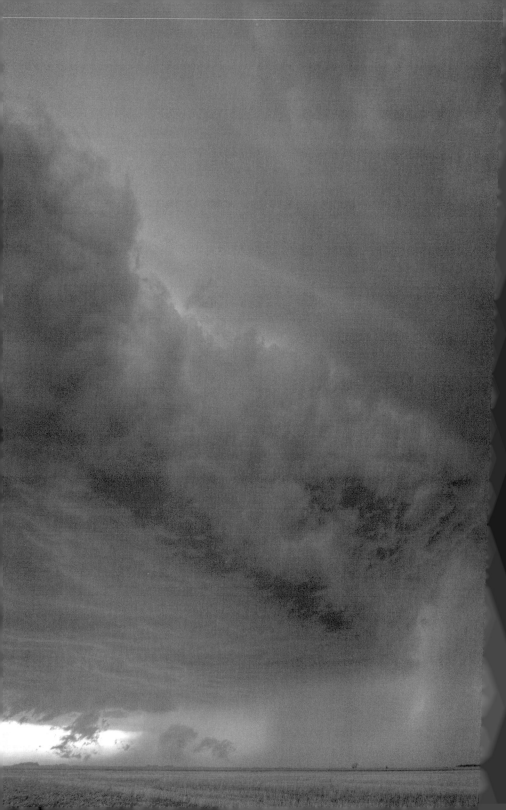

Contents

Acknowledgments

From the authors:

This project would not have been possible without the support, encouragement, and assistance of many people who made the endeavor possible.

From Roger:

I would also like to thank Peter Bronski, whose idea to pursue this book is what drove me to make it a reality. Your research and skillful, real-life writing has made the text seemingly come to life. Peter, you truly have been a blessing in my life.

Finally, thank you, my lovely wife, Caryn. Your encouragement and support throughout this process has always given me strength. Your assistance in my many chases each year make this a joy to do. Your love and constant standing by my side, helping me, pushing me, and sometimes carrying me has made this book and my life as a storm chaser possible. I love you from the bottom of my heart and with every breath I take. This book is for us.

From Peter:

First, my deepest gratitude goes out to Roger Hill. When I proposed the idea of *Hunting Nature's Fury,* you graciously and willingly laid your life bare for readers to see. You've given them, and me, a deeper insight into, greater appreciation for, and heightened knowledge of severe weather and storm chasing. You are a testimony to the rewards of finding and pursuing one's passion in life and an inspiration to everyone who has desired to follow his or her heart but hasn't had the courage to do so.

Second, thank you to my incredible wife, Kelli. You've tirelessly supported my writing—offering encouragement, a critical eye, honest feedback, and, above all else, unconditional love and support. It means more than words can express. Thank you, and I love you.

Prologue

Growing up as a child in the suburbs of Long Island, New York, I was always fascinated by severe weather. Usually, storms came out of the west. Washington Street, where my family's house was located, ran east-west, and I would stand on the curb and look westward to see what might be coming from over the treetops.

During the summertime, thunderstorms would boil up over northern New Jersey and western Long Island, and I would watch them advance, like an approaching apocalypse. The sky would grow ominously dark, and before the rain and thunder arrived, the leaves of the trees would begin to flutter in a way they only did before a big storm. A wall of rain would march down the road, engulfing yard after yard until it at last reached our house.

I would stand on the front porch, under the protective covering of the roof's awning, and watch the torrential rain and intense lightning. Sometimes, the wind would whip the rain in under the awning, and I'd seek shelter in the back corner of the porch. When the rain fell particularly hard and long, Washington Street would turn into a river, flooded by a creek at the end of our block that would overflow.

Inevitably, a bright bolt of lightning would strike a little too close for my comfort—most often in the tall, old oak tree directly across the street—and send me running back into the house. From the protection of its walls, I'd safely watch out the living-room window, peering over the back of the sofa.

I wasn't yet seven years old when Hurricane Gloria made landfall on Long Island in September 1985. But I remember my giddy excitement and eagerness as I helped my mom tape the windows and shop for extra water, nonperishable food, extra batteries. When Gloria smacked into the south shore of Long Island, she brought with her 100-mile-per-hour winds that gusted to 115 mph.

I assumed my usual spot on the living-room couch to watch the wind and rain lash at the trees and houses in our neighborhood. I imagined that this was what it would be like to be inside a washing machine. Then the eye of the hurricane passed directly over our house. Almost instantly, the winds ceased, and an eerie calm came over the sky. No wind. No rain. No loud noises of trees and debris hitting the house. It was a fascinatingly sudden transition.

My dad and I stepped out the front door to survey the damage. Power lines lay in the street. Trees were toppled over everywhere, and tree limbs, leaves, and other debris littered the neighborhood. We walked together for fifteen minutes, clambering over the fallen trees and visiting our neighbors. Soon, though, we returned to the house before the southern eye wall would arrive and the wind and rain would once again return.

In the end Gloria caused $1.6 billion in damage in 2005 dollars, and roughly half a million Long Islanders, including my family, were left without power. On a personal level, my fascination with severe weather grew deeper than ever.

But that was a hurricane, and this is a book about storm chasing. Mention the term "storm chasing" and I think that most people—including me—by default think of tornadoes, of close calls on the Great Plains, speeding down the road as a twister barrels down and demolishes a farmhouse before your very eyes. Yes, tornadoes define the penultimate severe-weather experience.

I experienced my first tornado in 1995, ironic as it may be, in those same suburbs of Long Island, almost ten years after Gloria. It was July 23, and I was at my uncle's home in Babylon for a barbeque. The whole family was gathered in his backyard, playing soccer on the lawn, swimming in the pool, and eating hamburgers on the deck. But then sometime in the early afternoon, the weather turned foul, and everyone retreated into the kitchen.

As we sat inside, the winds steadily grew in strength. Fearing that the umbrella over the picnic table would blow away, I ran out onto the deck to crank it down. While I stood beside the table, frantically working to take down ours, the umbrella in a neighbor's yard was plucked out of their table, sent flying through the air, and speared into the ground like a javelin. Had

I looked up before running back into the house, I would have seen a funnel cloud swirling overhead.

It touched down in Babylon only briefly as an F1 tornado, but when I returned home that night, I found that the same tornado had hit our house in South Farmingdale. The debris path was one-quarter mile long, some four hundred feet wide, and included our backyard. The twister ripped the chimney off a neighbor's house. Six trees were uprooted and toppled in our backyard, but miraculously, all six somehow managed to miss hitting our house as they fell. Incredibly, the folding chairs on our front porch hadn't even moved.

Five years later, unbelievably, our house was hit again. I was away at college, but my younger brother, Michael, saw the tornado come, this time through the front yard. It barreled down the street, and by his description, it looked black as night as it came steadily closer. As it neared the house, it felled the tall, old oak tree that I had watched get struck by lightning as a child. The oak fell toward our house, its thick trunk bisecting my grandparents' van, which was parked in the street. The uppermost branches of the tree tickled our front door, but amazingly, our house was once again spared.

Two tornadoes at my childhood home, but I hadn't seen either one. It wasn't until I moved to Colorado in 2004 that I saw my first tornado. It was a landspout, actually, a tornado that forms in the absence of a supercell thunderstorm, normally a prerequisite for tornado formation. I was sitting on a bus riding from Denver International Airport to downtown Denver, and I could hardly believe my eyes as I looked eastward across the plains. A long, slender, black funnel cloud churned across the stereotypical amber waves of grain.

In truth, none of these stories constitutes genuine storm chasing. In each instance, the severe weather has come to me. My fascination has made me an eager and willing observer, but I've never gone out in search of severe weather proactively. Even so, to the degree that I—and the general public—harbor a fascination with severe weather, I think there's a little storm chaser in all of us.

Just consider these facts: Attendance at the Denver Storm Chasing Convention has grown by some 2,000 percent since it first began informally in 1998. Viewership of The Weather Channel has grown from 9.4 million households in 1983 to more than 87 million households in the United States today. As of November 2007 three of the top one hundred grossing movies of all time—*Twister, The Day after Tomorrow,* and *The Perfect Storm*—are about severe weather.

We can't help but be drawn to the worst Mother Nature has to offer, even if it's from the comfort of our living-room sofas. We are armchair storm chasers, ready to live vicariously, but just as ready to hope that severe weather doesn't actually happen to us. Yet it does. Each year, an average twelve hundred tornadoes—and in recent times, as many as eighteen hundred—batter the United States. Most occur in Tornado Alley, a vast, weather-beaten swath of middle America that stretches from Texas north to Canada and from the Rockies east to the Appalachian Mountains. But in truth we all live in tornado country—tornadoes occur in every state of the Union and in dozens of countries around the world. Severe weather is forever in our own backyard, so it's no wonder we're fascinated by it.

True storm chasers, on the other hand, are another breed. They are a unique brand of individual that carry fascination to an extreme. When every instinct of a "normal" person says to board up the windows, to seek refuge in the basement, to evacuate his home or her community, storm chasers cut fiercely against the grain and embrace the worst and most awesome of Mother Nature. They get off their couches and go out to meet severe weather head on, face to face, up close and personal.

I met my first storm chaser in 2005. Having recently moved to Colorado from New Jersey as a freelance writer, I was looking for story ideas to pitch to *5280,* a regional magazine based in Denver. After hearing about the Denver Storm Chasing Convention, I emailed the event organizer, inquiring about whether or not there were any notable, famous, or accomplished storm chasers living in the Denver area. I thought such a person could provide a good local human-interest angle to a potential story. The email response from the organizer was simple: "Well, I suppose that would be me." His name was Roger Hill.

Whereas the vast majority of the general public, including me, occupies the armchair-storm-chaser category, Roger sits near or at the top of an exclusive group of elite storm chasers. Having witnessed well over three hundred tornadoes during the span of his career, Roger knows how to hunt these monsters better than most anyone. It was time for me to get off my couch and into Roger's van, to learn how he does so well what very few people have the bravery or knowledge or, some would say, stupidity to do at all.

I t was October, well outside prime storm-chasing season, but after turning Roger's storm-chasing invites down too many times because of schedule conflicts, I was finally prepared to say yes. His email the day before was unequivocal: "We are a go! The Kansas-Oklahoma border is looking very promising. Meet at my house at 7:00 a.m."

Bleary-eyed, I wake at 4:45 a.m. on Sunday morning, climb into my Jeep Cherokee, and drive to Roger's home in Bennett, east of Denver, in the predawn darkness. It's cold and snowing in the mountains, and a biting wind and steady rain have been falling at his house on sparsely populated ranch land on the High Plains.

Pulling into the driveway, I have two realizations.

First, it dawns on me that, for most people, a city like Denver is the gateway to the Rocky Mountains. From the city, people look longingly westward at the snowcapped peaks and envision hikes or climbs or skiing. Yet Roger turns his back on the mountains and gazes eastward, across the treeless expanse of the Great Plains, envisioning storms that have not yet formed but will by the day's end.

Second, I realize that unlike in mountaineering—my personal passion—where I am the expert and the decisions about risk are in my control, today my trust and safety are completely in Roger's hands. I offer up both to him implicitly and without hesitation, but it's still startling to realize that tornadoes are a beast I've never truly contended with before.

In a computer room off the side of the living room, Roger is reviewing weather maps and data from the Storm Prediction Center in Norman, Oklahoma. The outlook for the day remains promising.

We're joined today by Cathy, a petroleum engineer from the Denver suburb of Arvada. Cathy started chasing with Roger's tours in June 2005. She saw six tornadoes then and has been a regular client since.

Together, the three of us will "blast east," in Roger's words, destined for the still-distant Kansas-Oklahoma border. We clamber into the van, ready to head out onto the highway. Although it's only three years old, the van already has more than 264,000 miles. Mileage. One of the certainties of any season spent storm chasing.

The sides and roof of the van resemble the dimpled surface of a golf ball, showing the telltale signs of frequent encounters with large, damaging hail. Inside, a custom-built console between the front seats houses a weather station, GPS unit, radar receiver, power inverter, ham and CB radios, laptop computer, and wireless Internet receiver.

As we cruise east on Interstate 70, the day slowly brightens. Roger locks in the cruise control, and Cathy and I review the weather maps and data as we cross the state line into Kansas. Roger briefs me on his "green, yellow, red" chase protocol. The color codes refer to bathroom breaks. During "green" status, we'll break as often as needed. "Red" means we're in full chase mode, and we're not stopping for anything but the most dire emergencies. Understood.

I start to ask about the likelihood that we'll see a tornado today. Roger explains that I've just violated one of storm chasers' most hallowed superstitions. I used the "T" word. "Talk about supercell thunderstorms. Ask me about severe storms," he explains. "Those are okay. But we don't talk about the 'T' word. Not unless there's one on the ground." Also understood.

Chasing in October—and in spring or fall more generally—is counter-intuitive. Back in Denver the weather was cold and socked in with rain and snow. Hardly the type of conditions that would be expected to produce supercell thunderstorms and tornadoes. But drive far enough east, into the warm, moist air of the Central Plains, and it's a whole other story. Which is exactly what's happening. By 11:00 a.m. MDT, we're in west-central Kansas, and the skies are starting to clear. It's time for the atmosphere to go to work.

Unfortunately, radar reveals a squall line developing south of Hays, Kansas. Squall lines are what storm chasers call "string beans," and they hurt the chances of supercell development. Supercells are defined by strong cyclonic rotation, and the more linear a storm becomes—the more "string-bean-like" it becomes—the more difficult it is for that rotation to develop.

The day is still young, however, and by the time we load back into the van at 12:15 p.m. after a brief stop for lunch, things are starting to look a whole lot better. The Storm Prediction Center has issued a mesoscale discussion, storm-chaserspeak for "It looks like something might be starting to happen. Keep your eyes open." They're anticipating strong storms, damaging wind, and large hail over our target chase area. Perfect.

It's like a slow-motion drama unfolding on the computer screen, hour by hour, radar image by radar image, the outcome still uncertain.

We head south from Russell, Kansas, driving through Hoisington. A few years back, Hoisington was hit by a strong F4 tornado. It hit the high school on prom night and then barreled through a neighborhood. As we drive past the old path of the tornado, we're struck by the lack of trees and the conspicuous new houses built since. Each town we drive through in Kansas prompts Roger to recall a memory from a previous chase in earlier years. Every community has been touched by tornadoes, it seems.

Soon we're motoring through the town of Great Bend, whose main street looks like it was plucked straight out of the 1950s. The temperature–dew point split is currently at 70/62, much better than the 50/50 it was back in Bennett. If it approaches 80/62, we'll be in business for reasons I have yet to fully understand. Nonetheless, a storm is intensifying to our south-southeast near Medicine Lodge, and I feel a small spike in my adrenaline as we race to meet it.

At 1:20 p.m. the National Weather Service issues a severe-thunderstorm watch for our area, and we have our eyes on the Medicine Lodge storm, as well as a second storm forming farther south. They're showing hail up to one inch in diameter and very active lightning strikes.

By 1:30 p.m. Roger's adrenaline is starting to pump, too. "All right! We're in definite chase mode now," he says. Storms are exploding on radar. Suddenly, the day is looking a whole lot more promising.

"We're in the promised land now," Roger offers. "We have to get to Pratt and then get east." His eyes are fixed on the Medicine Lodge storm.

It's tracking northeast, and fast, and we want to get ahead of it—especially considering that it's now producing golf-ball-size hail. We're in chase mode "red," and Roger takes us east as fast as the road conditions and speed limits will allow.

According to Roger, we're chasing the best storm in the country right now, but even that may not be good enough for today. Weather maps continue to send us mixed signals, and at the moment it appears that too many storms are forming. They're interfering with one another, and no single storm is becoming dominant. With little other recourse, we head south on back roads, aiming for the tail end of the developing storms, where we'll have the best chance of catching an isolated cell that could truly develop into something.

Finally, we're on a supercell thunderstorm, but we don't yet know what it will give us. The storm responds quickly with rapidly intensifying rain. "Oh. We're going to get pummeled!" Roger says, following immediately with a maniacal laugh. "We're right in the path." As if on cue, marble-size hail starts falling as we speed in reverse down a dirt road. The hail falls so hard it turns into a veritable whiteout. "Now this is more like it!" Roger yells over the deafening noise of hail hitting the metal roof of the van.

We turn back onto a paved road and head east, punching through the core of the storm and working to get ahead of the rain and hail. The storm is tracking northeast toward Wichita, and the torrential downpour is blinding, making the landscape twilight-dark, except that it's only 4:00 p.m. local time.

We pull onto a dirt road that cuts between two open fields. A pair of volunteer firefighters from the community are there, too, storm-spotting in case a funnel cloud descends. The air is eerily calm, the literal calm before the storm. CG—cloud-to-ground—lightning is intense and close by. A man drives up alongside us in his pickup. "You guys lookin' for lightning pictures?"

"We're watching the storm," Cathy responds. "We're storm chasing."

Seemingly satisfied with her response, he drives off without another word. A strong shelf cloud advances toward us, and soon the rain and hail we left behind catches up with us. We pile back into the van at 4:40 p.m. and head to Wichita and then to the interstate that will carry us home. Our day of chasing is over.

Yet even as we pack it in, Roger looks and hopes for any sign that the storm we've been chasing will produce a tornado. It offers up two microbursts and a short-lived funnel cloud but nothing more. As we drive north and then west from Wichita, the rain falls hard, and the sky is like a strobe light from the flashes of lightning. Deep, thunderous "booms" rock the van.

Roger can't resist checking his radar one last time, confirming that the show is indeed over and that the storms that were too far away for us to chase today didn't develop into something spectacular. They didn't. By nightfall, a squall line stretches from Iowa to northern Texas, with nary a tornado to be found. But Roger's insistence on checking the radar "one last time" is a window into his passion-bordering-on-obsession, which is part of what makes him so good at what he does.

Drained and weary, we roll back into Bennett, Colorado, at 1:00 a.m., with 1,014 miles behind us, and a day's worth of stories to tell, tornado or not.

Severe weather affects all of us, some more than others. The communities we drove through in south-central Kansas know that acutely. But whether from hail, lightning, floods, hurricanes, tidal waves, forest fires, or tornadoes, we are all touched by severe weather. Storm chasers, for their part, just happened to be particularly determined to experience their fair share—and then some. And Roger Hill's piece of the pie is about as big as it can get.

Call it what you will. Passion. Hunger. Thirst. Obsession. Tenacity. Choose one descriptor, or choose them all—you've described Roger Hill. The remaining pages of this book chronicle Roger's journey as a storm chaser, seen through his eyes, captured and told in his own words. His is a dramatic story that unfolds across the Great Plains, and it begins in a tiny home in Topeka, Kansas, in 1966.

—*Peter Bronski*

CHAPTER ONE

A Boyhood Fascination

On the eighth of June, to Topeka the town
A twister came blowin', on the ground
Seventeen souls, they breathed their last
With splintering wood, and breaking glass

The rest came out, of their hiding place
Looked out and saw, the world's new face
With tears of grief, or prayers of relief
Breaking a path, to the neighbor's door

The long night passed, like a dreadful dream
With a cold west wind, and the sirens' scream
And the flickering candles, made a bright glow
Warming the souls, who heard the wind blow

The sun came out, on a battered land
Lighting the path, for each weary man
Found a child's smashed toy, scattered pieces of joy
Yesterday's home, now broken and blown

Lee Wright
"The 8th of June"*

1

On June 8, 1967—one year to the day after the 1966 tornado—the Daily Capital *sponsored a tornado-song-writing contest, with proceeds slated to benefit Washburn University. The contest was the brainchild of Lee Stone, then president of the Topeka Folk Singers Club and a reporter at the newspaper. The newspaper rented the Topeka Municipal Auditorium, and audience members paid to watch fifty-eight contestants perform their songs and parodies, many filled with heart-wrenching, first-person accounts of the destruction. But as the doors opened, the tornado sirens went off in Topeka, keeping many people away from the event. The newspaper was left with no money to donate to the university. Lee Wright's "The 8th of June" was one of those songs. (Lyrics reproduced with permission, courtesy of Lee Wright, "The 8th of June,"* Love to Love to Love, **http://www.myspace.com/ mleewright,** *copyright 2008.)*

S torm chasers are born counters. They count the number of tornadoes they've seen in their lifetime, the number of storms they've chased, the number of miles they drive chasing each year. Those numbers tell a story in shorthand—the story of a storm chaser's experience and history. Each story is unique, like a signature or a fingerprint. No two storm chasers chart the same course, literal or figurative, in hunting down Mother Nature's worst weather. But for every storm chaser, the story starts the same way, with Number One. Every storm chaser has a first tornado, and it is an experience that remains forever burned into memory.

I wasn't supposed to have a first. I wasn't even supposed to live in Tornado Country. But I did. And then, on Wednesday, June 8, 1966, in Topeka, Kansas, I almost died. I was nine years old.

Two years earlier, our family had moved to Topeka from Oahu, Hawaii. I was a military brat, born at Great Lakes Naval Air Station in Chicago on April 20, 1957. My father, Raymond, was a chief master sergeant in the air force, and was one of the first airmen to be promoted to the rank, which was new. His career of military service had started twenty-three years earlier, as a tail gunner in a B-17 bomber during World War II.

Together with my mother, Barbara; my older brother, Matt; my older sister, Christine; and me, Dad moved the family around the country as the military saw fit. One year after I was born, the family left Chicago for Selfridge Air Force Base, Michigan; two years after that, we moved to Macon, Georgia; and two years after that, to Hickam Air Force Base on Oahu, Hawaii. There we settled for the relative eternity of four years.

Then in June 1964 we uprooted once again and landed in Topeka, Kansas, less than sixty miles from Leavenworth, where my grandparents homesteaded on 240 acres of Missouri River bottomland. Life in Kansas was a world apart from Hawaii in so many ways, but above all else, I noticed the intense thunderstorms that seemed to be an almost daily occurrence during spring and summer.

Our family lived in a three-bedroom ranch in southwest Topeka, near the intersection of S.W. 30th Street and Gage Boulevard. The house was one of many that were part of a new subdivision, with small houses and even smaller trees packed in close together. The front yards had beautifully manicured green lawns, and every home, including ours, had a full basement. Almost all homes throughout Topeka did, so residents could escape the severe weather of the spring and summer seasons, and most builders would not offer a floor plan for a new home without one.

Every day, my father made the ten-mile commute to Forbes AFB, three miles south of Topeka proper. Today, the 4200-acre Forbes Field is home to an active municipal airport operated by the Topeka Airport Authority, commercial and state offices, an industrial park, and the Kansas Air National Guard. But in the years leading up to Dad's transfer to Forbes in 1964, the base played a pivotal military role for the United States during the Cold War. Six years earlier, in 1958, Forbes was selected as the central support site for a series of nine subterranean Atlas E missile silos that would be constructed in the surrounding countryside. By early 1961 the first missiles arrived on site, and by October of that year, all nine missile coffins had their Atlas Es.

Even before the Cold War, Forbes figured prominently in the nation's military history. The base was born as the Topeka Army Air Field (TAAF), authorized by an act of Congress less than two weeks after the December 7, 1941, attack on Pearl Harbor. Eight months later, the air base was complete, and in August 1942 the first troops arrived. By 1945 TAAF was one of three

B-29 hubs nationwide where crews picked up new Superfortresses, like the *Enola Gay*, and took off destined for the Pacific Ocean and the World War II assault on the Japanese islands.

Between 1947 and 1950, TAAF deactivated and reactivated four times and during that period was renamed Forbes AFB in memory of Major Daniel H. Forbes, a Topeka pilot killed on June 5, 1948, while testing the Northrop XB-49 "Flying Wing" jet bomber. Then, with the start of the Korean War in June 1950, Forbes reactivated and would operate continuously for more than twenty years, including during the mid-1960s, when our family arrived from Hawaii.

On the morning of Wednesday, June 8, 1966, Dad drove to Forbes just as he would on most any other day. I went outside and rode my bicycle around the neighborhood all morning. I always enjoyed riding up and down the streets and visiting the neighbors. Then, around lunchtime, I headed home. My mother, who stayed at home full time to take care of my sixteen-year-old brother, fourteen-year-old sister, and me, always fixed a great lunch. That Wednesday was no different, and I munched down a bologna-and-cheese sandwich with a side of potato chips and a glass of grape-flavored Kool-Aid.

After lunch, I went out to ride again. Not far from the subdivision was a small creek—Shunganunga Creek—where I would go to play. I stayed there until mid-afternoon, when I got tired. It was cool and cloudy outside as I rode back to the house. I was sitting down to watch television at home when the local news broke in to announce that the city was under a tornado watch. It was always exciting when the National Weather Service issued watches. I had always wanted to see a tornado, and perhaps even more so, I loved thunderstorms and the lightning and thunder the storms produced.

Around 5:00 p.m. Dad came home, and we all sat down for dinner as a family. Outside, the skies were still cloudy, and it was growing warmer and more humid, but otherwise the weather was quiet.

After dinner Dad and Matt drove into town while Mom and Christine watched television. I went back outside to ride my bike some more. Over the next forty-five minutes or so, the sky grew steadily darker and calmer. Soon, I heard thunder in the distance. Mom ran outside to find me—the news had warned of severe thunderstorms southwest of Topeka. I was hoping for a big storm, and it looked like I was going to get my wish.

A few minutes after Mom and I got back to the house, the tornado sirens went off. I stood outside by the front door, watching to the west as the sky grew darker and darker. Some people in the neighborhood ran inside to take cover; others ran outside in hope of seeing a tornado.

Dad and my brother, Matt, rushed home. They jumped out of the car, and Dad told us all to go into the basement. A monster tornado was less than two miles away and approaching our home, he said. As I stood on the porch, I heard a steady, low rumble—like constant distant thunder—to the west. Dad scrambled around the porch, gathering up any loose objects, while I just stared in shock at the sky. A huge, spinning, black mass was coming right toward us. It was the tornado, and my young eyes could see debris flying in the air all around it.

The wind blew stronger and stronger as I stood in amazement, my gaze fixed on the twister. Suddenly, my body jerked as Dad grabbed me and carried me quickly down the basement steps. Mom, Christine, and Matt, plus our black and white, five-year old springer spaniel, Missy, were already in the basement. Missy panicked and ran back up the stairs; I ran up after her to bring her back down.

At the top of the stairs, I looked outside and saw thousands of pieces of debris flying all around, hitting our house, our car, everything. The lone tree that stood in the front yard fell over. The noise was deafening. Hailstones the size of baseballs crashed to the ground and smashed into the house.

Dad ran up the stairs behind Missy and me and rushed us both back down into the basement. The rest of the family was already hiding under pillows, blankets, and mattresses. He shoved Missy and me under a mattress and put his arms around me. Then the tornado struck.

That morning had dawned cool and humid, especially for June, with temperatures slowly creeping into the mid-60s. What I didn't know as I rode my bike through the neighborhood, however, was that a moist warm front sitting to the south along the Kansas-Oklahoma state line had meteorologists worried at the National Weather Service office near Philip Billard Municipal Airport northeast of town. They were concerned that if the front to the south pushed northward and mixed with the cool air in Topeka, the atmosphere could become volatile enough to spawn tornadoes.

Most Topekans, my father included as he drove to Forbes, were oblivious to the concern. If anything, their attention focused on the news of the day. That day's *Topeka Daily Capital*, the local newspaper, said that actor Ronald Reagan was winning California's Republican gubernatorial primary race, that Dr. Martin Luther King Jr. was marching in Mississippi, and that Western Union employees were striking in Topeka. In Atlanta, Georgia, five hundred firemen were on strike. Apartheid in South Africa was making international headlines. The civil rights movement experienced a surge in energy when James Meredith, the first African-American student at the University of Mississippi, was shot on a highway while on a march from Memphis to Jackson. And in Vietnam, Americans had withstood an enemy attack, in turn killing 136 North Vietnamese soldiers.

As midday approached, meteorologists' fears were realized. The warm front had moved north of Topeka, and a strong cold front and dryline, the boundary between moist and dry air masses where tornadoes are often born, was moving in from the west. At 11:00 a.m. a tornado watch was issued for parts of eastern Kansas, including Topeka. Most Topekans—except maybe for me when I excitedly saw the news break into my television program early that afternoon—didn't pay much attention to the tornado watch, which was a common occurrence throughout Tornado Alley. Watches were a mere fact of life on the Great Plains, and they didn't always result in tornadoes, often ending uneventfully.

But around 6:00 p.m. things suddenly started to change in a very big way. At that time, a tornado touched down southwest of Manhattan, Kansas, nearly sixty miles to the west of Topeka. The tornado, whose winds were clocked in excess of 100 mph, started at the eastern part of Fort Riley and tracked northeast into Manhattan proper.

Thankfully, no one was killed. But as the storm barreled through town, it left sixty-five people injured, destroyed a hundred homes, and damaged more than three hundred. The entire city lost electricity. Radio towers for KSAC and KMAN were toppled, knocking both stations off the air. City officials estimated the cost of the damage at more than $5 million. The campus of Kansas State University alone sustained more than $1 million of that damage. One of the areas worst hit was Jardine Terrace, an apartment complex for married students. Fortunately, school was not in session, and the campus was relatively empty.

Meanwhile, in Topeka many people—including our family—were home eating dinner and watching television when they got word of the Manhattan tornado. But even a confirmed and damaging tornado virtually in our own backyard didn't give residents much pause. We had little reason to believe that a monster tornado could rampage through our city.

Topekans, sharing a belief held by the Native Americans who lived on that land before us, believed that Burnett's Mound, an Indian burial ground southwest of the city limits and Interstate 470, provided both literal and supernatural protection for the city. According to the long-held legend, the grave of Abram Burnett, a Potawatomi Indian chief, would guard Topeka from tornadoes as long as it remained undisturbed, the rounded hump of earth deflecting tornadoes around the populace and sparing Topeka the fate of so many other Great Plains communities.

And for decades the legend held true, offering peace of mind to people living in the heart of a region that is home to some of the nation's nastiest weather. But it was a false security. Little did we realize that, in a few short hours, our sense of comfort and safety would be shattered forever.

Slightly before 7:00 p.m., just one hour after the Manhattan tornado, a second twister descended from the sky. Eldon Thomas, a farmer who lived thirteen miles southwest of Topeka, in a far corner of Shawnee County, was the first to see it. He huddled his wife and their seven children on the floor of their mobile home as the tornado roared past. It was a monster.

Rated on the Fujita Scale of Tornado Intensity, it was classified as an F5, with winds estimated between 261 and 318 mph. Professor T. Theodore Fujita of the University of Chicago developed the scale. His seven-tier ranking system measures a tornado's wind speed, size, and on-the-ground damage, ranging from the relatively modest F0, with gale-force winds between 40 and 72 mph, to the F6, an unimaginable and hypothetical supertornado. Unlike theoretical F6s, F5s do happen, and they're a community's worst nightmare. Only 1 to 2 percent of all tornadoes ever achieve such intensity. And the tornado that touched down around 7:00 p.m. southwest of Topeka was one of those beasts.

The twister traveled northeast from the Thomas homestead, moving forward at almost 30 mph. Minutes later, with five miles of farmland behind it and just eight miles from Topeka, the tornado claimed its first two lives: Calvin and Clarice Wolf, a married couple in their early 60s, their bodies found in a car in a field a hundred yards from their demolished home.

On Burnett's Mound John Meinholdt, a volunteer weather watcher, and David Hathaway, a Topeka police officer assigned to watch for severe weather, saw the tornado touch down. Rain began to fall as the twister grew to mammoth proportions, appearing to fill the entire sky. Meinholdt radioed the National Weather Service from his perch atop the mound, and forecasters confirmed the tornado on radar. Hathaway notified his dispatcher, concluding his final transmission with "I'm getting the hell out of here."

By then hail was falling on the mound, and Meinholdt turned and "hightailed it" down the hill, he recalled thirty years later. On the way, he passed by the red station wagon of Rick Douglass, a nineteen-year-old WREN reporter on his way up the mound. Meinholdt jumped in his car and sped southeast on I-470, driving out of the twister's path and escaping harm.

Meanwhile, Hathaway, too, had reached the base of the hill and was helping motorists get under an overpass at I-470 and Gage Boulevard. Tornado researchers have since learned that highway overpasses are an exceedingly dangerous place to be during a tornado. The confined area under the overpass acts like a wind tunnel, accelerating wind speed and offering no protection from flying debris. An Oklahoma tornado thirty-three years later drove home the point: Of seventeen people taking shelter under an I-35 overpass, all but one were blown out by the wind; one was killed. A few miles away another person was dismembered and a dozen others suffered serious injuries: broken backs, severed body parts, and deep cuts from head to toe.

Reaching the top of the hill, Douglass suddenly realized that the tornado was dangerously close. He immediately turned and started downhill while making a broadcast, then drove his car to the east side of Gage, where he parked and radioed his station again. "I turned around and watched three houses get picked up and thrown around like a box of trash," he recalled during an interview twenty years later. The station asked him to stand by to give another report. Instead, Douglass threw down his microphone, turned, and sprinted for the overpass where Hathaway was waving, urging him to hurry. He never made it there.

The tornado's winds picked him up, battering him with debris. Air filled his nylon jacket, ripped the back open, and then blew it off his arms. "I was just floating," he recalled. "I remember getting off the ground and then back down again on the grass. I dug my hands in the ground and grass, but I was sliding backwards." The twister left him caked with mud, and he spent nearly a week in the hospital being treated for his injuries.

At 7:02 p.m. a tornado warning was issued. The Civil Defense (today known as the Civil Air Patrol) sounded Topeka's nineteen sirens. As the tornado bore down on I-470 and the Topeka city limits, it became abundantly clear that it was making a beeline for downtown, whether Burnett's Mound stood in the way or not, and with the Hill family's house squarely in its path. By the time it steamrolled directly over the mound, instantly crumbling the old legend, the tornado had grown to half a mile wide at its base. Its winds were so strong they ripped grass from the earth. Along I-470, three cars were plucked off the highway and stacked neatly blocks away on S.W. 29th Street. A long-time Topeka resident described "roofs flying hundreds of feet in the air and trees doing a weird fandango down the interstate."

Bill Kurtis, a newscaster for WIBW-TV, Channel 13, implored viewers: "For God's sake, take cover!" Topekans ran to their basements or scrambled to find shelter—they had ten to eighteen minutes' warning before the twister reached their homes.

Our family huddled in the basement as the tornado closed on our house near 30th and Gage, a short distance from where Douglass had been plucked from the earth. The tornado by then had metamorphosed into a giant black "stovepipe," a thick, violent column of swirling dirt and debris, spinning furiously and bearing down fast on our home.

As the tornado struck, the howling winds grew louder and louder until they sounded like a rushing waterfall. Suddenly, the basement windows shattered, sending pieces of glass flying. My ears felt as if they were going to explode as the pressure dropped. All I could hear was what sounded like a million things being ripped apart, breaking, shattering, crackling, whistling.

I was completely overcome with panic and fear. It seemed like forever before things quieted down. Then, as quickly as the violence erupted, it ceased. I could still hear things falling from the sky and hitting the ground, but the tornado had passed. Within minutes, it was totally quiet, the only sound being my sister's sobbing. Missy, our dog, was shaking like a leaf in my arms. I held her tightly, not truly sure of who was comforting whom, but I wasn't letting go of her. Dad lifted the mattress off me and Missy, blood dripping from his arm and leg. The broken glass from the windows was embedded in his limbs, but he didn't seem to notice. We all started crying and grabbed hold of one other. We knew what had just happened and were thankful to be alive.

The floor of the house was intact above our heads, but we didn't know if it was going to collapse on us or not. We had to get out of the basement. My father climbed over piles of debris that had blown into the basement and onto the stairs. He reached the door and pushed it open with a huge shove. Then he just stood and stared. From down in the basement, all we could hear him say was, "Oh, my God. Oh, my God."

Dad walked out into what used to be our yard as we came up the stairs after him. As I reached the doorway, I looked out in disbelief at what he saw. There was not a house standing undamaged on the block. The roof of our house was gone, and so were most of the walls. Almost everything in the house was either damaged or completely gone. The family car was missing.

Across the street, our neighbors' houses were unrecognizable. Several were completely gone—no roof, no walls, no floor, nothing. There were only concrete steps and a basement.

We walked down the street as a family to see if we could help our neighbors. The houses on our side of the street still had some walls. A select few even had roofs. But across the street, every house was gone, like a bomb had gone off. We found our car. It had been rolled down the street almost to the next block by the twister. The house at the corner of the block was nothing but a pile of rubble. In its front yard, lying on the lawn, was a birthday cake that said "Happy Birthday Patty." The only thing wrong with the cake was a few pockmarks where raindrops had hit it.

As the monster twister moved on from our block, it continued to do some of its worst damage, splintering homes to pieces. One block away, it moved across the intersection of 29th and Gage, where houses exploded, reduced to their foundations or to bare slabs. Huntington Park and Embassy, Topeka's newest luxury apartments, yielded to the storm's winds next. The entire second floors of the complex were blown away. All the buildings, totaling 150 apartments, were a total loss.

Three blocks away, the Taylor family was just sitting down to dinner when Jesse, the father, heard a roar and went to the front door. Nearby, he could see the funnel destroying the Huntington Park apartments. He and his wife grabbed their two sons, David and Chuck, and ran for the garage. They had just enough time to climb into the family's station wagon and crouch beneath the seats before the tornado hit. As it slammed into their house, rocks and other flying debris crashed through the garage door and into their car, leaving what looked like "great big bullet holes." The Taylor family survived, but their house (and their entire neighborhood) was completely destroyed. There was nothing left that could even be packed into a suitcase for the evening.

The twister marched on, setting its sights on the campus of Washburn University, founded in 1865. In MacVicar Chapel, named for former college president Peter MacVicar, who ushered the university through its early days during the late nineteenth century, about fifty people were attending a piano recital. The recital was moved to the basement because of the storm.

For many years, weather experts proclaimed that the southwest corner of a basement was the safest place to be in a tornado (this has since been proven untrue—it is more important to get away from windows, doors, and potential debris and falling objects than it is to situate oneself according to compass bearings). Nevertheless, owing to the wisdom of the day, university officials considered staging the recital in the basement's southwest corner. However, the piano there was out of tune, and the recital resumed instead in the southeast corner, using a piano that was in tune.

Suddenly, recital goers were struck by debris as stone and mortar exploded. No one was seriously hurt, but the basement's southwest corner—where they would have been save for an out-of-tune piano—was left filled with tons of stone, which likely would have seriously injured or killed many people.

Elsewhere on campus, nearly fifty high school girls were attending a regional baton-twirling clinic. They took cover in a basement and survived the tornado without injuries. The same cannot be said for the campus as a whole. Although no one on campus was killed, literally every building at Washburn University was either destroyed or seriously damaged. Today, the Fred and Julia Kuehne Bell Tower stands as the campus centerpiece and a reminder of the events of 1966. The concrete tower features a quartet of bells once housed in the clock tower of the Thomas Gymnasium, which was destroyed by the tornado.

Continuing its rampage, the twister roared through Central Park, leaving the Central Park Elementary School looking as though it had been bombed. On nearby S.W. Polk Street, a very pregnant Rosella Reece was home with her husband and three young children. They knew from the warnings that the tornado had hit Burnett's Mound and was coming across town. "I remember my husband telling me, 'It sounds like a train outside,'" she recalled years later. "And I said, 'There aren't any trains around here.' He realized, 'Oh, my God, it must be the tornado.'"

The Reece family ran downstairs and took shelter in their basement. The expecting Rosella and her three children climbed into a playpen, while her husband held them, laying his body over them like a protective shield. The tornado ripped the entire backside of the basement off the house and tore off the top of the two-story home. Rosella's husband sustained numerous lacerations from flying debris, but his children, huddled beneath him in the playpen, escaped unharmed. Twigs impaled the tires on the family's two cars.

The twister barreled onward, moving relentlessly into downtown Topeka. It failed to hit the Kansas Statehouse directly but left a scar on the capital's dome that remained for years. A Topeka police officer later reported that he saw what appeared to be a double garage hit the dome.

Darold Main, chairman of the Shawnee County Commission, was attending a meeting at the nearby courthouse. His wife called to say that there was a warning and to take cover. Main looked out the window and saw the monster roar past. "It was real quiet before," he recalled. "And when it hit, there was this roar. You could hear it coming like a train. Debris was swirling every which way."

The courthouse was spared, but Pla-Land Bowl, located down the block and around the corner, wasn't as lucky. As the tornado continued its assault on downtown Topeka, winds whipped several cars into a wall at Pla-Land, knocking the wall over and crashing it into a pool table. Pla-Land's owner, sixty-six-year-old Lisle Grauer, was under the table and was crushed to death. At the other end of the table, a bowler who was also hiding escaped injury.

The tornado crossed I-70 and headed into the Oakland community of Topeka, where homes and shops were destroyed. As the twister approached Philip Billard Municipal Airport and the National Weather Bureau offices nearby, the storm appeared to lose force but rose up once more in a final fury. At the National Weather Bureau, workers dove under heavy tables at the last minute. Airplanes were ripped from their moorings and scattered about the field. A loading ramp for Central Airlines was thrown two hundred yards across a runway and smashed.

The tornado crossed the Kansas River and left Topeka; the funnel cloud lifted off the ground and disappeared into the night sky. It was shortly after 7:30 p.m. The entire ordeal had lasted less than thirty minutes.

As the rogue tornado lifted into the night, it left behind a gruesome scene of death and destruction. But as hordes of stunned survivors, much like our family, stumbled out of the wreckage, they (and we) turned their gaze skyward and saw what one Topekan described as "as nice a clear blue as you can imagine." Hathaway, the Topeka police officer who survived the tornado as it charged past the I-470 and Gage interchange, noticed the brilliant scenery overhead as well. "After the tornado was gone, the sky was one of the most beautiful sights you'll ever see," he recalled. "The air was clear, and the sky was so bright and blue. It was gorgeous, with the exception of the awful devastation on the ground."

The scale of that devastation was almost unfathomable. The twister had laid down a swath of utter destruction that ranged from a quarter to a half mile wide along its length, stretched out over a twenty-two-mile path. "It was so awesome, I shed tears," Chuck Wright Jr., the city's mayor in 1966, recalled thirty years later. "It looked like somebody had taken a lawn mower, six blocks wide, and had gone through our city." Throughout Topeka, power lines lay in the streets, and overturned cars, uprooted trees, and the splintered remnants of former homes left the city in shambles.

Almost immediately, the search began for survivors, many of whom were seriously injured or trapped beneath rubble and debris. Topeka police and National Guardsmen worked side by side, concentrating their efforts in our family's neighborhood, at 29th and Gage, believed to be the worst damaged area in the city. A police officer radioed from the scene: "These houses are gone out here. They are just gone."

By 9:00 p.m. police issued an order to the searchers to check every house in the area looking for the injured. Searchers were to tie a white flag to each house to indicate that it had already been searched. Across the street from our house, a young girl whom I had seen many times around the neighborhood lay dead in the wreckage of her home.

Around the block on Twilight Drive, Hathaway heard the faint sound of a child crying softly, buried under the debris of a house. He dug through a pile of splintered wood to find five-year-old Craig Beymer, who was critically hurt. "I can remember that little boy so vividly," Hathaway recalled. "He didn't make it. I'll take that memory to the grave with me."

Hundreds of people across town were injured in the storm, and area hospitals—Stormont Vail, St. Francis, Santa Fe, Forbes Air Force Base, and Veterans Administration—opened their doors to triage the casualties. One woman had more than 170 shards of glass embedded in her body. She survived after spending many months in the hospital.

By late evening National Guardsmen with fixed bayonets and billy clubs, as well as Air Force, Marine, and Naval Reserve troops, were called in to protect communities from the rampant looting that was already taking place. Tom Noack lived on Twilight Drive, a short way from where Hathaway pulled young Beymer from the wreckage. "I could see cars stopped on I-470. People were getting out and running down toward the houses [looting]," he angrily recalled thirty-seven years later. "It made you sick." But he was able to laugh as he told the story of how one of his neighbors combated the looters: "He was sitting in an easy chair—that was about all that was left of his house—with a fifth of whiskey in one hand and a gun in the other."

Early the next morning—June 9, 1966—Shawnee County Commission Chairman Darold Main, who had survived the tornado from his position in the courthouse the night before, went up in a helicopter to survey the damage from above. "It looked like doll houses with their tops taken off," he recalled. "Just a strip clear across the city." Many homes were reduced to their bare slab or foundation.

Seventeen cities and counties sent equipment to help with Topeka's recovery efforts, including Kansas City, Missouri, which sent a convoy over a mile long.

In total, sixteen people lay dead in the tornado's wake. A seventeenth person died around 8:00 p.m. the same night in nearby Leavenworth County, the victim of a separate tornado spawned by the same storm. The twister's death toll—sixteen fatalities—made it the third deadliest tornado in state history. The only Kansas tornadoes to claim more lives were an April 26, 1991, twister in Andover that killed seventeen and a May 25, 1955, twister in Udall that killed eighty.

More than 550 people were injured. Eight hundred homes, including ours, were completely destroyed, while another twelve hundred were seriously damaged. In 1966 dollars, the devastation was valued at between $100 and $250 million, making it the most expensive tornado in United States history at the time. Accounting for modern-day inflation, the Topeka 1966 tornado still ranks as one of the costliest and most destructive in U.S. history.

In the days following the disaster, residents began the slow and painful process of literally picking up the pieces of their shattered lives. Carol Yoho, a young girl at the time, lived with her mother and father in a house southwest of Washburn University, centered in the tornado's path. "The garage had fallen on our little blue car," she recounted in 1999. "My uncles moved the debris. Four uncles picked up the car by the corners, lifted it, and set it down in the driveway. My dad got in and started the engine. The body listed badly to port, but the car ran. They drove it around the house twice, laughing."

Standing nearby talking with a neighbor, something in the mud caught Yoho's eye. She reached down and fished it out—it was her mother's wedding ring.

After the storm passed, Rosella Reece, who survived with her husband and three children in a playpen in their basement, went to the house next door, a three-story home that had its top one-and-a-half floors blown off. Four families, including Reece's, huddled inside, cleaning up broken glass and sheltering from cold winds that blew in after the storm. On June 12, four days after the twister, Reece gave birth, dubbing their child the "tornado baby."

My family and I went to live with my grandmother, Lilly, and my grandfather, Raymond Sr., on their farm in Leavenworth. That would be our home for the next several months while we slowly rebuilt the home in Topeka. After we finally returned to our neighborhood, it was never the same. The houses were all brand new. The trees were all gone. Many areas were totally stripped of vegetation and were left bare.

◉

Topekans had one of two (or both) reactions to the twister of 1966: Some were traumatized by their ordeal, fearful of living through another such tragedy; others were grateful, happy to be alive and recognizing that things could have gone very differently.

Chairman Main, for his part, was grateful. "I hate to say this, but it could have been a whole lot worse," he said. "If [the tornado] hit after people were in bed, there could have been really heavy casualties. Most people at that time were able to take cover. Really, the timing of it was pretty good." Many have echoed Main's sentiments, and Topeka's warning system became a model for other communities to follow.

Despite such a silver lining, many residents still bear the physical and emotional scars of a trying time. "I will always remember it," Reece said. "It was something to remember all your life, and nothing you want to go through again." Doug Franklin, an X-ray technician whose blind date cancelled on him when the tornado watch was issued, agreed: "I hope to never see such destruction again."

And then there was the reaction of a nine-year-old boy, the course of his life changed forever. Days after the tornado, when the *Topeka Daily Capital* was back up and running, the newspaper ran a photo of the young boy riding his bicycle down a street in a scene that, had the caption not identified it as Topeka, could have easily been mistaken for downtown Hiroshima, Japan, after the United States dropped the atomic bomb during World War II. Who that boy was, no one knows for sure. But it could have been me. I've often thought it was so, even though there's no way for me to prove it.

Regardless, my experience more than forty years ago could have—and maybe should have—scared me away from tornadoes forever. Instead it filled me with curiosity and wonder. How could that birthday cake have survived the storm's fury when whole houses couldn't? Why was I alive, and a young girl dead? The tornado and its aftermath gave me a yearning to learn more about tornadoes and the severe weather that spawns them. And ironically, it instilled a deep-seated passion to experience as many of such monsters as I can. In 1966 I was the hunted, the victim of one of Mother Nature's most awesome and destructive creations. Twenty years later, it was time to reverse roles. I would become the hunter and call myself a storm chaser.

CHAPTER TWO

The Science of Tornado Genesis

In one single act of devastating destruction, the 1966 Topeka tornado of my childhood toppled two long-standing tornado myths. One generations-old myth held that certain towns were protected from the wrath of tornadoes. Topeka counted itself in that list . . . until the myth was exposed as a falsity. Oftentimes, such "protected" status grew out of Native American legends, such as that of Burnett's Mound. But in truth different Native American tribes and nations have perceived tornadoes differently. Some saw tornadoes as positive events that wiped away the "negative" from the landscape. Others saw tornadoes as the preferred method of revenge of the Great Spirit. The Osage Indians believed that tornadoes would not strike at the place where two rivers joined. Interesting anecdotes, perhaps, but no community is protected from tornadoes more than any other. At least not on the merits of supernatural factors.

The second myth shattered by the Topeka tornado was that the southwest corner of a basement was the safest location within a building when a tornado was about to strike. The piano recital in the basement of Washburn University's MacVicar Chapel could have been enough evidence to dispel the myth. But Joseph Eagleman, a researcher with the University of Kansas, studied the 1966 Topeka twister intensely and proved the myth false beyond a shadow of a doubt. (The north side of a building, where you'll find the lowest wind speeds due to the tornado's rotation and overall direction of motion, is now known to be safest.)

Other myths, too, have fallen flat with the passage of time. Myth: Opening the windows of a home in order to equalize interior and exterior pressure will help in the event of a tornado. Such a philosophy is little more than wishful thinking. It's not the pressure difference inside and outside that matters. It's the 200-mile-per-hour winds slamming into your house. Myth: A tornado will suck the water from a swimming pool or well. Even in the largest tornadoes with the greatest pressure differences (and hence, the greatest suction), the forces simply aren't enough to suck up that much water that fast. Myth: Mobile homes attract tornadoes. An unfortunate form of discrimination? Maybe, in the case of the myth tellers. But as for the myth itself? Simply not so, although mobile homes are affected more easily by weaker storms. Myth: Tornadoes follow rivers. Nope. Myth: Tornadoes produce supersonic winds (winds faster than the speed of sound). Also nope. A tornado has yet to blow that generates its own sonic boom.

Myths like these have arisen, probably, because tornadoes have in fact done some very weird, and very confirmed, things.

In June 1953 a deadly tornado struck the industrial, working-class city of Worcester, Massachusetts. Sheets of plywood rained down onto two dozen towns. A waterlogged, frozen bed mattress was photographed floating in the Atlantic Ocean. Pink fiberglass housing insulation floated down from the sky and clung to clotheslines in Boston. A pair of pants with the wallet still in the pocket was blown twenty-five miles away. And a social security card was found on Cape Cod, ninety miles away from the home of its owner.

One of the single strangest tornado events took place in Great Bend, Kansas, on November 10, 1915. One farmhouse was leveled, killing two people that were inside. Yet, nearby, five horses were found unharmed and still hitched to the same rail, after being carried a quarter mile by the tornado. The house of resident Charles Hammond had its roof stripped off. Only when the family went outside to check on their neighbors did they realize that their own home had been hit. At the store of local Grant Jones, an entire wall was blown down, but the canned goods stored on shelves against that wall didn't move. A necktie rack with ten ties still attached traveled some forty miles. And a four-page love letter from a guy to his girlfriend was carried seventy miles. A canceled check was found 210 miles away in Nebraska and for seventy-five years stood as the longest-known distance tornado debris has traveled. (A personal check also holds the current record for longest-known distance debris has been carried by a tornado. In this instance the event—confirmed by the University of Oklahoma's Tornado Debris Project—was an April 11, 1991, tornado that whisked a check 223 miles from Stockton, Kansas, to Winnetoon, Nebraska.)

The confirmed oddities as a result of tornadoes don't end there. In one instance a barn door was blown open, the wagon blown out, turned around, blown back in, and the barn door blown shut. Another time, a live chicken was found inside a dresser drawer (due, in all likelihood, to the improbable but real possibility of a chicken and a dresser being caught up in a twister, a dresser drawer blowing open, the chicken blowing into that drawer, and the drawer subsequently being blown shut).

On February 9, 1859, in Mountain Ash, England, fish literally fell from the sky. Many were kept alive and put on display in a London zoo, the entire circumstance verified by the media, a scientist, and a minister. Almost a century later, on April 22, 1949, fish fell from the sky in Louisiana, as reported in the journal *Science*. A bank employee and several merchants were struck by falling fish while walking to work, and two biologists from the state Fish and Wildlife Department, who happened to be in town, collected samples.

Predictably, stories of chickens plucked of their feathers by tornadoes are ubiquitous. It does happen, commonly, probably due to tornadoes instigating chickens' flight molt, a fear response that causes the birds to drop their feathers or at least causes the feathers to loosen considerably (allowing a tornado's winds to do the rest).

Of course, livestock and people alike taking flight are often heard of. Such flights are indeed common (relative to the very uncommon instance of tornadoes and people coming into direct contact). Typically, people are carried by tornadoes on the scale of hundreds of yards. The longest confirmed "flight," however, was just over one mile. Lawrence Kern and his family were caught up in a tornado in Kickapoo, Kansas, on May 1, 1930. Lawrence was thrown over one mile and buried into the ground head first up to his shoulders. Both he and his wife died, but the children survived. More than two thousand people attended his funeral service in Leavenworth, where, thirty-six years later, the Topeka storm would claim its seventeenth life and where I would go on to graduate from high school.

As strange and unlikely as such stories are, the tornadoes that give rise to them are at least as improbable. By some estimates just one in every thousand thunderstorms will produce a tornado. Less than 1 percent of the United States population will ever be in the path of a tornado (storm chasers excepted). In Tornado Alley in particular, a home is hit on average just once every thousand years. The frequency of destruction of a home (depending on your definition of " destruction") is even less: once every ten thousand to one million years.

And yet, in what can only be called a cruel twist of irony or fate, in Logan County, Nebraska, only two homes have been leveled in the last hundred years. Both homes sat on the same homesite. And in Eastwood, Missouri, when his home was destroyed by a tornado, owner Leon Morgan put a mobile home on the site. Just twenty-two days later he was killed when a tornado struck the same spot.

Tornadoes, it seems, defy basic categorization or description. They've been called a giant serpent, the finger of God, an elephant's trunk searching for food. They are mysteries, enigmas of nature. Which begs important questions. When do they form? What are they? How do they form? And why? In one succinct question: What's the story behind tornado genesis?

They are questions scientists have been asking for at least 160 years. The acquisition of tornado knowledge has been a slow evolution that started first with forecasting and warning. Before scientists cared about *how* and *why* tornadoes formed, they first wanted to know *when* tornadoes formed so they could issue accurate forecasts and warn the public. Protecting the public from loss of life, limb, and property was the utmost priority. When should people keep their eyes trained on the skies, watching in advance of potential danger?

For more than a century, the United States had no formal warning system and no method of forecasting severe weather and tornadoes. Then, in 1847—two years after the telegraph went into public use—the Smithsonian Institution started a volunteer national weather-observation system. The system initially included 150 stations, eventually expanding to some 500 by the outbreak of the Civil War in 1860. That first weather network included a specific special request for thunderstorm and tornado observations.

In 1874 the U.S. Army Signal Corps took over responsibility for weather observation and issued basic forecasts known as "outlooks." John Park Finley, who joined the Army Signal Corps in 1877, systematically studied tornadoes in what is today considered the birth of tornado climatology and forecasting. By 1882 then Sergeant Finley advocated the establishment of a tornado-reporting system to be based in Kansas City, Missouri. He began to enlist volunteer tornado reporters, and by June 1884 those reporters numbered 957.

In that same year Finley transferred to Washington DC, where he began making daily predictions, dividing the country east of the Rockies into sections. A prediction of "no tornadoes" was considered as successful as a prediction of tornadoes, and since twisters are very rare, "no tornadoes" happened quite a lot, giving Finley a 97 percent accuracy rate. Even so, if you look only at those forecasts for which tornadoes were affirmative, he was right 28 percent of the time, a notable achievement, since it's been estimated that only one in ten documentable tornadoes were actually reported at the time. During this period Finley also developed an empirical method for forecasting tornadoes—looking for low pressure, humidity, a northward curve of temperature lines (today called a thermal ridge), and a cold front (a weather feature not officially identified until 1920).

By 1887, in what has been called the "dark era of tornado reporting," Finley's methods had been abandoned. The Army Signal Corps, not wanting people to panic during a warning, banned use of the word "tornado" from public forecasts (the ban would stand for sixty-five years). The Corps' rationale—unbelievably—was that the harm done through predicting was worse than that of the tornadoes themselves. Ten years later, in 1897, official documentation of tornadoes ceased and would not resume until 1916.

Finally by 1920 things had slowly started to turn around. Balloons and kites were used for atmospheric observation, and by the 1930s, more advanced weather balloons came into use. But it was an outbreak of sixty killer tornadoes in 1942 that caused a public uproar, demanding better forecasting and warning systems.

One year later, in 1943, experimental tornado-warning systems were set up in Wichita, Kansas, and in Kansas City and St. Louis, Missouri. Networks of spotters and warning systems utilized existing airfields and military facilities to carry out their work. Then, on March 20, 1948, a tornado hit Tinker Air Force Base near Oklahoma City, destroying more than $10 million in government and military property. That event finally prompted the federal government to develop a reliable forecasting system. Edward Fawbush and Robert Miller developed that system, based totally on correlation, rather than causation. It didn't matter to them how tornadoes formed. It only mattered under what atmospheric conditions tornadoes could be expected to appear; it was a matter of correlation, rather than causation.

At last, on March 17, 1952, the U.S. Weather Bureau issued its first public tornado forecast. Two months later, in May, the bureau created the Severe Weather Unit to focus on tornadoes. And in 1953 meteorologists "discovered" the hook echo, a characteristic radar signature of severe thunderstorms that are about to form or have formed tornadoes.

April 11, 1965, however, revealed a flaw in the forecasting and warning system. The event is known as the Palm Sunday Outbreak, in which nineteen violent tornadoes killed 256 people in six states. In retrospect the tornado forecasts were accurate. The Achilles heel proved to be getting that information to the public in time. The hard lessons learned on Palm Sunday 1965 spawned the SKYWARN spotter program, the NOAA weather-radio system, and other early-warning information systems. That year the Severe Weather Unit also became Severe Local Storms or SELS. (SELS, in turn, would become the National Severe Storms Forecast Center—NSSFC— which would then become the Storm Prediction Center—SPC—upon its move from Kansas City to Norman, Oklahoma, in 1997.) In 1966 the terms "watch" and "warning" came into use, borrowing from hurricane terminology that had started in the 1950s.

Over the course of the 1970s and 1980s and in more recent times, technological advances—namely, weather satellites and Doppler radar—have shifted meteorology into the era of modern-day forecasting. That forecasting has two parts: (1) anticipate the potential for tornadoes (what *can* happen?) and (2) recognize thunderstorms that can produce tornadoes (what *is* happening?).

Evaluating the potential for severe weather and tornadoes assimilates three important pieces of information: pattern recognition (large-scale weather patterns), parameter evaluation (basic information about temperature, humidity, wind, etc.), and nowcasting (what's happening literally outside at the present moment, on the order of a single countywide area or smaller).

Forecasting information is then divulged to the public in three stages: outlook, watch, and warning. Outlooks are issued early on the "day of" and include an assessment of the risk for severe weather on the scale of an area spanning roughly ten states. Watches—for either severe thunderstorms or tornadoes—are issued two to seven hours in advance of the anticipated weather event, cover about twenty thousand square miles, and indicate that conditions are favorable and that potential exists for severe thunderstorms or tornadoes. Lastly, warnings are issued in real time, lasting less than one hour and on the scale of individual counties. A tornado warning indicates that a funnel cloud has actually been sighted or that one has been strongly indicated by radar. Residents should take cover. Warning time for towns can range from just seconds to half an hour, depending on where communities sit along the storm's track.

In contrast to the forecasting—understanding the "when" of tornadoes, the science of tornado genesis—understanding the "what, how, and why" of tornadoes, began roughly in 1887. What are tornadoes? What are their life cycles? How do tornadoes actually form? Why do they actually form the way they do? Before scientists could understand tornadoes, though, they first had to understand the thunderstorms that gave birth to them.

In his book, *Tornadoes*, Finley postulated that tornadoes begin after "two clouds come together." Yes, this was the same Finley who started early forecasting and warning systems and whose efforts were abandoned by the

Army Signal Corps in the same year that his landmark book was published. Two years later, in 1889, William Ferrel first postulated tornado rotation, suggesting that they form when a thunderstorm's updraft encounters a "gyratory wind field." Thanks to the "dark era," no significant leaps in understanding tornadoes were made for more than half a century, and it would take some seventy years for scientists to identify the source of Ferrel's "gyratory wind field."

Then in 1946 the Thunderstorm Project was born. It was the first multiagency field experiment on severe storms and the start of large-scale, federally funded, peacetime weather research. Scientists hypothesized a three-stage concept for thunderstorms: towering cumulus phase, mature phase, and dissipating phase. Three years later, in 1949, Edward Brooks at St. Louis University proposed that certain large thunderstorms have a small area of rotating low pressure called the "tornado cyclone" that produces destructive twisters. (Ted Fujita, a pillar of tornado science and creator of the Fujita Scale of Tornado Intensity, later renamed the "tornado cyclone" the mesocyclone, since tornadoes didn't always form in that region of the storm.)

April 9, 1953, proved a pivotal date when a tornado struck Bismarck, Illinois. In nearby Champaign, electrical engineer Daniel Staggs was testing new weather radar for the state Water Survey office. Staggs captured an image of the storm's "hook echo"—the now-signature radar hook shown to be associated with a tornado (actually the rain and hail sweeping around it).

The mid- to late 1950s saw a series of further developments. Tornadoes in 1955 and 1957 in Nebraska and Texas, respectively, were widely photographed and videotaped by the public. That robust pictorial information allowed scientists to study in detail funnel development of tornadoes. Later in 1957, Fujita studied a tornado that hit Fargo, North Dakota, and coined several new terms in popular use today: wall cloud, collar cloud, and tail cloud. Then in 1959 a tornado hit Wokingham, England, after its parent storm first formed over France, crossed the English Channel, and then tracked across Great Britain. Weather student Keith Browning studied the storm, observed the "chaotic" storm entering steady state, and coined the term "supercell."

In the early 1960s Neil Ward, a researcher with the National Severe Storms Project in Oklahoma, drove to a storm and photographed it. His was one of the first modern-style storm chases. More significantly, he noticed striking similarities between this storm and that of the Wokingham supercell. These storms were different from regular thunderstorms.

Beginning in the late 1960s and continuing through the early 1970s, the Florida Keys Waterspout Project became an unlikely contributor to Great Plains tornado science. Joseph Golden, a meteorology student and summer employee of the National Hurricane Center, conducted his doctoral dissertation on waterspouts. That dissertation immediately preceded and laid the groundwork for the understanding of the life cycle of tornadoes. Then, on May 24, 1973, the National Severe Storms Laboratory and the University of Oklahoma fully documented the life cycle of a tornado. Joseph Golden was on the team of researchers.

Since 1973 the science of tornadoes has continued to advance incrementally, in part due to the advent of Doppler on Wheels (DOW)—mobile radar. And although tornadoes still hide some of their mysteries, we know more about them today than ever before.

But understanding tornadoes, as I've mentioned, first starts with understanding the thunderstorms that give rise to them. Thunderstorms, like tornadoes, go through stages of development: the cumulus, towering cumulus, cumulonimbus (Cb), and dissipation. A normal Great Plains thunderstorm will complete this cycle of growth and dissipation in a thirty- to forty-five-minute time period.

Thunderstorms are born of heat and humidity. When the sun's rays hit the surface of the earth, the land warms and, in turn, so does the air above it. But that warming process takes place unevenly from place to place, causing some pockets of air to be warmer than others. Warmer air is naturally less dense than the air immediately around it and rises in bubbles or parcels (like a hot-air balloon, which rises because the air inside the balloon is warmer than the surrounding air). Pockets of warm air and hot-air balloons both will rise only as long as the air within is warmer than the air without. If the two temperatures are equal, the air is in equilibrium. If the "interior" air is cooler than the exterior air, it will sink.

As air rises, it naturally cools—at the rate of 3–5 degrees Fahrenheit for every thousand feet in altitude gained. Cooler air has less capacity than warmer air to store moisture in the form of water vapor, which is where humidity comes into play. As air cools, it will eventually reach a point of saturation (the dew point), below which water will begin to be "squeezed" out of the air. That water condenses in the form of water droplets that become visible as clouds. The beginning stage of a thunderstorm—the cumulus stage—is comprised of these forming clouds as they rise in currents of warm air called updrafts.

The strongest solar heating of the day occurs in early to midafternoon, during which time many cumulus clouds typically form. By late afternoon, however, that heating starts to subside. In turn, so do most smaller cumulus clouds, which dissipate after losing their primary source of energy. Cumulus clouds built upon the largest and most powerful updrafts, though, can remain. If enough instability is present—if they have enough potential to grow—these larger, taller cumulus clouds will continue to grow upward, entering the second phase of thunderstorm development: towering cumulus.

The continued growth of towering cumulus clouds is typically inhibited by one of two factors, though. In one instance, as the air within the cloud mixes with the cooler, drier air outside the cloud, the air will reach a point of equilibrium, which will cause the cloud to stop rising and will squash further growth of the cloud. Alternatively, the cloud may encounter a capping inversion or, simply, a cap. A cap is a layer of warmer air at midlevels of the atmosphere, around ten thousand feet above ground level. It can form for a variety of reasons, but what's important is what it does to cloud development. Remember that clouds (and their updrafts) will rise only as long as their air is warmer than the air around it. But if a cloud encounters air warmer than itself—say, in a cap—it can grow no higher, and its further development will be immediately halted.

In a developing storm of sufficient strength, a towering cumulus cloud may be able to overcome both inhibitions and then can continue into the third phase of thunderstorm growth: cumulonimbus (Cb). In the case of a cumulonimbus cloud, the cloud's upward growth is limited only by the gradual cooling of its air as it rises in the atmosphere. Upon reaching equilibrium, the cloud can grow no higher and instead spreads out laterally, forming the storm's anvil. Anvils typically form at an elevation of thirty thousand feet or more above sea level, and the cloud at that altitude is typically composed of ice crystals rather than liquid water droplets, because of the cold temperatures.

This is the mature phase of a thunderstorm. During this phase, the updraft will carry water droplets upward, sometimes at speeds of hundreds of feet per second. Such droplets stick to one another and grow into droplets of ever-larger sizes, until they are so big that they can no longer be held aloft and fall to the ground as rain. The area of the storm where rain and hail fall to the ground is known as the downdraft. Every thunderstorm has both an updraft and a downdraft—what goes up must come down.

Downdrafts can contain strong, heavy rain, large hail, and high winds. But they can also be the self-inflicted downfall of the storms from which they grew. As the downdraft descends, its rain-cooled air gets pulled back into the storm's updraft, weakening the updraft by diluting its warm, moist air. In a worst-case scenario, the rain and hail may fall directly through the updraft, effectively killing the storm.

For severe thunderstorms to develop, certain elements are needed beyond the basics of heat, which provides lift, and humidity, which provides moisture. A third required element is instability, which can be measured in a multitude of ways. The most important thing to note is that instability is a measure of the atmosphere's potential: As a storm begins to develop, is it likely that it will accelerate through the growth process, or is the atmosphere in a mood to return to equilibrium and "relax"? The fourth crucial ingredient in the severe-thunderstorm and tornado equation is wind shear.

Wind shear provides the essential element of rotation, so necessary for severe thunderstorms and twisters. Wind shear comes in two flavors: speed shear and directional shear. In speed shear wind speed changes (typically increases) with altitude; for example, it could be 30 mph at the surface, 45 mph at fifteen thousand feet, and 60 mph at thirty thousand feet. In directional shear wind direction changes with altitude. For example, winds could come out of the southeast at the surface, out of the south at five thousand feet, out of the southwest at fifteen thousand feet, and out of the west at thirty thousand feet. In an ideal scenario a growing thunderstorm will encounter both forms of shear.

Wind shear has three net effects on a growing storm. First, it can push a thunderstorm into a tilted aspect, as opposed to a perfectly vertical orientation. This causes the updraft and downdraft to be displaced from one another, allowing the storm to remain stronger for longer periods of time. Second, wind shear on a grand scale can cause the initial rotation of a thunderstorm, like wrapping a length of string around a top and pulling it. Third, and perhaps most important for tornado potential, is wind shear's effect on a storm's vorticity.

Wind sheer gives rise to vortex tubes, horizontal areas of rotation near the surface of the earth, akin to laying a pencil flat on a table and spinning it in place. These vortex tubes don't exist in a literal sense—you can't see them or measure them explicitly. They're an approximation of what the atmosphere is doing. Updrafts—the same updrafts that give rise to thunderstorms—can then "lift" these vortex tubes into a vertical position. The resulting vorticity plays a large role in a severe thunderstorm's overall rotation.

Every thunderstorm is different. Each has a unique fingerprint, a character and personality all its own. They are alive in the atmosphere—breathing, eating, doing what they can to survive. Even with such individuality, though, all thunderstorms can be grouped into one of three classifications.

Single-cell thunderstorms are the simplest and least severe of the thunderstorms. They have one updraft and one downdraft and are relatively short-lived. Multicell thunderstorms, the most common type, are storms containing multiple updrafts and downdrafts. They are evidenced by multiple cumulus towers (updrafts) and multiple rain bands (downdrafts). Multicell thunderstorms can live for several hours (compared to forty-five minutes for a single cell) and can produce large hail, heavy rain, damaging straight-line winds, and the occasional weak, brief tornado. The third and most violent classification of thunderstorms is the supercell. It is the most rare but also the most responsible for violent severe weather. Supercells can persist for long periods of time and are built upon a single, rotating, intense updraft, coupled with multiple downdrafts that attempt to compensate for the updraft. They are self-sustaining, forming in isolation and pulling in moisture and instability from the untouched air around them, while their downdrafts suppress the formation of other nearby storms.

Classic supercells are defined by their overall rotation, as well as by an area of stronger rotation within called the mesocyclone. The meso isn't something you can observe. It is recognizable only on radar. It is the vertical manifestation of the vortex tubes born by the wind shear. In a classic supercell, wind shear tilts the updraft forward, and rain and hail falls from the upper portion of the storm, which leans downstream (in front of) the base. On the Great Plains the precipitation core is typically to the northeast. That precipitation causes cooling and a strong downdraft known as the forward-flank downdraft (FFD). When the FFD hits the ground, it spreads out laterally. The leading edge of that spreading is called the gust front, the rush of cold air you feel preceding an approaching storm. Near the rear of the storm exists the updraft base (or the rain-free base, although it may not be truly rain free). Here, the storm receives warm, moist air from the south and southeast. That air is sucked up into the updraft, where precipitation is held aloft by vertical winds that can exceed 100 mph. Meanwhile, counterclockwise-rotating air circulation around the updraft will direct a portion of the storm's FFD to the back edge of the supercell. That downward cascade of cool air near the back of the storm is known as the rear-flank downdraft (RFD). Like the FFD the RFD spreads out upon reaching the ground, wrapping cyclonically around the supercell. The strength of the RFD alone is often enough to blow cars off the road and to derail train cars. The RFD also erodes clouds away from the rear of the storm, resulting in a distinct, cloud-free, clear slot.

At the interaction between a supercell's updraft, FFD, and RFD, conditions are ripe for a tornado. In its most basic form, a tornado is simply an upward spiral of fast-moving air. The air enters at the base and exits at the top. It can extend for up to five miles into the parent storm, though we often only ever see 10 percent of the tornado—that part which exists between cloud base and the ground. An average tornado is some fifty yards wide and has an on-the-ground path length of one mile. In extreme circumstances, though, tornadoes have reached two-and-a-half miles wide, had winds in excess of 300 mph, and remained on the ground for hundreds of miles.

Like the supercells that give birth to them, tornadoes go through stages of development: beginning, organizing, mature, shrinking, decaying. In the beginning stage, known as the dust whirl, you'll observe swirling on the ground, as well as a short funnel hanging from the base of the cloud above. Note that if both are present it means that the circulation is continuous from cloud to ground and a tornado has formed, even if the debris cloud and the funnel cloud haven't "connected." During the organizing stage the tornado's vortex becomes visible as the condensation funnel cloud appears to descend. At this stage the tornado can increase in size and intensity or vanish. During the mature stage the tornado is at its greatest size and is vertical or only slightly tilted. As a tornado enters the shrinking stage, its diameter decreases and the funnel tilts, often with the lower end lagging behind the upper end. Note that wind speed can *increase* as the funnel shrinks, as when a figure skater pulls in her arms in order to spin faster (conservation of angular momentum). In the last stage—the decaying or rope stage—the rear-flank downdraft wraps around the tornado and fully cuts off the inflow of life-giving warm, moist air. As the tornado thins out into a rope or even segmented pieces of funnel cloud, dust or dirt may linger in the air, and debris will fall back to earth.

Not every tornado behaves strictly according to these guidelines, and stages can overlap, be skipped, or repeat themselves. And of course when a tornado strikes—as it did in Topeka in 1966—it doesn't much matter what stage it was in or how it formed. What matters is the story it leaves behind, told in the lives and landscapes of the people and places it touched.

CHAPTER THREE

A Storm Chaser Is Born

A s the summer of 1966 marched on, we tried picking up the pieces of our
life in Topeka. Our house at S.W. 30th and Gage was rebuilt. But our
home remained broken, and we ultimately left Topeka behind. Dad retired
from the air force that same year, and we settled in tiny Beverly, Missouri, on
the eastern banks of the Missouri River directly across from Leavenworth,
Kansas, where the storm had claimed its seventeenth life.

Despite the death and destruction left behind in the wake of the tornado,
I remained fascinated with watching storms. Anytime a thunderstorm
rolled through Beverly, I would go out onto the porch to watch. I simply
couldn't resist gazing skyward.

Near our house, Bee Creek flowed into the Missouri, and the stream was
often loaded with catfish. Early one morning when I was fourteen, I grabbed
my bicycle, fishing pole, and some liver for bait and set off with Missy
trailing behind. We were constant companions, our human-dog bond
forged stronger than ever from the time we spent together huddled under
the mattress in our basement in Topeka as the tornado roared overhead.

No sooner had we left our house in Beverly than a lightning bolt struck
a mere thirty feet from us, seemingly out of nowhere. The shock from the
bolt threw me off my bike and knocked Missy to the ground. Both of us
scrambled to our feet and ran back into the house, once again shaking like
leaves. Neither one of us was hurt, but our nerves were sorely rattled. No

catfishing in Bee Creek that day. Even though the early morning sun was still shining, storms were building to the south and moving north over Beverly. Best we stayed at home, in the house.

That fall I went to high school. Mom and Dad divorced, and Mom remarried. With each of them trying to settle into their new, separate lives, and with me and my siblings caught in a custody limbo between them, my high school years were spent moving around, as if we were still a military family like when I was a child: freshman year in Weston, Missouri. Sophomore year in Oskaloosa, Kansas. Junior year in Valley Falls, Kansas. And finally, senior year in Leavenworth.

Upon graduation from high school, I followed in my father's footsteps and enlisted in the air force. In 1975, the same year I graduated from Leavenworth High, the air force sent me to Offutt Air Force Base in Nebraska. Over the next ten years, I bounced from base to base: Mountain Home Air Force Base in Idaho. Ramstein Air Base in Germany. Grand Forks Air Force Base in North Dakota. Finally, in 1985, I landed at Lowry Air Force Base in Colorado as a master sergeant. One year later I started storm chasing.

Throughout my twenties—the years leading up to 1986—storm chasing was something few people did and even fewer heard about. Across the plains, people would go out onto their porches and watch a storm, but nobody that I knew of actually went out and drove *to* a storm. Nobody except for a very small number of hearty souls who were beginning to hit the roads in pursuit of severe weather. The pioneering storm chasers. Guys like Chuck Doswell, Gene Moore, and David Hoadley.

Today, Doswell is a senior research scientist for the Cooperative Institute for Mesoscale Meteorological Studies in Norman, Oklahoma. But back in the early 1970s, he was a graduate student at the University of Oklahoma, something of a breeding ground for budding storm chasers. Sporting a thick, black goatee and sleeveless T-shirts, Doswell chased in a car he called the "white elephant," a 1967 Pontiac Tempest. A storm chaser couldn't have asked for a more aptly named vehicle. He went out on his first chase on April 18, 1972, and later that same month, on the 30th, he caught his first tornado.

Gene Moore, who today makes his home in San Antonio, Texas, after more than thirty-five years of storm chasing, was part of the University of Oklahoma crew, too. He'd head out with teams from OU and from the National Severe Storms Laboratory nearby.

And then there was David Hoadley, who started chasing in North Dakota in 1956. Doswell and Moore were just grade schoolers then, and I wasn't even born. Storm chasing wasn't even in an infancy. He had no data to go on and chased solely on observers' reports from area airports. By the 1960s Hoadley was focusing his chasing on Kansas, and on May 25, 1965—one year before the Topeka twister of my childhood—he saw his first "big one."

But while these pioneers of storm chasing were out on the roads, I was still on my front porch. Not much had changed since Beverly. I did have questions, however. I wondered what made big storms tick. What caused a tornado to form? What would it be like to be in a big hailstorm? How close did you have to be to a lightning strike to feel the electrical charge? How "cool" would it have been to be Dorothy in *The Wizard of Oz*, my favorite movie?

Even more than having questions, I wanted to have *answers,* and I soon found myself getting into the car and driving—just a few miles at first—to get closer to a storm. I would sit on the hood of my car, a 1984 white Chevy S10 Blazer, lie back against the windshield, and watch lightning streak across the sky. More than simply watching, though, I was observing and trying to understand. At what point would a storm produce more cloud-to-ground lightning than cloud-to-cloud? Where in a storm would a tornado form, and where could I go to watch it happen?

Year by year my curiosity deepened until finally I had to do something about it. I hit the road. It was 1986. I went out only a few times each year at first and never beyond Colorado's borders. Venturing far afield chasing storms was something not many people did. Frankly, we just never thought of going out of state to chase a storm back then. Even if we did, I was still on active duty with the air force. So I chased when I could—after work, on weekends, whenever I could get away—but never more than a hundred or two hundred miles from home.

With a weather radio in one hand and a camera in the other, I would watch for storms to form over the Rocky Mountain foothills west of Denver and then move out onto the plains. Those storms didn't always last, but they almost always gave birth to new storms on the eastern plains. My goal was to get in front of those new storms and watch as they intensified.

I always loved the lightning and the color variations of the clouds. But the real treat was hearing hail strike the ground in the distance, which caused a low but very audible roar from miles away. With the strongest storms I could even hear hail roar—the sound of the hailstones smashing into each other while they were still up in the clouds rising and falling, getting tossed around by the intense updrafts. Their rumbling sounded like a constant thunder.

I'd stay with the storms as they pushed eastward, but once they moved across the state line, I would call it a day; it just didn't make sense to chase storms into other states hundreds of miles away. How things would change!

Back in 1987 I didn't have much need to travel for storms anyway. The storms once again came to me. After transferring to Lowry in 1985, I moved off the base and settled in Green Valley Ranch, near present-day Denver International Airport. A three-bedroom, split-level house with a great view of the Rocky Mountains became home for me and my family — my wife, Allison, and our children, Adam and Nikole.

Besides the view, we soon discovered that Green Valley Ranch had another special attribute: It sat squarely in Colorado's own mini–Tornado Alley. It was an area known as the Denver Convergence Vorticity Zone, or the DCVZ (and also called the Denver Cyclone). The DCVZ ran—and still runs—from north to south, beginning near Fort Morgan, running past Denver International Airport and Green Valley Ranch, and terminating over the Palmer Divide somewhere near Kiowa. The Palmer Divide is an east-west ridge that separates the Platte River basin to its north, and the Arkansas River basin to its south, and it has a reputation for making its own weather.

As the southern anchor point for the DCVZ, the Palmer Divide is the first place where warm, moist air flowing up from the southeast collides with hot, dry air blowing out of the west. At the boundary line—the place where these winds crash into each other—the air mixes and rises. The mixing causes areas of swirling rotation to form, while the rising causes storms to develop. If those two ingredients happen in sync, the DCVZ comes to life.

The first week of June in 1987, however, wasn't showing many signs of activity—in the DCVZ or anywhere else in the country for that matter. The weather was relatively quiet.

On Tuesday, June 9, the skies over Denver were clear. It was noticeably more humid than usual, and a welcome change. The unusually hot and dry days immediately preceding it had caused problems with fires, especially at a racetrack northwest of the house, where piles of tires caught fire and billowed a thick, black smoke. They burned for what seemed like an eternity, until finally extinguishing themselves when there was nothing left to burn. The humidity of June 9 would help decrease the fire danger.

I spent the day at home, working in the yard. Around 2:00 p.m. puffy, white towers of cumulus clouds started to grow over the DCVZ. Finished with my yard work, I retreated into the house to relax, cool down, and find respite from the heat of the day. Hour by hour, the popcorn-shaped clouds continued to grow, and by late afternoon thunder rumbled out of the north.

I stepped outside and gazed northeast, where a particularly large thunderstorm had developed. It had a very dark, flat cloud base, and periodically bolts of cloud-to-ground lightning would streak from earth to sky. Bands of heavy rain and hail painted the sliver of sky between cloud base and ground.

Unable to resist, I ran into the house, grabbed my camera and car keys, and prepared to chase the developing storm. My excitement was building. It was just one year into my life as a storm chaser, and I was still searching for my first true, big "catch." I wasn't yet out the front door when eight-year-old Adam and four-year-old Nikole distracted me from the chase.

Suddenly Allison called out, "Roger, there's another tire fire out there." I ran outside to look. It was no tire fire—just three miles from the house, the debris cloud from a full-fledged tornado was getting bigger by the minute before our very eyes. As I prepared to set off on the chase, Adam and Nikole shouted out from the house; they wanted to come along.

"This is dangerous," I told them. "The storm may be very scary. Are you sure you want to come with me?" They were certain. We would chase the tornado together.

I drove north on Tower Road as the tornado continued to churn away at the countryside. Without warning, a second tornado formed just east of the road, some six miles to our north. The thunderstorm I originally intended to chase was farther to the northeast still, and the sun kept trying to break through the clouds to the west. With the combination of sunlight from the west and the dark storm in the background, the tornadoes took on a ghostly white hue. I virtually held back tears at the beautiful sight.

I didn't have time to ponder my emotions, however. Yet another funnel cloud formed farther to the east. It seemed that funnel clouds were descending from the storm all around us, and that more tornadoes were forming minute by minute! I pulled over onto the side of the road so we could simply sit and watch the scene unfold.

As we pulled back onto Tower Road and crept north, the first tornado weakened, the second strengthened, and the third developed a debris cloud that spun wildly. When we arrived at the south side of Barr Lake, near the town of Brighton along Interstate 76 and northwest of Denver International Airport, I decided to stop.

The first tornado was a mere quarter mile from us, quickly approaching a farmhouse. The homestead was spared, but lawn chairs and a trampoline were hurled into the air, and a shade tree next to the home was stripped of its leaves.

"The tornado's coming directly at us!" Adam yelled. Nikole sat in the front passenger seat, crying. "The tornado is moving to the north," I reassured them. I slid into the seat next to Nikole and held her in my arms; her sobs slowly faded. "We're safe here. I won't let anything happen to us," I told her.

Her crying stopped, but she wanted no part of getting out of the car to watch the tornadoes. Confident that she was okay, I grabbed my camcorder—a Hitachi VHS model—and filmed the tornado as it became a long, skinny rope. Then, nearing the edge of Barr Lake, the tornado died. A cloud of dirt hung in the air as television station helicopters circled in the very space where the tornado had been. They arrived minutes too late to catch the action.

Mesmerized by the dissolving cloud of dust, I sat and watched for a few minutes longer before realizing that one of the other tornadoes was still on the ground to our east. Climbing back into the car, I drove east on the tornado's tail, until I noticed another funnel cloud nearby to our southwest. It was a long, white, snaking funnel cloud that extended roughly one-third of the way to the ground from the base of the thunderstorm.

Nikole's crying resumed, peaking in intensity each time we spotted a new tornado and waning each time the "action" slowed down. I did all I could to console her, while continuing to watch the tornado and its parent storm at the same time. I was hooked. Not even the cries of my child could fully pull me away from the storm.

This storm was my gateway drug. I had no idea at the time how addicted I would become. But when it opened the door to more intense storm chasing, I walked through that door and started down a slippery slope. Like any "fix," the more you do it, the more you need *more* and the more hooked you become.

A debris cloud from this newest funnel appeared only briefly, and then the funnel disappeared. In all, seven tornadoes descended from the sky over the United States that day, all of them in Colorado, all in the DCVZ swirling around me.

I pulled over on the side of the road and just sat, watching as a succession of storms developed over the DCVZ boundary. I stepped out of the car and craned my neck upward, taking in the scene—cumulonimbus clouds, cloud-to-cloud lightning, cloud-to-ground lightning. The claps of thunder rumbled so loud they reverberated deep inside my chest. I stood there for what seemed like hours with Adam by my side, watching, listening, filming, photographing.

Realizing that the television helicopters had arrived on-scene too late to capture the action, I called local TV stations to inquire whether they wanted some video of the tornadoes. One station—KCNC, Channel 4—said yes. They sent out a satellite truck to meet me on location and upload the video to be fed to the station for use on the air with that night's news broadcast. I didn't want any money for the video, I told them, just my name on the air. It would be my fifteen minutes of fame, I thought. Or at least however many minutes or seconds of video they decided to air.

Around 9:00 p.m. that night, Adam, Nikole, and I returned home, tired from our afternoon and evening of chasing. As I pulled into the driveway, Nikole slept peacefully in the back seat of the car, as if nothing frightening had ever happened that day. Adam, always a bundle of energy, chattered nonstop. What caused tornadoes? How did they form? Did you have to have lightning to have a tornado? Perhaps another storm chaser in the Hill family was emerging.

Improbably, that night the first-ever video I shot as a storm chaser was broadcast on television. For a novice storm chaser like me, it was a thrill. It was my first big break. To this day a copy of that footage marks the first entry in my video archives.

The years following that first big break didn't offer much opportunity for storm chasing, however. As an instructor in the air force, I had a very short supply of free time to spend chasing. Long periods of time spent on the road and away from chasing territory—in Montana, Washington, Nevada, Arizona, California, Utah—compounded the difficulty of chasing.

Nevertheless, the June 9, 1987, tornado was a true beginning, the beginning of what would eventually become the focus of my career and my life. And when the air force transferred me to San Antonio, Texas, on a new assignment in 1992, storm chasing once again became the focus. From my home in the small town of Seguin, Texas, east of San Antonio, I could chase Texas-size storms. It's been said that everything is bigger in Texas, and that's often true of its storms. They are bigger, badder, nastier monsters than what I'd seen in Colorado in the late 1980s. Colorado's storms were photogenic but small. Texas's storms, by contrast, proved to be mammoth, sometimes growing to proportions that spanned several counties.

I had caught the bug. Intercepting—"catching"—that first tornado simply made me thirst for more. I was hungry. I wanted more storms, more lightning, and, above all else, more tornadoes. I wanted more of the worst Mother Nature could dish out. Thoughts of storms filled my mind. I dreamt about them. I obsessed about them. Storm chasing for me was as addictive as anything I'd ever known. It superseded all else and would soon come to exact a heavy toll on my personal life.

CHAPTER FOUR

Work and Play Collide

In 1995, three years after transferring to San Antonio, I retired from the air force. I returned to Colorado, where the City of Aurora offered me a job as a buyer purchasing service and commodities contracts for the city. The move to Colorado thrilled me to death, not only for the state's beautiful scenery but also for the storm chasing.

During my first year back, I didn't have the opportunity to chase much. But storms were virtually in my backyard, and I chased close to home when I could. On May 30, 1996, I was working on the deck of my house in east Aurora. Around midafternoon, I noticed a large area of towering clouds developing east of town. By late afternoon those clouds had coalesced into a monster tornadic supercell thunderstorm near the town of Elba that ultimately spawned a mile-wide tornado.

I thought about chasing the storm but focused on the deck project instead. It was one of a million decisions every storm chaser makes in his or her lifetime of chasing. To go or not? What storm to chase? How long to wait?

Some questions don't have a right or wrong answer. Others do. Regardless, every answer, every choice has a consequence. And at the very least, every chaser must live with that consequence, with the outcome of a decision. Just as certainly, every chaser in the world has days he wishes he had chased but didn't. May 30, 1996, was such a day for me.

To this day it still bothers me that I let this storm get away, that I didn't chase it. Missing a big event like the mile-wide twister near Elba hurts. You think about what you missed. You agonize over what you could have seen but didn't. Shock sets in first—learning about what actually happened in your absence. Shock then gives way to anger. I *should* have been there, and I'm mad that I wasn't. A deep depression follows, filled with a sense of loss over an opportunity not realized. The depression then transitions to a sense of detachment from the event, coupled with an analysis of why you didn't chase the storm. Did I botch a forecast? Was I too tired? Did I focus on the wrong storm? Was it beyond my control?

Finally, if you're lucky, you get over it. Maybe. Sometimes it takes years. And sometimes you never get over it. Life presses on, though; no storm chaser can catch every tornado, and if one thing is certain, it's that there will always be more tornadoes to chase. By the end of 1996, however, my season total included just seven tornadoes. It was more than many Americans will see in their lifetimes, but for me it simply wasn't enough—not nearly.

The following year didn't start off much better. Storm chasing opportunities were few and far between. My job at the City of Aurora kept me too busy for my liking. More specifically, it didn't allow for me to take off on a moment's notice and indulge the strong yearning in my heart—storm chasing.

There was the occasional opportunity to take leave time and chase, however, and it was during one of those breaks from work at the city—and some ten years after I saw my first tornado as a storm chaser—that I finally captured video of a truly giant twister. It was May 25, 1997.

It looked like it was going to be a good tornado day, and I woke early in Aurora, Colorado, and set out for Wichita, Kansas. Sure enough, a very intense supercell thunderstorm formed near the Kansas-Oklahoma border southwest of the city. It spawned several tornadoes, including a beast that touched down in Harper County, Kansas, and tracked directly east into Sumner County. What would come to be known as the "Wellington Wedge" was born south of Argonia and moved east, barely missing the town of Perth and destroying several homes just south of Wellington, which in turn is directly south of Wichita.

By the end of the day, thirty-seven tornadoes touched down across the Great Plains, clustered in three very specific areas. An east-west line of tornadoes ravaged central Kansas. A second grouping of twisters terrorized southern Oklahoma all the way to the Texas border. And of course there were the Harper-Sumner County twisters—including the Wellington Wedge—that rumbled across the Kansas-Oklahoma state line. I caught the Wedge on video.

To this day, I still don't know how they knew, but the folks at The Weather Channel called me. They had heard that I had captured video of the twister and wanted to buy the footage. Happy to make my first sale, I rushed to a nearby television station and uploaded the video. One month later a check for $350 arrived in the mail.

I certainly wasn't going to retire on that kind of money, but it did pay for the cost of the trip and then some. More importantly, it was my first glimpse of the fact that there's money to be made in storm chasing.

The following year, 1998, I captured several impressive storms and a couple of tornadoes on video. I sold every one to The Weather Channel. Yet even with those growing sales, there just wasn't enough income in the tornado-video business to support my family and me, and storm chasing remained a hobby.

By 1999 opportunities to chase had become more abundant. I had left my job at the City of Aurora and taken a position with CH2M-Hill, a major engineering consulting firm in Denver. I was a contracts manager in the construction division of their operations, handling a large U.S. Army Corps of Engineers project in the northeastern United States. The job kept me on the road often.

Because of the time demands of the position and my frequent time spent on the road, when I was in town, my boss allowed me to keep the hours I wanted. It was a perfect arrangement. It allowed me to work, to bring in needed income. But just as importantly, or perhaps more so, it allowed me to chase.

With such a flexible schedule, on April 2, 1999, I found myself in western Oklahoma, where I captured a nice tornado—one of forty-one that hit the plains that day—and an intense hailstorm on video. It was a learning experience, the first time I sustained significant damage to my vehicle. Common sense dictates that getting out of the way of an approaching tornado is a must. But I found out the hard way that getting out of the path of baseball- to softball-size hail is equally important.

Hailstones form in huge cumulonimbus clouds (thunderheads), the same storms that often give birth to tornadoes. The clouds contain much energy, evidenced by the updrafts and downdrafts within. These vertical winds can reach speeds of more than 110 mph. Inside the main updraft of a thunderstorm, the cloud is composed primarily of supercooled water (water that remains liquid even at temperatures below 32 degrees Fahrenheit). Supercooled water droplets require something on which to freeze—ice crystals, frozen rain drops, dust. When the droplets and one of these hosts collide, the supercooled water freezes, creating a new hailstone or enlarging one that already exists. This process will continue—with hailstones growing larger and heavier—until the updraft can no longer support the stone, and the hail falls from the sky.

The largest hailstone ever documented was found in Coffeyville, Kansas, in 1970. The huge stone weighed 1.67 pounds and was 5.67 inches in diameter. An updraft of well over 100 mph would have been required to hold it aloft until it fell. It was such a large stone that there is no category for it on the hail chart index. Marble-size hail is up to .5 inch across and requires a 35 mph updraft. Quarter-size hail, 1 inch across, 49 mph. Golf-ball-size, 1.75 inches, 64 mph. From egg size to tennis ball, baseball, grapefruit, and softball, the hail size grows from 2 inches across to 4.5 inches. The Coffeyville hailstone was quite literally off the charts.

When it does fall, hail rockets toward earth in paths called "hail swaths" that can vary in size from just a few small acres to large belts ten miles wide and a hundred miles long. In August 1980 a hail swath in Orient, Iowa, dropped so much hail that it drifted six feet deep and had to be cleared with snowplows.

The hail swath that I encountered in western Oklahoma on April 2 shattered my windshield, broke the wipers, knocked out the headlights, and put more dents in the van's body than I could count. But I was relatively lucky. In July 1990 softball-size hail in Denver caused $625 million in property damage. More importantly, such mammoth hail can and does kill people.

For my part, I ended up with a new windshield, a bill for the repair service, and a great story to tell when people asked about my hail-dented van later that chase season. The video of the twister and the hail that came with it earned me $400. It would have paid for the chase, if not for the $3000 in damage to the van. Insurance didn't cover the damage, either. It was, and still is, nearly impossible for storm chasers to obtain comprehensive coverage for their vehicles. Insurance companies argue that when you see a tornado or a severe storm you're supposed to drive away from it, not toward it.

Not even two weeks after that tornado, I was once again in western Oklahoma, this time near the town of Carrier. And once again it was looking like a tornado day. All the ingredients were in place for the development of tornadic supercell thunderstorms. There was strong deep layer shear (a change in wind direction and an increase in wind speed with altitude). Dew points were high, indicating good moisture content in the atmosphere. Strong instability and strong atmospheric lifting completed the developing weather profile that day.

I arrived near Pond Creek, a small community in north-central Oklahoma west of Interstate 35, and waited for storms to form. As the afternoon evolved, a few storms did form, but as they moved northward into cooler air, the colder temperatures robbed them of their energy, and they died. I needed to move farther to the south and southwest. Only there might I be able to catch storms that would have the opportunity to fully mature before racing off into colder air and fizzling out. I set my sights on Carrier, Oklahoma.

A supercell thunderstorm developed later that afternoon, and at 3:45 p.m. Central time, a tornado touched down four miles southwest of town. It moved to the east-northeast, heading directly for the town of Carrier. The path of the tornado was just 150 yards wide at that point, but as it approached town, its width grew to 500 yards, and it grew in strength, reaching F2 status, with winds estimated between 113 and 157 mph.

I was to the south of the tornado and the town, but I could make out the twister's tapered cone shape. But then the rain and hail wrapping around the storm obscured my view, just before the storm smacked into Carrier, where the tornado ripped the roofs off numerous houses.

I decided to journey north and east in an attempt to get ahead of the storm for a better view, where I could shoot some good video. This soon turned out to be a bad idea. As I drove through the core of the storm, racing to get into position, I once again encountered large hail up to golf-ball size. For the second time in just two weeks, my windshield was destroyed. By the time I emerged from the hail and regained my view of the storm, the tornado had dissipated. As it left the town, the tornado weakened, its path contracting to two hundred yards wide. At 6:05 p.m., four miles northeast of Carrier, the tornado lifted into the sky and vanished.

In total, eight homes and businesses were destroyed, fourteen sustained major damage, and another nineteen had minor damage. Total estimated cost: $1.5 million.

I stayed with the storm for a few hours longer as it tracked northeast across Oklahoma and then drove the entire way back to Denver. During the drive back I called Dan Watson, an assignment editor at The Weather Channel. "I have some killer video you guys are gonna love," I told him. "I caught the Carrier tornado on tape, as well as some huge hail falling."

"We don't have any video from that storm," Dan told me. "If you can get to a station to upload, we'll buy it."

Utterly exhausted, I arrived in Denver around sunrise the next morning, 6:00 a.m. or so. Snow was falling heavily in town. When I arrived at the teleport station on the south side of Denver to upload the Oklahoma footage, The Weather Channel asked if I could also shoot video of the snow, people, and traffic in Denver. I agreed, and TWC significantly upped its pay rate, nodding to the extra footage I'd provide.

My relationship with The Weather Channel was starting to take on new meaning. Soon they were calling me to shoot video of all kinds—sunny days, rain, thunder, mountain scenery, wind. It was a wonderful way to make some extra money.

When I went in to work at CH2M-Hill, I was in no condition to concentrate on my job. As this pattern repeated, it didn't take long for coworkers to figure out that storm chasing was becoming more than just a passing fancy for me.

Storm chasing was pulling me away from both work and family. I was so singularly focused on chasing storms that I was going to chase regardless of what my wife, my boss, or anyone else said. I didn't see the effect it was having on my personal and professional life. My wife, Allison, did.

Chase by chase, she grew more resentful. It's hard to maintain a good relationship with a spouse when you're apart from one another the way we were. But I had to chase. I had to see more storms and more tornadoes. Nothing would stand in my way. Not work, not family, nothing. I chased instead of being with Allison. I skipped church. I called in sick to work. I missed social commitments. Finally, Allison confronted me. "Your priorities are all wrong," she told me angrily. "Roger, you're obsessed." She was right. I probably was obsessed.

Soon I was chasing constantly. Every time it looked like there was a possibility of severe weather, I went out to chase it. I hit the road whenever I could get time off from work and on the weekends. Every free moment was spent chasing.

On June 3, 1999, my daughter, Nikole, and I chased an incredible storm in northwest Kansas near the town of Almena. The plains were alive with tornadoes that day. A smattering of twisters rumbled through North Dakota, and three large clusters of tornadic storms erupted across Kansas. In all, forty-two tornadoes ravaged the plains that day, and the storms dropped hail up to 4.5 inches in diameter. One of the best storms of the day, though, was the Almena supercell we chased.

It produced several large tornadoes, including a giant F3 with winds between 158 and 206 mph. At its largest the twister was one kilometer wide! Of particular note about this storm was its conspicuous lack of cloud-to-ground (CG) lightning. Large, intense supercells like the one over Almena typically have CG rates that match or exceed one flash per minute. But the unusual Almena storm produced just 17 CG flashes during its entire lifetime. Over the 4.5-hour lifespan of the storm, that equates to a CG rate of only 0.06 per minute. Hardly the one-per-minute rate such storms are known for.

I had caught the entire life cycle of the F3 twister on video, another first for me as a chaser. I called my new best friends at The Weather Channel, and as luck would have it, they had a satellite truck nearby where Jim Cantore was broadcasting. He wasn't yet a household name, but for fans of The Weather Channel, he would be soon, known for his animated, in-your-face field coverage, which viewers saw firsthand during the intense hurricane season of 2004.

When I arrived Jim, friendly and outgoing, greeted me with a firm handshake. I uploaded my video, and after a few minutes of conversation about the storm, we were both back to business.

For me, "business" was increasingly about not just chasing storms but about chasing storms and selling the video to TWC. It seemed that every video I shot TWC bought. I loved it! The additional income allowed me to upgrade my camera equipment. I studied and practiced and refined my method of shooting weather video. Soon I wasn't only selling to TWC but also to the major television networks: CBS, NBC, ABC, CNN. One by one, I amassed a growing media contact list, the storm chaser's equivalent of a Little Black Book filled with names and numbers you don't share with anyone.

When I started storm chasing, I didn't know where it would take me. Except, of course, on a wild ride across the Great Plains. Now it was taking me—or at least my footage—into the televisions and living rooms of millions of Americans. Maybe it was a case of "when you're hot, you're hot." Everything was going right, and it felt like nothing could go wrong.

In truth, though, everything was going wrong, both at home and at work. At CH2M-Hill, the office environment grew tenser from all my chasing. My desire to chase had become so strong that I began cutting down on my work hours in order to spend more time out on the road chasing storms. When I was in the office, I spent countless hours on the computer, checking weather Web sites on the Internet. I would wander around the offices, looking out the windows to see if anything was forming close by. I was constantly distracted, paying more attention to the weather than to the contracts I was hired to manage.

Finally, during the spring of 2000, the tension between chasing and work inevitably climaxed. My boss, Karen Sharp, called me into an office.

When I walked into the office, Karen was sitting in a chair off to the side of a desk. Behind the desk sat Russell Boyd, CH2M-Hill's regional manager. They both looked expressionless, even stern.

"Roger, please sit down," Karen said. I settled uncomfortably into a chair in front of the desk, directly across from Russell.

"We're extremely concerned with your job performance," Russell chimed in. "You've been gone a lot chasing storms." As I sat quietly, listening, I realized that they were offering me an ultimatum.

"Something has to change, Roger," Karen continued, "or I'm afraid you won't have a job here anymore." Essentially, I had to choose between the job and the storms. For me, the choice was clear and easy.

After a short period of silence, I gave them my answer. "I think it would be best if I just leave," I told them. I walked out of the office and down the hall, prepared to gather my belongings and say goodbye to the office and my colleagues. But doubts crept in. Was this the right decision? How would I pay the bills?

The money at CH2M-Hill was good. But even beyond the conflict with storm chasing, it wasn't the right place for me. With my military background, I thrived in a structured work environment. As a consulting firm with a casual and relaxed atmosphere, though, CH2M-Hill didn't offer the structure I craved. The chance to leave and pursue something different didn't seem like such a bad idea. Sometimes you have to free yourself, to let go of what's holding you back, to truly discover yourself.

Before I walked out of the office for the last time, Russell, the regional manager, tracked me down. "I think you can make a good 'go' of storm chasing," he offered, wishing me luck. "Sometimes you have to let go of one profession to go on and do something you enjoy, your passion in life." He was right. Storm chasing was the main passion in my life now. Only one question remained. Could I make it work? Could I survive and make a decent living doing what I enjoyed more than anything else in life?

My job at CH2M-Hill was a thing of the past, but so was my income. It was time to embrace storm chasing full time, to pursue my true passion. But how could I make a living while doing so? The answer to the question plagued me. Selling storm chasing videos to the media provided some, but it wasn't nearly enough—not enough to pay the bills and certainly not enough to live comfortably. Storm chasing had to do more for me financially; I had to think of what that could be.

Developing a storm-chasing company that would take paying clients out onto the Great Plains in search of tornadoes was the way, I thought. In the early 1990s a gentleman named Marty Feely had founded Whirlwind Tours; he was probably the first commercial storm-chase tour operator in the country. He showed that it could be done, and developing my own company became more than just a passing afterthought. I wanted to act on the idea, but how?

How do you develop a company that has inherent danger at the core of its business model? What risks are truly involved? How do you deliver on clients' dreams of adventure? How do you even begin to obtain insurance or financing to purchase equipment and vans? Where and how do you advertise? Ultimately, how do you become successful? These were all unanswered questions for me, but I knew who had the answers.

Shortly after leaving CH2M-Hill in 2000, I contacted David Gold, a Texas-based atmospheric scientist. Two years earlier David had founded Silver Lining Tours, a fledgling storm-chasing business catering to the general public. David and his then-business partner, Bill Gargan, a forecaster for the National Weather Service in Lubbock, Texas, started the company as a way to fund their own storm-chasing addictions, the way a mountaineer becomes a climbing guide in order to spend more time in the mountains. It was a brilliant idea, and one that was operating in a small, niche market that until then had belonged, more or less, only to Marty Feely and Whirlwind Tours.

Soon Silver Lining Tours shared a three-way coexistence as one of the premier storm-chasing tour operators in the country. In 1996, two years prior to Silver Lining's beginnings, Cloud 9 Tours formed, founded by Charles Edwards, a product of the University of Oklahoma storm-chaser incubator. In 2000 Tempest Tours was formed by Martin Lisius, who also founded the Texas Severe Storms Association.

David, for his part, was a well-established and respected name in storm-chasing circles by the time I contacted him. He had earned a BS in meteorology from the University of Oklahoma—thus, two of the top three chase operators in the country had their roots at OU. But David also went on to earn an MS in meteorology and a PhD in atmospheric sciences from Texas A&M University. He began chasing in 1988 and along the way managed to involve himself in some high-profile projects: a National Severe Storms Laboratory experiment, the IMAX filming of *Stormchasers* in 1993, and National Geographic's *Twister Tours,* released in 2000. Such credentials heightened Silver Lining's legitimacy and drew me to David.

Our first correspondence was via email, and communication by communication I picked David's brain about the chase tour business. He graciously answered my questions. But then one day David's email contained a question of its own: "Roger, why don't you try out the tour business by working with me as a tour guide under the Silver Lining Tours banner?" Rather than start my own outfit, I accepted David's invitation and became a tour guide in 2000. It was an opportunity to see how the business ran, to see what made it successful. Just as importantly, it also put a few extra dollars in my pocket, which were sorely needed at the time.

With no source of income other than storm chasing, times were tough, and my finances were on the lean side. Bills were often paid late. When a check came in, it was immediately spent. I was living paycheck to paycheck, and by extension so was my family. I was my own boss, but the paychecks only came in when the storms cooperated, so in a sense Mother Nature was my true boss. Working as a tour guide for Silver Lining would moderate Her feast-and-famine ways.

Joining Silver Lining proved an opportune time for another reason. Despite the success of the movie *Twister* in 1996, storm-chasing tours in the late 1990s just weren't as popular with the general public as operators like Silver Lining, Cloud 9, and Tempest had expected. Commercial storm chasing was just beginning to gain a foothold in the market. But David believed in the concept, and by the time I came on board in mid-2000, his determination was paying off.

CHAPTER FIVE

Tornado Therapy

My first tour as a guide for Silver Lining began on May 9, 2000, in Oklahoma City. It was a ten-day tour, scheduled to conclude on May 18. I arrived from Denver a day early to finally meet David Gold face to face. Until that point our relationship had been restricted to emails and phone calls.

Early on the morning of May 9, there was a knock on my hotel-room door at the Holiday Inn near the Oklahoma City airport, our base hotel; it was David. He greeted me in tennis shoes, shorts, and a Silver Lining Tours T-shirt, his usual chase attire. A wide grin extended from ear to ear, and his right hand extended out in a preemptive handshake.

I took his hand in a firm grip, thanking him for the chance to be a tour guide on his tours. Extremely intelligent and highly proper, he articulated each word that came from his mouth. We talked about chasing, about family and friends, about this tour, and about our respective thoughts on the forecast and severe-weather outlook for the next ten days of chasing.

"We're also going to be joined on this tour by National Geographic Europe," David explained. "They're filming a program called *Twister Tours*, and an English couple with us for this tour—David and Sheila Winn—are going to be the focus of the show." The National Geographic crew was headed up by Executive Producer Alister Chapman, David continued. Alister had made a name for himself as a professional cameraman and editor, producing programs for not only National Geographic but also CNN, the Discovery Channel, and the BBC. He ran a United Kingdom–based storm-chasing group and was even an internationally competitive motor-rally driver in his earlier years.

Later that morning David and I walked down the hall to the Holiday Inn's conference room, where the tour clients were all expected to gather. Bill Reid, our driver for Van 2, was there, as were the National Geographic crew, headed up by Alister and his Sony Betacam video camera, a huge and expensive shoulder-mounted behemoth that ran on half-inch tapes. Alister planned to shoot the orientation meeting.

As the clients gathered together, I soon realized that each of us in that room chased for different reasons. Some came to get out into the wide-open plains, where they could watch majestic supercell thunderstorms roll across the countryside. Others came for the camaraderie, to meet other people with the same passion, to talk about storms they've seen, and about the prospect of storms yet to be seen. All came for the ultimate prize, the tornado.

Most people will never summit Mount Everest or swing a baseball bat on the hallowed grounds of Yankee Stadium, or fly a fighter jet at Mach 2. But in storm chasing anyone can experience the ultimate prize firsthand. Tornadoes are within anyone's grasp, and the job of Silver Lining Tours—my job on Tour 1 in 2000—was to deliver that ultimate prize safely. They, the clients, came for different reasons, but they all shared a fundamental goal—to see one of the most awesome and phenomenal forces on the face of the earth and to be able to live and tell their stories of an encounter with a tornado.

Like the clients on the tour, I had my own reasons for storm chasing. Some of it was simply indescribable, as if the desire to chase was genetic instinct or subconsciously imprinted in me in some way. And yet other reasons were clear as day. Some of those reasons were linked to that defining moment when I was nine years old in Topeka and a true monster tornado nearly took my life. Some of my desire to chase stemmed from my fascination with weather. And I wanted to meet the people who lived on the plains, as I did in my youth, and hear their war stories of survival in the face of atmospheric adversity.

But if one thing haunted me about my storm chasing, it was the death and destruction often left in the aftermath of a tornado. It was the dark side of the profession. People felt that storm chasers thrived on such macabre scenes. That was never the focus for me. I chased for the beauty of the storm and the adrenaline rush of getting close to a big tornado. I wanted to see the storm in all its majesty, not what it left behind. But too often, a tornado did leave something behind—a tale of lives and communities forever changed. The good and bad of storms were thus inextricably linked. Like a yin and yang, they coexisted and were inseparable. And every storm chaser wrestled with balancing a storm's angels and demons.

Another client on Tour 1 in 2000 was battling demons of her own. Cathy Adams came on the tour not because she loves storms but because she was terrified of them. Her greatest fear in life was thunderstorms, and she wanted nothing more than to put that phobia behind her. Her husband, Steve, gave her the tour as an anniversary present. He figured the best way for her to overcome her fear was to face it head-on, experiencing thunderstorms, hailstorms, tornadoes, and any other severe weather they could experience over the course of those ten days.

We all settled into our seats in the conference room as David began his briefing about the potential weather pattern for the tour. It looked as if two major systems would provide excellent opportunities for storm chasing, with the potential to produce many tornadoes. Exactly where and when that would happen weren't possible to predict that early. There would be a few down days over the course of the tour, during which people could relax, do laundry, and generally catch their breath, but at least half the days on tour were expected to be chase days, which was about average. May 10, David explained, would take us to northern Nebraska and Iowa. If nothing else, it would put us in position for what May 11 might bring.

On the morning of May 10, we met in the hotel lobby and then piled into two vans, with the National Geographic crew trailing behind in a rental sedan. As expected, it was a positioning day—the weather over the Great Plains had been quiet on the 9th, and the 10th was looking even tamer (only two tornadoes were reported that day, in Pennsylvania and Virginia). This was nothing out of the ordinary, as the atmosphere often cycled between "calm" days and "chase" days.

Our plan was to head north on Interstate 35 destined for Omaha, Nebraska, some 460 miles and seven hours distant. Once checked into our hotel late that afternoon, we grabbed dinner at Johnny Sortino's Pizza Parlor in south Omaha on L Street. I had eaten there many times while in the air force, and in the years since it had become a must-stop destination during my storm-chasing adventures. The pizza was incredible, and the casual environment offered an opportunity for all of us to get to know one another better. We were all excited about the next day, which was looking more and more promising.

On the morning of May 11, David and I sat at our computers at the hotel in Omaha analyzing the forecasting models for the day. Then we came together to compare notes. Two heads were always better than one in this game, and David was an experienced and gifted forecaster. We agreed that north-central and northeastern Iowa had the best potential for the day. Our chase target was set.

A low-pressure center at the surface was forecast to strengthen across northeast Nebraska. Its counterclockwise rotation would pull warm, muggy air into Iowa from the south. The air was looking extremely unstable, and if a storm developed, it could be explosive. Even better, there was strong wind shear—change in wind direction and speed with height. If a storm developed, it would rotate rapidly thanks to the shear, fostering tornadoes.

There was one possible fly in the ointment, however. It looked like there might be strong southerly winds at higher elevations. If those winds aloft transported warm air into the mid-layers of the atmosphere, it could put a "cap" on the atmosphere and squash thunderstorm development. Thunderstorms develop—with their intense updrafts—as long as the air can rise. The air, in turn, only rises as long as the air within the thunderstorm is warmer than the air around it. It's the same principal that allows a hot air balloon to fly. The point where the air within the storm becomes equal to or cooler than the air around it is known as the cap, and the thunderstorm can grow no higher. And if warm air settled into the mid-layers of the atmosphere, that cap would be too strong and too low to allow truly big storms to grow. Hopefully, that wouldn't happen and the storms we were expecting would come to fruition.

Even so, setting our sights on Iowa was a risky decision. North-central and northwestern Nebraska was also looking promising, especially for thunderstorms. We were faced with heading to Nebraska, where we'd be assured of good storms, or with heading to Iowa, where we might catch the best tornadoes of the year—or nothing at all. It's a tension every storm chaser faces. You have to decide whether you'd be satisfied with simply a good storm or if you wanted to go, in essence, for double or nothing. Our decision was made. We would follow our gut instincts and our forecast and head to Iowa.

We drove through western and central Iowa, and by noontime when we stopped for lunch, we were in Des Moines. From there we went north to Ames and then east toward the Waterloo area. As we drove, with me in the driver's seat in Van 1 and Bill Reid captaining Van 2, David downloaded updated data from the Internet via a slow, dicey cell-phone connection. By early afternoon we had rolled into Charles City, the scene of an intense F5 tornado back in the 1960s.

Everyone piled out of the van and immediately stepped into incredibly humid air. It was like soup, the kind of air you felt as if you could swim through. We were just north of an approaching warm front, and the skies were mostly cloudy. The temperature–dew point split was 82/77 degrees Fahrenheit. With the dew point so high and so close to the actual temperature, it was confirmation of the incredible humidity each one of us felt the instant we got out of the van. Winds were light out of the east, another indication that we were just north of the warm front. To our southwest, behind the warm front, temperatures soared to 100 degrees Fahrenheit.

As we sat by the roadside, patiently waiting for storms to form, clients—including David and Sheila Winn from England and Cathy and Steve Adams—threw footballs or baseballs, played Frisbee, or just lounged in the shade trying to stay cool. The skies cleared a bit, which was actually a good thing. Clear skies allowed the sun to heat the earth, and that heating in turn caused rising columns of air that would ultimately become the thunderstorms we hoped to chase. By 4:00 p.m. towering cumulus clouds were developing over the area, and a select few were even producing rain. It was the atmosphere's first attempt at storm development. Perhaps the growing storms had the strength to overcome the cap we had been so concerned about earlier in the day.

At 5:00 p.m. that wish came true. The Storm Prediction Center issued a tornado watch for our chase area. The watch mentioned the cap but also said that the cap was eroding. As the cap eroded, the SPC expected rapid supercell thunderstorm development, almost by the minute. We watched the skies and waited.

One hour later David downloaded a fresh radar image. Our first real storm of the day was developing west-southwest of Waterloo. It was situated right along the warm front and was headed northeast. We clambered back into the vans, and the chase was on. It wouldn't take long for the storm to become an intense supercell.

We blasted south from Charles City on Highway 218, heading toward Waterloo. We maneuvered around Waverly—a small town north of Cedar Falls and Waterloo—and continued southbound. Out the front window of the van, I could see the storm developing and growing stronger with each passing minute. The storm's anvil—the flat, spreading top of the thunderstorm—was razor sharp. Soon to the west the updraft base—the dark, horizontal bottom of the storm—became visible. To the southwest the rear-flank downdraft—rapidly moving, clear, dry air—wrapped around the back of the storm. It was fast becoming a classic supercell.

The National Weather Service came over our onboard weather radio with a tornado warning for our storm, which was now directly to our west. As we continued south past Janesville, a truncated, cone-shaped tornado formed three miles to our west, heading directly for us. We pushed onward through driving rain, rushing to get south of the twister.

"Oh, yeah, baby!" I hollered through an excited laugh. "It's a beautiful tornado. Look at it wrapping up!"

A dark blue-gray funnel extended halfway to the ground, while a translucent debris cloud stirred at ground level. "Look at it going to town. It's not far from us here," I continued. From the back of the van, Cathy Adams nervously asked, "How far, exactly?"

"Two or three miles, maybe," I estimated.

At that point, with hail crashing down, David realized that Van 2 had fallen far behind us. "We've gotta get going if we're going to get south of the tornado," I told David. Van 2 hadn't responded to David's earlier radio transmissions. Now the situation was serious.

"It's only 1.5 miles west of our road," he told me. Then, he jumped on the radio to implore the second van. "If you're going to go, you've gotta go now! It's coming fast. Haul ass!"

We screamed through a residential neighborhood, realizing that in all likelihood these houses were in the path of the tornado. David's transmissions over the radio continued. "We're in danger. It's a large tornado. It's humongous, and it's right to the west of us." Still no response from Van 2. And we were about to get cut off from one another by the twister.

My cell phone rang, but I was too focused on driving through the rain and hail, and away from the tornado, to answer it. The tornado, now very close, marched through a treeless farm field and then smacked directly into north Waterloo.

"How far south do you want to go?" I asked David.

"Get south of this damn thing," he said sternly. "I don't want to die."

Some of the tour customers, including Cathy, were somewhat freaked out by David's comment. They were experiencing a true taste of exactly what they'd gotten themselves into.

By now we were just north of Highway C57, where a police officer flagged us down. "There's a tornado coming," she told us, stating the obvious. "You have to get south and get out of the way."

"We're storm chasers. We're planning to stop here," David said.

"Well, fine," the officer responded. "I am getting out of here."

She sped off, leaving us alone on the side of the road. We inched southward just far enough to get out of the tornado's way and to get out of the rain and hail. I pulled our van onto a dirt road and threw it into park. Looking behind us, we could see that the funnel cloud was by then a giant stovepipe extending from cloud to ground. The clients, including Cathy, tentatively climbed out of the van and took pictures and shot video of the tornado and of one another. The Winns from England were awestruck. Cathy was beside herself, standing next to David and repeatedly yelling, "Oh my God! Oh my God!"

"I'm not so convinced we're out of danger here," I said to no one in particular.

"We're okay," David said, calming the group's fears. "The tornado is moving northeast." I watched carefully for a few moments and realized he was right. Good.

But I also realized that the winds from the rear flank downdraft were wrapping around the tornado and headed straight for us. They sounded like a huge, rushing waterfall coming right at us. "Here it comes!" I yelled, warning everyone to brace for the strong winds. Most of the clients ran back into the van, but I stood outside with the National Geographic crew, ready for the blast to hit.

"Oh my goodness, look at this!" I told the NG crew as the RFD winds began to pick up. The wind was strafing across the land. Brown dirt hurtled across the ground. Green crops were bent over into a horizontal position. The crew was struggling to stand upright. Then the true RFD blast hit, with 70- to 80-mph winds. "Hang tight!" I yelled over the roar. "Look out! Hang on!"

The tornado crossed the highway right in front of us. "The houses we came by are not going to be there when we go back," I told the crew. It was a somber realization. "There's gonna be nothing left."

The RFD was so strong that telephone poles seemed to be bending under the force of the wind, and nearby power lines, whipped by the winds, were swinging and swaying wildly, like jump ropes held between each pair of poles. We were getting plastered with hail, tree branches, debris. The NG crew and I ran off the road to take shelter on the lee side of a building. "That is a monster," I told them. "It's going to go on for a long time."

From our protected spot next to the building, we watched as the tornado churned across the countryside less than a mile to our north. A few cars stopped in front of us, their occupants pausing to gape at the immense twister. Power flashes near ground level gave evidence of the tornado's wrath each time it hit a house or ripped a transformer or power line from its pole.

Incoming rain bands wrapped around the storm, and our view was about to become obscured. With the tornado still on the ground, we climbed back into the van and drove east from Waterloo, determined to stay with the storm and ahead of the tornado.

The van was silent as I drove, save for my chatter with David. The clients seemed too shaken to talk about what they had just seen. Our goal now was to stay with this violent F3 tornado as it moved east across Highway 63 and into farm country. We dropped south to Highway C66 and then headed east, with the smoky gray tornado at our nine o'clock. We sped down the white-gravel road as fast as was safe, but as we caught up with the RFD that hit us earlier, visibility dropped to zero, and the road became engulfed in a total brownout from the blowing plume of topsoil.

Cathy screamed from her spot in the back of the van as I slowed us to a crawl. "Keep away from these power lines," David said. We were seeing just the tip of the iceberg of this tornado's wake of destruction. "I don't even want to see what kind of damage this thing causes," I told David.

And then, as quickly as the tornado had formed, it weakened and dissipated. We slowed down and stopped for a moment, both to catch our breath and to see what the storm would throw at us next.

We were about four miles west of the small town of Dunkerton, watching a suspicious area of cloud motion, when the radio chirped to life. It was Van 2. They were one mile east of Dunkerton and in a safe position. When they got cut off from us by the tornado, they changed course and sped away on an eastbound road to stay ahead and out of the way of the tornado.

As we were making plans to reunite the vans, a debris cloud suddenly appeared to our southeast. A funnel poked out of the dark cloud base. "Tornado number two!" David and I exclaimed in unison, causing several passengers in the van to break into laughter. David and I were like two boys on Christmas morning, overcome with our eager enthusiasm.

The new tornado was less than a mile from us. Cathy and Sheila sounded frantic in the back of the van, a definite sound of distress in their voices. "Dave, can we get east of Dunkerton? Will this road take us all the way there?" I asked.

As David checked our road maps, the black debris cloud grew in size. It's relatively weak right now, but it will strengthen, I tell the van. "Strengthen?" Cathy said incredulously. "It looks strong enough to me, don't you think?"

"Oh, yeah," I agreed. "Believe me, that could kill you."

"It's a big son of a bitch," one of the men in back added.

We drove closer to the twister and then pulled over onto the side of the road to watch as it crossed the highway ahead of us. While we sat watching, another car drove past us, headed straight for the tornado.

"I don't know if I'd be driving there," someone said. "I wouldn't either," I added.

As if he heard us, the driver slammed on his brakes and came to a screeching halt, stopping his car in the middle of the road, a few hundred yards shy of the tornado as it crossed the highway.

The twister marched onward toward Dunkerton, with its white funnel and black debris cloud making a continuous snake from ground to cloud. The folks in Van 2, from their position east of Dunkerton, had a fantastic view as the tornado moved away from us and toward them.

I repositioned the van, and then we all unloaded to film the scene. It was eerily calm and quiet. The dark twister appeared to swirl in slow motion, while a lone bird flew across the foreground of the scene. Then the town of Dunkerton got hit. We wouldn't find out until later the storm's actual toll on the community.

Less than twenty minutes after it formed, the tornado fizzled and died. We drove east of Dunkerton on Highway C66 to its intersection with Baxter Avenue, where we at last reunited with Van 2. Together we watched the sky. The storm's mesocyclone was still rotating, with lots of sloppy scud clouds—loose, ragged fragments of cloud—swirling around the base of the storm. "This thing is not done yet," I told everyone.

A wall cloud—a localized, abrupt lowering of the cloud base—developed and started to rotate rapidly. It didn't take long for the third tornado of the day to form. The funnel cloud stabbed at the ground, like a drill press digging into the earth. Flashes of light filled the sky. It was either lightning or yet more power lines going down. The dark funnel churned across Baxter Avenue to our north. It nearly steamrolled over a solitary white farmhouse that sat in a small stand of trees on the edge of an open field. The house was spared.

We all stood fixated on the scene, filming with our cameras. It was then that I looked over and saw Cathy. She was standing in front of the tornado, smiling as her husband, Steve, took her picture. It was only our first day of storms on the tour, but perhaps her phobia was already a thing of the past.

"You can hear it!" David Winn exclaimed as Alister filmed him and his wife in front of the twister. "This is Mother Nature at her finest," I chimed in. "But be ready to jump in the car."

As we all watched, a bolt of lightning shot directly through the funnel, piercing it like an arrow shot from heaven, eliciting a hearty round of oohs and aahs from everyone. Then, with the tornado having crossed the highway, we planned to head north to examine its debris path, and then stair-step on roads going east and north and east again to stay with the storm.

The tornado dissipated as we chased on its heels, leaving a cloud of dirt hanging in the air where the funnel once spun. Even so, the show was far from over. As the evening wore on, the sky glowed a dull orange behind the dark storm. Intense CG lightning sparked out of the storm's anvil. The third tornado, which we thought was dead, reformed as a renewed funnel cloud—slender as a needle—extended down from the storm, built a debris cloud, and grew in strength.

We stopped both vans so everyone could get a good view and take pictures. It was an incredible sight! As the clients filmed the reinvigorated tornado, a very large multiple-vortex tornado formed farther west. Suddenly, we had two tornadoes in one single scene—not at all a common sight! It was 8:11 p.m.

Our excitement overflowed. David and I stood off to the side, soaking up the spectacular storm and the joy of our clients. The clients, for their part, were now acting as if they'd been chasing storms their whole lives. They chatted incessantly. Their enthusiasm bordered on frantic. Maybe it was to calm their nerves or to release excess energy. But one thing was sure—they all, including Cathy, seemed to be enjoying themselves tremendously.

Soon both tornadoes were gone. One became obscured in rain and hail and disappeared from view. The other roped out and dissolved into nothing but a memory.

As darkness fell we still stayed with the storm. Although our daylight was gone, and with it any potential view of a twister that might form under cover of nightfall, the lightning was tremendous and nothing short of spectacular.

Flashes occurred every second or two. Some lightning bolts spidered across the sky overhead, crawling through the storm's anvil. Other bolts streaked to the ground. Crashes of thunder constantly filled the air.

Ancient Greeks believed that lightning was the weapon of Zeus. Scandinavian mythology held that Thor, the Thunderer, hurled lightning bolts at his enemies. But thanks in part to Benjamin Franklin's legendary kite-flying experiments during 1752 and 1753, storm chasers today know that lightning is essentially a giant static-electric spark that releases when the differential in charge between earth and sky becomes great enough for a lightning bolt to "bridge the gap" in a ninety-thousand-mile-per-second journey from cloud to ground.

Storm chasers know, too, that lightning represents one of the greatest dangers while chasing. In a typical year nationwide, lightning causes more deaths—sixty-seven people on average—than tornadoes, hurricanes, or any other weather event except floods. Between 1959 and 1994 lightning accounted for more than thirteen thousand casualties (deaths and injuries combined), with nearly 25 percent of those being fatalities.

For a "normal" person, the Great Plains are a pretty safe place in terms of lightning. Because of their low population and well-used warning systems, the nation's central states rank fairly low on the "danger of being killed by lightning" scale. But the central plains also have some of the highest lightning-flash densities in the country, second only to the deep Southeast and especially Florida. And storm chasers put themselves in the direct path of storms that produce some of the biggest bolts of lightning in the country.

A typical lightning bolt superheats the air around it to 50,000 degrees Fahrenheit, three times hotter than the surface of the sun. An average lightning bolt also carries with it 20,000 to 40,000 amps of electricity, enough energy to light a 100-watt household incandescent light bulb for three months straight. By comparison, an arc welder uses 250 to 400 amps to weld steel; an average single-family home uses about 200 amps of peak current (imagine turning on all your electrical appliances and lights at once), and it takes just 20 milliamps (one fiftieth of an amp or one millionth of the amperage contained in a lightning bolt) to cause a person's chest muscles to contract, stopping breathing. Quite a different situation from simply being caught "breathless" at the sight of a monster tornado.

Every year, an average 30 million ground points across the United States are struck by lightning. And as we drove east into the night, it seemed that the area around Dunkerton and Waterloo was doing its part to add to that count for the year 2000. The electrification of the storm remained phenomenal. Off to our north, we could still make out the updraft base of the storm, and the dark silhouette of a final tornado that formed and sauntered off into the countryside.

We were all tired. The storm was wrapped in rain and hail. It was well after 9:00 p.m., hotels were beginning to fill for the night, and it was time to find a place where we could rest our heads. The next day we planned to chase in southern Illinois, and an overnight stay in Dubuque near the Iowa-Illinois-Wisconsin border seemed best. David found us rooms at a hotel downtown, and we called it a night and made our way to Interstate 80.

By the time we arrived at the interstate, it was time for a well-deserved and much-needed bathroom and snack break. We had been in "chase mode" for hours. It had been difficult, if not impossible, to stop—not that any of us really thought about stopping anyway, even if we needed to. With the chase over, though, we could let down our guard and take care of our most basic needs—or at least those needs beyond survival, the primal need and instinct of any storm chaser.

Together our two vans resumed the eastward journey on Interstate 80. The storm we had chased for so many hours earlier in the day continued with strobe lightning. Other storms formed behind it, even as the night wore on. The rain returned as another tornado-warned storm approached from the southwest. "I think this is better than sex!" exclaimed David Winn. His wife, Sheila, elbowed him in the side as the rest of our van exploded with a roar of laughter.

Around 11:00 p.m. we at last arrived at our hotel. As we all checked into our rooms, the day's tornadoes were still the topic of discussion on everyone's lips. We hadn't eaten a decent meal since lunch, so I ordered pizzas for the group, along with a round of beer at everyone's insistence. We sat together, unwinding from the wild day and strengthening the bond we all shared as storm chasers.

Just as we prepared to retire to our rooms for the night, the tornado sirens went off in Dubuque. We rushed to the lobby as one last storm taunted us for the night, producing nothing more than heavy rain, lightning, and wind. No other tornadoes occurred in Iowa that night.

But Mother Nature had already spoken. Our tornado count ended at eleven for the day. In all, fourteen confirmed tornadoes, and possibly as many as twenty-six, ravaged the United States on May 11, 2000, most of them clustered in northeastern Iowa within our target chase area. True to the SPC's predictions, storms like the supercell we chased "exploded," transitioning from initial radar pickup to tornadic in less than fifty minutes.

Dunkerton received the worst of the tornadoes' fury. Three successive tornadoes—at 6:03 p.m., 6:55 p.m. and 7:20 p.m.—each left a mark on the town. City hall was completely destroyed . . . for the second time. Just one year earlier city hall also had been destroyed, that time by a flood. On the outskirts of Dunkerton, the farmstead of Polly Mills, an elderly widow, was hit by one of the twisters. Her farmhouse was shredded, but sixty miles away on a farm east of Monona in Clayton County, someone found one of Polly's letters. As the twisters rumbled through the densely populated town center, numerous people were badly injured, including one woman who lost an arm and a hand and died seventeen days later. Sadly, it wasn't the first, or the last, time tornadoes claimed lives in 2000. A total of fourteen killer twisters hit the United States in 2000, including the F3 we chased through the Waterloo–Cedar Falls–Dunkerton area. Twenty-four significant tornadoes—those ranking F3 or higher on the Fujita scale—hit the United States in 2000. The F3 Dunkerton twister ranked fourth most violent on that list.

As Tour 1 of the 2000 chase season continued, David's initial prediction about two major clusters of storms with a break in between proved true. On May 12, one day after the Iowa outbreak, twenty tornadoes were reported (thirteen confirmed), many of them in south-central Illinois, where we chased from our overnight rest in Dubuque. Then for five straight days the plains were quiet. There were no tornadoes and little weather—severe or otherwise—to speak of. But as Tour 1 was winding down, Mother Nature delivered her second act. On May 17, thirty-two tornadoes erupted across the High Plains, strung out between northeastern Colorado and central

Nebraska. We caught many of the Nebraska twisters, including a massive F3 that ripped through the town of Brady, causing three-quarters of a million dollars in damage. Thanks to footage from storm chasers like us, the tornado got major coverage in the national media. Then one day later Tour 1 concluded.

It was a tour none of us would soon forget. Our tornado outbreak, of course, was nothing like the historic outbreaks that have become the stuff of legend—outbreaks like the Palm Sunday Outbreak or the biggest outbreak of them all: the Super Outbreak of 1974. In a twenty-four-hour period spanning April 3 and 4, an unfathomable 148 tornadoes erupted across thirteen states. If you added the path lengths of all those tornadoes together to form a single line, they would stretch out for twenty-six hundred miles. In less than eighteen hours, the twisters decimated nine hundred square miles of American heartland.

Our outbreak had its own outcomes. Cathy Adams overcame her fear of thunderstorms. David and Sheila Winn became the stars of *Twister Tours,* which went on to be broadcast and rebroadcast on every major television network around the world. David Gold and I solidified a friendship and a business relationship; we had spent time in the trenches together, seen one another's forecasts, validated our respective reputations as storm chasers. And whether client or tour guide, we all walked away from the tour sharing one important common denominator—we had experienced one of the most intense supercell thunderstorms to hit the United States in all of 2000.

CHAPTER SIX

Too Close for Comfort

B y 2002, with two previous seasons under my belt leading tours for Silver Lining, my chase routine was well established. Tour after tour would depart and return with military-like precision. The Silver Lining Tours schedule allowed for one "down" day between tours, and I used that day to its full advantage. Getting to know my wife, Allison, again. Resting. Servicing the vans. Doing paperwork. Looking at the forecasting models for the next tour. Meeting the new clients who would begin their tour the next day. June 22, 2002, was no different.

Tour 5 had just concluded, and Tour 6 was scheduled to depart the next day. I awoke on the 22nd to a warm, sunny day. After a quick breakfast I went into town to get my van serviced—oil change, tire rotation, exterior and interior wash—and then headed home to complete Tour 5's end-of-tour accounting. I hadn't yet given a thought to the weather pattern for the next tour that was about to begin, but it was time to look at the models.

During the afternoon I sat at my computer, poring over forecasts from the Storm Prediction Center, National Weather Service, and a series of other resources I used. It became increasingly apparent that the first day of Tour 6 would require us to make a very long drive to get into position for what looked to be an explosive day right out of the gate. Every forecast model showed the classic ingredients for a tornado outbreak: extreme atmospheric instability, strong wind shear, abundant moisture, and good lifting. All those ingredients were coming together over far northeast South Dakota, where three large air masses were forecast to meet.

I almost blew off the thought of trying to get the group up before daybreak to make the long haul. From Denver to northeast South Dakota it was a good seven hundred miles and ten-plus hours of driving. It hardly seemed possible to even make it to the chase area in time.

What's more, it would be a big investment for what might be a "high risk–high reward" situation. The forecast included a strong cap in the atmosphere—warm air in the mid-layers—that might prevent thunderstorms from forming at all. Of the four forecast models I reviewed, two called for the development of storms. Two did not. However, as with Iowa in 2000, if a thunderstorm did manage to form, I knew it had a superb chance of becoming a supercell and spawning tornadoes.

In the end I determined that the drive was worth it. Clients paid a lot of money to be taken to the areas that had the best potential for severe weather. If that area happened to be in northeast South Dakota, then that's where we were going to go.

At 7:00 p.m. I met the tour group at a hotel near Denver International Airport. During a group dinner at a nearby restaurant, we introduced ourselves and got acquainted. Unlike my first tour in 2000, when I drove the van and David Gold called the shots from the passenger seat, I'd be the one calling the shots on the tour. Scott Landolt, a meteorologist, would be my driver. Our group also included Claire Bailey, a young lady from England; Ed Schoenborn, a wealthy gentleman from North Carolina; and two others.

I stood up at the end of the table to give my pretour speech, setting expectations for the tour, explaining the dos and don'ts of tour etiquette, and reviewing the weather pattern. As I began to speak, the group went quiet, seemingly focused on my every word. They eagerly anticipated what type of weather pattern they'd experience on the tour. I told them about the four forecast models for the next day and then laid out the risks and rewards of making the journey to South Dakota. No one was hesitant about driving long hours for what could be a "feast or famine" storm situation.

That was good, I told them. I only expected us to get two or three days of chase time on the tour. High pressure was forecast to build throughout the plains, which would end the threat of severe weather from day four of the tour onward. It was best we go for broke on day one!

At the ungodly hour of 4:30 a.m., I crawled out of bed and stumbled into the shower. It was déjà vu. It seemed like I had repeated those motions so many times that spring and summer already, and I had. The tours had thus far driven nearly thirty-two thousand miles that year crisscrossing the plains to get to severe weather hot spots. June 23, 2002, would be no different, adding to the mileage tally. At times it almost seemed as if the atmosphere was purposefully pulling us from one state to another, laughing at us as we raced from Oklahoma to South Dakota to Colorado to Kansas.

With my hair still wet from the shower, I went to the computer to check the morning forecast models from the SPC and from the local National Weather Service offices in Aberdeen and Sioux Falls. The scenarios they forecast looked very similar to those from the night before, with one major difference: There was no longer disagreement. They all predicted storms in our target chase area! All of sudden, my heavy eyelids didn't feel so heavy anymore. The Storm Prediction Center issued a moderate risk for severe storms, with a good threat of tornadoes and large hail. On the SPC's scale of five levels of risk, the moderate rating is the second highest. Excellent news for storm chasers. The local National Weather Service offices, for their part, warned that if the atmospheric cap dissipated things could get potentially dangerous. In all, the weather setup was strangely similar to the May 11, 2000, tornado outbreak in Iowa.

I was ready and motivated to hit the road. The van's diesel engine roared to life, and I pulled up to the hotel lobby at 5:45 a.m. To my surprise, all the guests were packed, waiting, and ready to go. At 6:00 a.m. we rolled onto Interstate 76, cruising through northeast Colorado and destined for South Dakota, with no time to waste.

Cell-phone reception was spotty, but finally, near Ogallala, Nebraska, I was able to obtain a signal strong enough and for enough time to download updated radar and satellite images of the target area. A huge complex of thunderstorms was rolling across eastern North Dakota and into Minnesota.

Those storms were pushing cool air south along the Minnesota–North Dakota border and toward South Dakota. If the cool air moved too far south, it could dampen the tornado outlook. But if that cool air stalled, it could actually provide more focus for thunderstorms to form. The interface between the cool air from the thunderstorms to the north and the warm, moist air coming up from the south is what storm chasers call an outflow boundary. New thunderstorms often develop along these boundaries, and the situation made us even more determined to get north quickly.

We blasted north on Highway 83 toward Valentine, Nebraska. Along the way, we passed through Thedford, and I told the group how a monster tornadic supercell thunderstorm had roared through the community just three years earlier, producing multiple tornadoes on the ground at the same time, on the very road we drove on. I thoroughly enjoyed sharing such past tornado stories with my tours. It immersed them in the "tornado landscape," placing their tour into a regional and historical context. And it heightened their level of excitement.

But on that day there wasn't yet any visible sign of the destructive forces of Mother Nature. The skies were blue, with white pillows of cumulous clouds rising into the atmosphere.

We crossed into South Dakota and continued north through the Rosebud Indian Reservation, heading toward the state capitol of Pierre. It was early afternoon, and as we approached the city, I regained enough cell reception to check the Internet for new weather data. The models continued to call for explosive thunderstorm development by 6:00 p.m. The cool air coming down from the north stalled along the South Dakota–North Dakota border. And just to the east of Highway 83, the atmosphere developed a north-south dryline, an invisible boundary between moist and dry air. To the east of the dryline, air coming up from the Gulf of Mexico was warm and moist. To the west, winds out of the arid Southwest carried very hot, very dry air.

Like an outflow boundary a dryline is often the location of thunderstorm development. The only thing better than a dryline or an outflow boundary was having *both* a dryline *and* an outflow boundary. The place where those two invisible boundaries meet is called the triple point and often produces the most violent storms seen on the plains. On June 23 the triple point was in Brown County, just northwest of Aberdeen, South Dakota. We were en route and still had several hours before storms would form, but it would take us every available minute to get there.

From Pierre we continued north toward Mound City and could clearly see a line of cumulus towers growing along the outflow boundary. With the outflow boundary running roughly east-west and the dryline running north-south, we wanted to get to the southeast of the triple point, where those two lines intersected. Scott, our driver, turned us east on Highway 10 toward the tiny town of Leola, in the heart of South Dakota's Glacial Lakes and Prairie region. We were still in the hot, dry air, but as we drove we could see hazy, humid skies to the east on the other side of the dryline. We were almost to the Promised Land.

Around 5:30 p.m. we arrived in Leola, and everyone unloaded from the van to stretch their legs and marvel that we had made it to our chase target area in time. The air was warm and muggy, and we climbed back into the van for a short drive to the outskirts of town, from which we could watch the skies. The cumulus towers hovered to the north, and almost overhead you could see the dryline, where the sky went from hazy brown to a bright, clear blue. My eyes followed the dryline north until it intersected the line of cumulus towers. That was ground zero, and it was about to become the wildest place on the planet.

I wanted to jockey for even better position, and we clambered into the van yet again to reposition, driving north from Leola on Highway 19 and then east on Highway 8 to its intersection with Highway 23. This put us just where we needed to be, a few miles southeast of the triple point.

By 6:00 p.m. several thunderstorms attempted to grow, but each time they moved northeast into the cooler air, they died. Storms needed to stay in the warm, muggy air in order to survive. Weather radar showed that the triple point was stationary, which was good news. But it also showed supercell thunderstorms—including one that produced a tornado—in western and central North Dakota. Had I made the wrong choice? Did we target the best chase area? Should we stay put and play the waiting game, seeing what the atmosphere delivered?

In storm chasing, you don't leave your target area unless you have a very good reason. You'll never catch every supercell or every tornado, but it can be easy to fall into a "grass is greener" mentality. But I had learned to trust my instincts and my forecasts. It was best to stay put.

Around 6:30 p.m. an area of large cumulus towers grew directly to our southwest. From our vantage point in north-central South Dakota near the North Dakota border, we could sit back and watch the towers grow, looking like the mushroom cloud from an atomic bomb as the clouds boiled upward and outward, rising skyward at hundreds of feet per second. Unlike the earlier storms those thunderheads didn't race off into the cooler air. They seemed anchored in place, and their location in the warm, muggy air meant that we'd have a significant storm soon. That cell became our first chase focus of the day.

We drove south, and inside the van, everyone was quiet. Soon we hit the first precipitation from the storm—large raindrops, followed by nickel-size hailstones. Still, there wasn't yet a single flash of lightning. As we emerged from the rain and hail, I could see a beaver tail on the storm, a long, narrow band of clouds streaming into the base of the storm's updraft. The point where the beaver tail and the storm's updraft base meet is often the specific location where tornadoes form.

Scott pulled the van over on the side of the road so we could unload, watch, and shoot video. The storm's base looked pregnant, bulging downward. The field in front of us was treeless, with short brown and light green grasses, providing a colorful contrast to the dark storm cloud. Ed, from North Carolina, handed his camera to another chaser. "Take my picture, but don't tell me when you're going to do it," he instructed. "I don't want a 'Here I am in front of it' kind of picture. Make it candid, and make me look good."

Suddenly, at 7:18 p.m., a dirt swirl appeared at ground level beneath the lowest part of the storm's base. It danced across the countryside for a minute and then disappeared. "Was that a dirt devil?" Ed asked.

"I think it was a weak tornado," I told him. Scott agreed.

Moments later the dirt swirl reappeared, bigger and taller than last time. In the cloud above, a funnel cloud tried to form. It was tentative at first, and the debris cloud at ground level was faint. Slowly, the debris cloud grew taller, pulled up into the tornado's vortex. Like using paper and charcoal to take a rubbing from a gravestone, the debris made visible what was already there but couldn't be seen. We had a tornado. Number One was officially on the ground as it spun through fields of wheat and hay and the occasional stand of trees.

The funnel cloud continued its descent, a sharply defined cone poking down from the cloud base. Finally, it linked with the swirling tendrils of debris cloud. "Woohoo!" the clients cried out, nearly in unison.

The storm intensified as a bright bolt of lightning struck a few hundred yards away, immediately followed by a thunderous boom. The tornado crossed Highway 23, churning eastward a half mile to our south but still north of east-west Highway 10. As it sucked up soil from an empty field, the funnel—then three hundred yards wide—turned coal black.

We jumped in the van as quarter-size hail and windblown rain pelted us, pinging off the roof of the van, and drove south on 23 and then east on 10 to stay with the twister and watch as it moved across the prairie. "Be careful," I told Scott. "We have to get very close to its path."

"This is the best tornado of the year, folks," I said, turning to the guests sitting in the back of the van. "It rivals any tornado that's been seen this year."

The debris cloud was five times wider than the funnel, and during times when the debris cloud momentarily faded, we could see the funnel cloud nested within it. After thirty-two minutes, though, the twister began to lose strength. It weakened into a slender, elegant elephant trunk and soon thereafter completely dissipated.

But just as the first tornado vanished, a second came into existence, some two miles farther east. We approached it from behind and then stopped to watch it form. Above, the supercell thunderstorm had a classic "Liberty Bell" shape. A ghostly white funnel cloud descended from its base as a brown debris cloud rose up to meet it. It quickly grew from an elephant trunk to a fat stovepipe.

Once again, it was perfectly calm and quiet where we stood, while a monster raged not far away. We all stood watching, filming with our cameras atop tripods, soaking up the beauty of the green wheat fields dancing in the wind with the tornado churning just behind them. The right side of the storm looked as dark as an apocalypse.

The rear–flank-downdraft winds were on their way toward us, and I could hear them coming. The tornado moved southeast, heading toward a distant highway. Even though it was more than a mile from us, I could hear its roar, louder than even the oncoming RFD winds.

Suddenly, a second tornado formed just north of the first, almost a satellite of the much larger primary tornado. "Look! A second tornado!" yelled Ed. Claire just stood in silent disbelief as the first tornado grew even bigger. The storm above looked like a living, breathing creature, morphing before our very eyes. I took a quick moment to step in front of my own cameras and film myself in front of the unbelievable scene. But rain was approaching from behind the twisters, and it was time to pack up and head east to get ahead of the storms and the tornadoes.

To do so we'd need to go east on Highway 10, then jog north on US 281 before going east again on the continuation of Highway 10. But that route would take us directly into the path of the twisters, and I wasn't 100 percent sure we could make it before being cut off by the tornadoes. It was a race; if we didn't get ahead of the storm now, our chase day would be over. We'd forever be behind the storm, trying in vain to catch up with it.

After rushing east on 10, we turned onto US 281 north. "Gun it, man," I told Scott. "We gotta get ahead of this thing. It's right next to us, coming right at us." The van's engine raced as we sped north. "Never mind! Stop! We're not gonna make it," I yelled. "Stop at the top of this hill. I don't want to take a chance." From the back of the van, one of the clients added: "Neither do I."

At the crest of the hill, I saw the base of the tornado just a quarter mile to our north, at the van's eleven o'clock. A strong inflow jet—a band of winds screaming into the base of the tornado—raced across the road ahead of us. I thought twice about driving through it. But we weren't out of danger. The tornado was still heading straight for us, on a collision course with the van.

"Go! Go! Go!" I yelled.

The van sped north, with the tornado seemingly right out the left-hand side of the vehicle. "We have debris!" someone called out. Debris from cornfields and from structures the tornado had already hit were falling from the sky around us and flying through the air. The sky grew dark overhead. I could feel the twister looming, just three hundred yards away, and closing fast.

Scott squeezed as much speed from the van as he dared, and after a few very tense moments, I realized that the tornado was behind us. "We got it," Scott told the van. "We've made it."

"You came close to death there, folks," I added in all seriousness, my heart pounding in my chest.

A half mile north of our brush with death, we stopped to get out and look back. It was relatively peaceful, considering the close call, as we watched the tornado spin, silhouetted in black, while the sun began to set behind it.

Wanting to find a safer location from which to observe, I ordered everyone back into the van. Heading east on the continuation of Highway 10, which had turned into a gravel road, we sped past a farmhouse where a middle-aged couple stood out front, waving their arms, inviting us in to take shelter. Not wanting to stop yet, we continued two miles farther down the road before stopping.

We leaped out of the van and watched as the monster crossed the road we had just driven on—Highway 10. The clients hunkered down by the roadside. "Be ready," I warned. "We've gotta get in the car soon." I could see power poles getting snapped off at ground level and trees getting pulled up by their roots, as the tornado bore down on us again, growing ever closer.

The couple and their farmhouse disappeared behind the funnel, which had widened to nearly a mile across. Even at such a monstrous size, the tornado only moved across the landscape at 20 mph. "This is one of the best tornadoes I've ever seen," I told the group.

As the tornado slowly dissipated around 8:18 p.m., I couldn't resist waxing poetic about what we had just seen. "What a day," I said. "This will go down in infamy in Silver Lining tours." Dirt lingered in the air where the tornado had just been. Chunks of debris, mostly pieces of houses and farms that were hit along the roads we just drove, came falling back down to earth. The field next to us undulated in green, flowing waves from gentle winds flowing into the storm's updraft.

The storm wasn't done yet, however. We moved farther east, to a point just south of Barnard. To our north, another tornado—our fourth—formed and quickly intensified, growing from an initial debris swirl to a full-on tornado in moments. A satellite twister formed just to its south but quickly fizzled, leaving the main tornado to grow in strength. We drove east to get ahead of it.

"Be careful," I told Scott for the second time that day. "It's coming right at us. If this road comes to an end, we're dead."

All of a sudden, the nice gravel road disappeared into a farmer's wheat field, becoming nothing more than a pair of ruts. We couldn't turn around. And with the tornado on our heels, if we stopped or got stuck, we'd be in serious trouble. We continued driving east over the rough ground, bouncing from rut to rut, clients being tossed around in back of the van. None of us—except for Scott in the driver's seat—took our eyes off the tornado, which had become a "wedge," as wide as it was tall.

None too soon, our track reemerged onto a gravel road. We reached a "T" intersection, turned south and evaded the twister. At a small lake just east of Barnard, we stopped to regroup and watch the tornado. The supercell thunderstorm was just across the lake from us, and as we watched the main twister that had chased us through the wheat field, funnel after funnel descended from the cloud base. Each one formed a brief debris cloud and then faded, as if in deference to the biggest tornado. "What a day," I whispered to myself.

We moved north and east one final time to watch the tornado die. The sky was on fire in the west, glowing orange and yellow. The giant tornado spun directly to our west. As it churned, it eclipsed the sun. The tornado continued onward, slowly revealing the sun once again. First just a sliver of light. Eventually, the sun and tornado became like a ring, with the sun a jewel set atop the band of the tornado. With the sun behind, the tornado stood in dark silhouette, with its fringes catching the sun like a true silver lining. Far in the distance towering cumulus clouds and radial rays of light framed the scene.

As it continued to spin, the tornado grew thinner and thinner, like a baker pulling a roll of dough. From where we stood, it was calm and quiet, and no one spoke to preserve the sanctity of the scene before us.

Finally, the tornado roped out until it was too thin to hold itself together. A few final wisps of cloud, and it was over. We were left with nothing but the setting sun behind the towering thunderheads. It was 8:54 p.m.

Initial reports said that only two tornadoes hit the United States that day, but the final official tally ended at nine. Seven of those twisters hit Leola and Barnard. The outcome of our "high risk—high reward" gamble was clear. We had placed our bet, and we had won.

The strongest tornado of the day was an F4 that hit Barnard, with estimated winds between 207 and 260 mph. It was the first F4 ever recorded in Brown County, one of only a few to ever hit South Dakota and one of just five to hit the United States in all of 2002. Power lines were ripped down. A pickup truck was tossed a hundred yards into a stand of trees. Numerous houses were completely destroyed. Yet, thankfully, no one died. Twenty-eight killer tornadoes hit the United States that year, but on June 23, 2002, destruction wasn't measured in human lives. Only dollars and cents.

We spent that night in Sioux Falls, South Dakota. During the drive down Interstate 29, conversation came in spurts. At times we drove in utter silence, people reflecting on what they had experienced. At other times, the chatter went on nonstop, the excitement and released tension pouring forth. I later heard from the couple that had tried to wave us in to their farmhouse as we drove past racing away from one of the twisters. They and their home were spared. Their letter included several photos from the storm. One of those photos showed a large tornado bearing down on their house. In the foreground, our chase van raced east right in front of the twister. It was one moment frozen in time from a chase none of us would ever forget.

CHAPTER SEVEN

Lost and Found

Year by year, tour by tour, storm by storm, I spent more and more time on the road and at the same time grew further and further from my wife, Allison. She saw the marriage imploding—long before she told me about my "backward priorities" in April 1999—and soon I saw it happening, too. But our marriage hadn't always been on the rocks.

We first met in early 1978 in Omaha, Nebraska, during my first assignment with the air force after graduation from high school. To bring in a little extra income, I worked part time as a manager at the Washington Inventory Service. Allison was hired later, and I became her trainer.

It didn't take long for sparks to fly between us. We dated for six months and then moved in together. In November 1978 we were married.

As with most newlyweds, our marriage was great at first. We did everything together and never wanted to be apart. But when the air force transferred me to Germany, Allison got a job working evenings, and I worked days. It was then that our marriage first started to go downhill. By 1985, when I landed in Colorado at Lowry Air Force Base, the marriage had stagnated. We were growing apart.

Both of us looked outside the marriage for fulfillment. Allison found religion. I found storm chasing.

Her life became totally dedicated to Jesus. Allison consulted God before doing anything. She tried thrusting Christianity on me, too, but that only succeeded in pushing me further away. She was "born again." But I was born to chase.

Storm chasing, among other things, was my outlet from a failing marriage. Allison was okay with it at first, never complaining in the years before it became an all-consuming passion for me. But by 1998 things had changed. She grew resentful of the time I spent away from her. She also grew jealous—I sometimes chased with friends, some of whom were college-age men and women. The younger women, in particular, troubled Allison. Although nothing inappropriate ever happened, my time with these "groupies," as Allison called them, was problematic.

Nonetheless, I chased more and more. And the more I chased, the further away I became. I didn't even realize how far I'd drifted until it was too late. Allison tried coming with me to storm chase a few times. It was her attempt to bring us closer together, to spend time as a couple, to save our marriage. But it simply didn't work. My feelings had changed. A marriage is about devoting yourself to a true love. For me that true love was storm chasing. Mother Nature was the woman in my life. Soon there'd be another.

During the 2002 chase season, I spent time some time on an Internet Web site searching for an old high school friend, Danny Edwards. I didn't find Danny, but I did stumble across my old high school sweetheart, Caryn Dolph. Caryn and I met during my sophomore year of high school in Oskaloosa, Kansas. I hadn't seen or spoken to her in twenty-eight years.

She was as surprised to hear from me as I was surprised to see her name on the Web site. A flurry of emails flew back and forth as we caught up on one another's lives. I soon learned that she was living in Vermont, married, with one son, Colton. She revealed that her marriage, too, was on the decline. I told her about storm chasing, and she told me about her horses— her personal passion was showing quarter horses. It didn't take long for our emails to take on a romantic tone as old flames reignited anew.

In late October 2002, after the conclusion of the 2002 chase season, we decided to talk on the telephone. Her voice hadn't changed a bit, and I felt an excited flutter in the pit of my stomach as we chatted. We both secretly worried that we might fall in love with one another.

We decided to meet. I, for one, had to know whether the chemistry we had over the phone would sustain itself in person. In early December we rendezvoused in Springfield, Massachusetts. We talked about goals, hopes and dreams, likes and dislikes, hobbies and passions. Of course, I couldn't help talking about storms, and Caryn shared her excitement to chase with me. When we shared a first kiss, I knew my marriage with Allison was over. Caryn was the woman I wanted to spend the rest of my life with.

Back in Denver I told Allison everything—about Caryn, about the affair. I wanted a divorce. "According to God we will always be married," Allison told me. In the end that comment was as much resistance as she offered. Perhaps she also felt that the marriage couldn't be saved. If storm chasing was the nails in the coffin of my failing marriage, then Caryn was the hammer that drove those nails in. The divorce was finalized in the spring of 2003.

I had sacrificed a lot in my life. Maybe too much. In 2000 I left my old professional life behind and stepped into a new skin as a full-fledged storm chaser. Now, I was giving up another tie to my old life—my marriage. I had wiped the slate clean and was starting from scratch. My children were the only tie to the life I once led.

I was on my own, and times were tough. I was in Colorado, and Caryn—still married—was in Vermont. Money was tighter than it had ever been. Although the video sales and commercial tours were bringing in greater and greater income with each passing season, I still hadn't crossed the threshold into financial self-sufficiency. As much as I loved storm chasing, I still had to keep my bank account in the black. Debtors knocking on my doorstep wouldn't care about the great tornado I saw last week. And while the checks poured in—relatively—during the chase season, during the winter months my financial outlook was about as bleak as the weather. Threat of severe weather and tornadoes: near zero. Income: the same.

To combat the winter financial doldrums, during the previous two winters I went to work for the City of Aurora in Colorado. An old friend, Robert Conway, the city's purchasing manager, hired me. Bob and I knew one another through the air force; we had been stationed together during the 1980s. The city needed a procurement agent, and I was the man for the job. It fit my needs perfectly.

In the world of government purchasing, the busiest months are those at the end of one fiscal year and the beginning of the next. Otherwise known as winter, the dead time for severe storms. The city's overworked employees needed help; hence, Bob brought me on board. It was seasonal work—I was only needed during those busiest months. It filled the income void.

By early March in Colorado, however, clouds start developing each day as the sun heats the High Plains and the Front Range. This shift in weather patterns signifies the coming of spring and the start of the storm-chasing season. Increasingly I spent more time checking weather Web sites and gazing out the windows, longing for my next tornado. The sky was calling to me. As April approached I said goodbye to the city to embrace the storm-chasing season. I would return to the city in the late fall.

It was the perfect world. But would it last? Or could it? The answer came too soon. Budget cuts at the city precluded my coming back on board for the 2002–2003 winter, the same time Allison and I went our separate ways. Suddenly, finances were looking pretty lean. Fortunately, that wouldn't last for long.

Simultaneously with the city's budget cuts, David Gold and I began discussing how we could make Silver Lining Tours better than it already was. I had an idea. All of SLT's tours until that point had been ten-day tours, which basically required clients to take two weeks off from their jobs for a vacation. What if SLT offered a six-day tour that clients could complete in one week of vacation?

We unveiled a host of six-day storm chasing tours based out of Denver, and as the 2003 storm chasing season approached, this new format was clearly our most popular tour. Hopefully, the added revenue from those tours would make up for my lost revenue from the City of Aurora.

With the chase season looming, Caryn's divorce finalized. I asked her to marry me, and without hesitation, she said yes. We were engaged. We made plans for her and Colton to move to Colorado from Vermont later that year, after the conclusion of the SLT tours. But that span of time seemed much too long to wait until I saw her again. She had expressed an interest in joining me storm chasing. I also knew that, thanks to her work with quarter horses, she could drive a thirty-two-foot-long horse trailer and maneuver it on a dime. Would she be my driver for Tours 6 and 7?

Caryn, by then my fiancée, flew out to join me on June 15. It was wonderful to see her, and I also eagerly anticipated the chance to take her chasing. She enjoyed storms, though not with the same fervor that I did. Regardless, driving across the High Plains together in search of tornadoes was my version of paradise. The experience would leave Caryn either wanting more or running in the other direction. I prayed for the former.

The weather pattern for Tour 6, though, was anything but conducive to severe weather. We had sunny skies and little to chase. For Caryn it was a good introduction. She could get comfortable driving the lead van without the stress of severe weather and tornadoes. As was customary when the weather wasn't cooperative, we toured the region's cultural sites—Devil's Tower, Mount Rushmore. It was a meaningful way to pass the time until Mother Nature decided to wake up. On day three, Wyoming offered up a small supercell, and on day five, Nebraska gave us a supercell with a tornado warning. But Tour 6 ended without a single tornado, and we returned to Denver with our proverbial tail between our legs.

Tour 7 started on June 22, 2003. We had two vanloads of clients. Caryn would be with me, driving the lead van. Unlike Tour 6 this tour had a great potential for a serious tornado outbreak. Everyone—Caryn included—was excited.

Day one took us to central Nebraska, where the potential for supercell thunderstorms was good, but the potential for tornadoes was not as promising. Still, it was the best place to be. By midafternoon we had arrived in O'Neill, Nebraska, and did our usual waiting game. Around 4:00 p.m. cumulus towers rose to our south, and off we went to chase the developing storms. As we arrived in Central City, rain started to fall. An intense supercell was nearby to our southwest, moving east. My plan was to head straight south, punching directly through the core of the storm, and then watch for tornadic conditions. I thought the worst of the hail would fall to our southwest, but as we drove south, golf-ball-size hail rattled the van. Caryn didn't even flinch. She was a natural storm chaser.

By the time we emerged from the southern edge of the storm, it was already weakening. That evening we returned to O'Neill for the night and only then learned of the mammoth hail we narrowly avoided. Just four miles west of where we drove through the core of the storm, record-setting hail fell near the town of Aurora. A hailstone measuring 7 inches across plummeted to earth, becoming the largest hailstone to ever fall in the United States. It eclipsed the previous record—the 5.67-inch Coffeyville, Kansas, hailstone from 1970. Thank goodness we hadn't driven south farther to the west. We would have lost every window in the van, and Caryn might have walked off the tour that night!

Day two kept us near O'Neill, where the threat still looked good for severe weather. Alas, the "action" didn't get started until well after dark, when an F4 tornado touched down east of town. We decided not to chase it—it was late, and chasing after dark, when you can't clearly see the tornado you're chasing, adds a whole other element of danger to an already risky game. Instead, our group sat in an open field east of town, watching millions of fireflies flicker off and on, while the tornadic supercell unleashed dramatic lightning bolts in the distance.

On the morning of June 23—day three—it was looking like it was going to be a big day; there was a significant threat of large and destructive tornadoes. The clients were excited and anxious, and so was Caryn, though I thought I saw a hint of concern behind her grin.

By noon we had loaded into the vans and cruised north out of town. Near the South Dakota border, cumulus towers were developing. As we sat and watched, Sean Casey drove up in his TIV—Tornado Intercept Vehicle. It's a car that's been retrofitted with a stronger engine, steel armor plates, and bulletproof glass. Casey's idea was to drive it into a tornado while filming. He hasn't yet put it into a twister, but who knows what will happen if he ever does? Regardless, the TIV has appeared many times on the Discovery Channel, and our clients were excited to see it and get a personal tour.

In early afternoon my weather radio squawked with the severe-weather tones from the National Weather Service. There was a tornado watch from our location northward into east-central and southeast South Dakota. The warm front we were shadowing had moved north into that area, so off we went to stay with the boundary. We blasted north on Highway 281, east on

Highway 18, and then north on Highway 37.

A large thunderstorm was developing along the boundary, and as we raced toward it, the NWS issued a tornado warning. We were still thirty miles from the supercell, but I could clearly see the wall cloud hanging down, hugging the ground. A tornado would form soon, and we had to get there as soon as possible.

Caryn pushed the gas pedal to the floor. Minutes later, as we raced to meet the supercell, a tornado touched down just southwest of Mitchell, South Dakota. We were still twenty miles away, but we could see it morph into an elephant trunk. Farmhouses, silos, and barns whizzed past the van's windows as we closed on the twister.

"Let's get up close and personal with it," I told everyone. "Let's get to know it well."

Ten miles from the tornado, I saw that it continued to strengthen and grow bigger. "That thing is nowhere near dead," I said.

Minutes later another wall cloud descended east of the first, and moments after that, a second tornado touched down. Two tornadoes on the ground at the same time! And they were both Caryn's first. The structure of the storm was jaw-dropping—with its strong circular rotation, it looked like a soda can stacked on top of the twisters.

As we pushed to within five miles of the twin tornadoes, they each roped out and died, fading in the distance behind a pair of silos. "The show is probably nowhere close to being over," I told the van. The van sounded like a busy restaurant on Saturday night—you could hardly hear yourself think over the loud, energetic conversations taking place.

Caryn pulled the van over, and we idled on the roadside north of Mitchell, still on Highway 37. We watched as the storm marched off into the distance and disappeared from view. Flashing red and blue lights caught my attention in the van's side view mirror. A South Dakota Highway Patrol officer pulled up behind us to ask about the weather. As I stood outside the van chatting with the officer, an atomic bomb–looking updraft exploded to the northwest. "That's where your next tornado is going to form," I said, pointing toward it.

I climbed back into the van, and Caryn drove us to a position five miles southwest of the town of Woonsocket. As we cruised along a country road, a funnel cloud began descending from the wall cloud beneath a bell-shaped supercell. Our view darted in and out of trees lining the road. A tornado warning over the radio—issued by the Sioux Falls office of the National Weather Service—broke my concentration. "Take cover now," the robotic voice instructed. In town, tornado sirens blared, urging residents to heed the warning.

"We need to get north and get closer to it," I told Caryn. The tornado seemed to be taking its time to form fully. "You gotta talk it down," I instructed the group.

"Nice cone," someone offered. "Do what tornadoes are supposed to do."

The curving funnel cloud looked like an inverted shark fin or saw blade. As the tornado neared Woonsocket, the condensation funnel cloud nearly reached the ground. "It's definitely a tornado now," I explained. "The funnel's to the ground with a debris cloud."

The tornado was almost directly at our twelve o'clock, and traffic on the highway puttered along at a snail's pace, watching the tornado ahead. "We're going to get so close you may feel and hear it," I said. "Better than the last one, no?"

Clients spilled out of the van to video the scene. The tornado was a big, fat stovepipe, and I ran across the road with my camera in hand, answering clients' questions as I went. Looking into the viewfinder and then pulling my head up to look with my own eyes, I saw an enormous debris cloud. "Oh, I hope it didn't hit Woonsocket," I whispered to myself. "It may have."

The tornado, a homogeneous charcoal gray along its length, was far enough away that it seemed silent and calm where we were positioned, while we remained close enough to see the violent rotation in great detail. I called Caryn over. She had gotten distracted chatting with customers and snapping their pictures with them in front of the tornado. "What do you think?" I asked, gesturing toward the twister.

"Woohoo!" she responded, offering me a thumbs-up and a wide smile.

The tornado churned northeastward, with tons of debris in the air around it. A herd of cattle moseyed across the field in front of us, seemingly oblivious to the destruction sweeping across the landscape in the distance.

One of the men on the tour grabbed my attention over the sound of camera shutters clicking. "Way to go, Roger," he said. "Thanks for getting us here."

Just then Caryn blurted out, "Where's the horses? Let's get married!"

"I suppose we have the tornado. Now we just need the horses," I hollered back. Two people, and two passions, becoming one—we had joked about getting married on horseback in front of a tornado.

"There's cows. Will they work?" one customer chided.

"I'm a justice of the peace; I could perform the ceremony," offered another customer, stepping forward.

I just laughed, knowing Caryn and I couldn't get married then and there. But the exchange did become the talk of Tornado Alley later that season.

"I hope nobody got hurt," I said, returning my attention to the dangerous beast not far from us. The tornado began to rope out, dissipating two miles away from us. As it did, tons of debris still hung in the air, soon to come down. "Don't want to be under that stuff," I continued.

Another cloud lowering began forming to the north. It could be a cyclic supercell, one that reforms and spawns tornado after tornado. While we waited for that to happen, several appreciative clients pulled me aside. "Thank you, sir! You're awesome! You're relentless. What a show!" they offered. Their sincere gratitude humbled me, and I was glad to be able to share my passion with them.

The storm began to disintegrate, perhaps putting too much of itself into the tornado we just witnessed. But to the east another supercell—dark as night—dropped two side-by-side funnel clouds. We drove to the junction of Highways 39 and 6A in Kingsbury County and stopped. "It's a tornado-fest!" I yelled, unable to contain my excitement.

The pair of funnels tried to form tornadoes but to no avail. Yet another wall cloud descended, though, and soon we had another tornado, a long snake that reached out in front of the wall cloud and pawed at the earth. We were far enough away to get out of the van and actually turn off the engine. The storm above rotated like a merry-go-round. Tornado after tornado descended and eventually lifted back into the sky.

"I have a feeling this thing is going to drop a massive tornado," I told the group. As I finished speaking, a customer spoke up: "Oh, my God. Look at it." Multiple vortices danced around one another at the base of yet another twister.

"I wish we were closer to it," I mumbled to myself. But the roads wouldn't allow it. From our location, we would need to go six miles north before heading east, and with the current track of the storm, that route wasn't a possibility.

Instead, we drove to the town of Iroquois and went east from there on U.S. Highway 14. Radar indicated that we were in the "hook echo" of the storm, a hook-shaped extension of the thunderstorm where tornadoes often form. The rain, wind, and hail grew more intense the farther into the hook we drove. As we got east of Iroquois, the rain was so intense we couldn't see. We forged on, however. Just beyond the hook echo, the rains should let up in an area of the storm known as the Bear Cage. But like entering a literal bear cage, heading into it would be flirting with disaster. Our visibility would improve, but there was also a good chance we'd come face to face with a monster twister, with little time to react.

All of a sudden, Caryn cried out, "Oh, my God!"

I looked up from my computer to see the largest tornado I had ever seen in my life, a mile-wide wedge tornado, filled with the flying debris from a town it had just obliterated. "What a tornado!" I yelled.

"Where?" came a question from the back of the van.

"It's everywhere!" Caryn hollered back, waving her hand back and forth across the van's front windshield. The twister filled the entire field of view. It was dangerously close to the road, churning away at our eleven o'clock. We were just a quarter mile away from an F4 tornado, its howling winds at somewhere between 207 and 260 mph.

"Slow down, Caryn," I instructed. The tornado was moving to the northeast, away from us. I wanted to cautiously follow it.

One of the men seated in back chimed in. "I had seen a TV special with you in it, Roger, where someone said that chasing tornadoes is better than sex," he said, referring to David and Sheila Winn and the National Geographic *Twister Tours* special. "I think he may be right!"

"Holy shit," a woman interrupted. "It's not going to turn around and get us, is it?"

We pulled over on the side of the road behind another storm chaser whose car was equipped with a large roof-mounted weather station. A police car sped past with its lights flashing. Small pieces of debris floated to the ground around us, while in the middle of the road, two cars sat parked, their drivers sitting on the hoods, watching in awe. Just ahead—squarely in the tornado's path—was the town of Manchester, South Dakota.

As the tornado rampaged into Manchester, we inched back out onto the road. "We've got power lines down," Caryn cautioned. She began to ask if it was safe to drive over them, but we already had. A guide wire jumped up off the ground and wrapped around the van's front bumper.

"Quick, throw me a coat," I asked the van occupants. I jumped out of the truck, and with the tornado roaring just ahead down the road, I grabbed the wire with my coat-covered hand and unwound it off the bumper so we could continue driving. As I climbed back into the passenger seat, my eyes met Caryn's, and it was then that I realized what I had done. If that power line had still carried electricity, I would be dead.

We crept forward, into what was once Manchester. Propane tanks spewed gas. Trees were completely uprooted or snapped off near the base of their trunks. The few trees that were left standing were stripped of their leaves and branches, leaving only naked trunks behind. Not a single house was left standing undamaged. Many were totally destroyed. *I wonder if anybody got hurt or killed,* I thought.

On the east side of town, we made our way around the debris and downed power lines and onto County Highway 14 north, which confusingly intersected at a right angle with east-west U.S. Highway 14. Already, the first ambulances were arriving on scene in Manchester to look for survivors.

One mile north of town, we stopped to watch the tornado shrink from a wedge into an elephant trunk. It was smaller, but only slightly, and remained very destructive and dangerous. Telephone poles still snapped like matchsticks under the force of its winds. Finally, it roped out into a slender, snaking tornado and dissipated. Before it breathed its last breath, customers snapped their "glory shots"—photos of themselves in front of the monster. I couldn't help, though, but think about what may have happened to tiny Manchester.

My attention immediately refocused on the weather around us, when the storm unleashed another large, multivortex tornado three miles to our east. At first it seemed unsure if it wanted to form or not, the funnel cloud flirting with the idea of descending. Then, it seemed to suddenly make up its mind, and the funnel definitively dropped down, the spike of the funnel stabbing the earth.

We returned to U.S. Highway 14 and sped east toward De Smet, South Dakota, the childhood home of Laura Ingalls Wilder, of *Little House on the Prairie* fame. "That's the beginning, folks," I said, looking north out the left-hand side of the van. "It'll get bigger than this."

A debris cloud grew, while police cars sped past us with their lights flashing and sirens blazing. "Tomorrow's going to be a bitch to match this," one customer blurted out. "This was the Mother Lode."

"Let's just go back to Denver and party the rest of the night!" I joked. The customer was right. This truly was the Mother Lode. We'd seen more tornadoes in one afternoon and evening than most people will see in a lifetime.

This latest tornado formed into the by-then-familiar elephant trunk. "I promise we won't get as close as we did on the last one," I reassured the group.

"Is that the closest you've been?" one woman asked.

"It was close. That's for sure."

Five miles west of De Smet, the tornado roped out. But the storm still had something left to give. We drove into town and then north out of town, staying with the supercell. Another solitary tornado formed, appearing stationary from our vantage point. It churned in place over a fixed point on the horizon.

"It is unbelievable!" someone exclaimed.

One customer pulled out his cell phone. "I'm watching tornado number seven! I'm sitting here watching it! It's my seventh one in the last two hours. I'm in South Dakota. It's unreal. Okay, Dad. I gotta go."

In one final show the storm coughed up two more tornadoes before breathing its last gasp. We turned around and charted a course back to De Smet. Along the way, the chatter in the van spilled over in excitement. What pictures and video did we catch? Like the one customer earlier, many in the group pulled out their phones to call friends and family, unable to contain themselves. They had to share their experience *now.*

By the end of the day, our group incredibly had seen sixteen tornadoes. It was what most storm chasers would consider a career day.

Another storm chaser had a career day of his own. While we chased the storm primarily from the south, traveling north and east to stay with it, my friend, Tim Samaras, came at the storm from the north.

Tim and I met through a mutual storm-chasing friend back in 1998. He worked as an electronics research engineer in Denver and, like me, was fascinated by the twister from the movie *The Wizard of Oz* when he was a kid. In 2002 Tim burst onto the national storm-chasing scene when he did what no storm chaser had been able to do before: place a custom-made probe directly in the path of a tornado. National Geographic took notice and funded Tim to try to do it again in 2003, that time with more and better probes.

Called "turtles," the forty-five-pound probes were squat and made of metal, embedded with a series of sensors to measure a tornado's wind speed and direction, barometric pressure, humidity, and temperature—scientific data that could help forecasters understand tornadoes better and in doing so save lives.

As residents ran for their lives from the F4 Manchester twister, Tim placed himself directly in the line of fire to deploy his probes. With his chase partner, Pat Porter, driving the van, Tim would jump out—with the tornado only one hundred yards away—and set a probe in the road. They'd drive a little farther down the road and release another. But the tornado was virtually on top of them; just eighty seconds after Tim deployed the probes, two of them took a direct hit. He came closer to a monster twister than possibly any other storm chaser ever had . . . without getting sucked into the funnel himself.

Later, when Tim retrieved the probes and downloaded the data, he discovered a one-hundred-millibar drop in barometric pressure, the greatest ever recorded. It was a feat that landed Tim in the *Guinness Book of World Records.* Such a drop in pressure is the equivalent of being plucked from a sunny beach in Florida and being immediately dropped into the center of a Category Five hurricane.

Back in Manchester the town's six residents were in shock. Four were injured, but everyone survived. Considering that their homes were stripped to the foundation by an F4 tornado, it was nothing short of miraculous. Nearly 75 percent of tornadoes are relatively weak F0s and F1s. Just one percent become violent F4s and F5s. However, more than two-thirds of all tornado-related deaths are caused by that one percent. Of the twenty-three tornadoes in 2003 that caused fatalities, most were weaker F3s or below. And of the thirty-seven significant tornadoes of that year, the Manchester F4 ranked the third most violent. By those two measures, the twister should have taken lives, but it didn't. The residents of Manchester were lucky. Or perhaps they had more than luck on their side.

June 24, 2003, was an unfathomable day on so many counts. Initial reports said that 54 tornadoes ravaged the plains, stretched out along a southwest-to-northeast line spanning Nebraska, Iowa, South Dakota, and Minnesota. That initial estimate was later upwardly revised to an official tally of 106 tornadoes. Sixty-seven of those tornadoes occurred in South Dakota, tying the United States record for the most tornadoes to hit one state in a single twenty-four-hour period.

It was an intimidating introduction to tornadoes for sure, but my fiancée, Caryn, handled it like a pro. She later admitted that she was nervous at times—as anyone would be, me included—but she stayed calm when it mattered most. She survived her initiation and became a true storm chaser that day.

She survived June 24 in South Dakota and, undeterred, said she still wanted to marry me. As the 2003 chase season came to a close, we set off for Las Vegas, where we got married in the Little White Chapel on August 13. Her son, Colton, was my best man. For the first time in my life—aside from an impromptu chase years earlier with my then young children, Adam and Nikole—storm chasing became a family affair. We were a modern-day Bonnie and Clyde, and our bounty was tornadoes.

CHAPTER EIGHT

We're Gonna Die!

May 22, 2004. The blare of the bedside alarm clock roused me from my sleep around 5:00 a.m. Out the window of my hotel room at a Holiday Inn near the airport in Oklahoma City, Oklahoma, the eastern sky was just beginning to brighten with the first light of day. For now, the heavens were cloudless. But I expected that to change.

Next to me, Caryn, by then my wife, lay asleep, her golden hair tousled as if by the wild winds of the Great Plains. She was finally resting soundly after my tossing and turning kept her up most of last night.

I slid out of bed and silently headed for the shower, but the weather images on my laptop's computer screen stopped me in my tracks before I ever made it to the bathroom. The forecasts from the Storm Prediction Center were calling for strong to violent tornadoes to our north, along the Kansas-Nebraska border. Butterflies filled my stomach. Only one thought crossed my mind: getting north, quickly.

I rushed through the shower, grabbed my laptop and cameras, plucked the van keys off the nightstand, and leaned over to kiss Caryn tenderly on the forehead. She stirred ever so slightly, and I slipped out of the room. It was just 6:00 a.m.

Down the hall, I knocked on the door to Tim Kozier's room. Tim, in his mid-forties with a robust mustache and a receding hairline, was my new van driver for the chase season. He'd seen me on storm-chasing television shows and wondered if he could drive for me. After test driving during some chases before the start of the season, he officially signed on and had been with me for only two weeks. He was a great driver, but with relatively little chasing experience, he panicked easily when the weather got rough.

Tim had seen the same weather forecasts I had.

"What a day this is shaping up to be," he said with a hint of concern. "I don't know whether to be excited or scared. Could be some big tornadoes."

"I know. I can't believe the forecasts. If it goes, it will be a wild ride! Let's grab our goodies and get moving," I said, tossing him the van keys. "Everything is pointing to the Kansas-Nebraska border north of Concordia. This is one day [when] we don't want to be a minute late."

"I'll get the van," he said distractedly. Then, almost as an afterthought: "Boy, am I nervous."

"I hear you. I didn't sleep worth a crap last night. Was up most of the night thinking about what could go wrong."

"You told me it'd be like that on the big days," Tim said.

"Now we just have to get up there and into position before all hell breaks loose."

"And we have to stay safe," he added.

"You can trust me, Tim," I reassured him. "We've already been through a few tornadoes together this year. Have I ever gotten you into a place where we couldn't escape? Let's rock and roll!"

I walked to the hotel lobby to find everyone waiting. "Everyone" in this case was made up of five paying clients who joined Tim and me on this chase. They'd all chased with me before—Jacquie Kukuk: a slight-framed business owner in her early fifties from Yuma, Arizona, the social butterfly on tours; Adam Fleischer: a twenty-year-old college student from Midland, Texas; Tim Lamoille: an almost-six-foot, two-hundred-pound construction supervisor from Levittown, New York, who buys anything storm related as souvenirs from tours; Richard Mason: a stereotypical British gentleman from London with an insatiable thirst for cigarettes and severe storms; and Colton Hull: my fourteen-year-old stepson, overcoming his fear of storms ever since a lightning bolt struck a little too close to home when he was living in Vermont before Caryn and I married. We all exchanged early-morning pleasantries and shook off the fatigue of a short night's sleep.

Tim, meanwhile, pulled the van around front. Our motley crew stumbled out the hotel's front doors and loaded up. Our destination was four hundred miles distant, and we had no time to lose. We merged onto I-35 North and set a course for Concordia, Kansas.

We weren't supposed to chase that day. May 22 was to be a rest day between commercial tours. The first tour of the season had ended a day earlier, on May 21, and Tour 2 was to begin two days later on May 23. But throughout the day on May 21, the weather conditions over the central Great Plains were morphing into a setup I had seen before, a combination that could produce a classic tornado outbreak, with northern Kansas and southeastern Nebraska at the epicenter.

A low-pressure system moved eastward over the Rocky Mountains and onto the plains. Ahead of that system, a second low-pressure system tracked along the Kansas-Nebraska border, following a warm front that extended east into southern Iowa. Meanwhile, subtropical moisture raced northward from the Gulf of Mexico, destined for the epicenter. Their combined effects made the atmosphere over Concordia, Kansas, incredibly unstable, and it looked as if the entire region would explode with tornadic supercell thunderstorms by mid- to late afternoon on May 22.

The Storm Prediction Center issued a high-risk alert for severe thunderstorms and tornadoes. In the storm-chasing world, that's as good as it gets. It was a classification reserved only for those forecasts that called for a potential tornado outbreak.

From the SLT office in Texas, David Gold called customers who were scheduled to chase with us on Tour 2, asking if they could arrive a day early. May 22 was going to be spectacular, he said. Most couldn't adjust their schedules, but five could. They trickled into Oklahoma City throughout the night of May 21.

Caryn was to have been the lead van driver for Tour 2, with me navigating and forecasting. But we agreed that she would stay behind on May 22 and wait for the rest of the chasers to arrive. I wished she could have come with me, but Tim would fill in for her as my driver instead.

While we waited for the five clients to arrive, Caryn and I sat in our room, but I wasn't much company. On the eve of a predicted major weather event, as I expected May 22 to be, it's nearly impossible for me to focus on anything but the weather. I check and recheck the data incessantly, making sure I haven't missed some slight change in conditions that would affect our plan for tomorrow. I always want to chase the best storm of the day. There's nothing worse than choosing the wrong storm to chase or choosing the wrong target chase area, and then later that day hearing reports from other chasers about the "other" storm I should have seen but didn't.

I sat at the computer, waiting, anticipating, contemplating, forecasting. Finally, sometime close to 1:00 a.m., I fell into a fitful asleep. Tornado dreams raced through my mind. In my dreams, as in real life, I want to get close to these beasts. I want to experience their winds. To hear the sounds. To feel the rumble in my chest. To see the storm develop and evolve. To experience a monster storm is to experience a living, breathing, destructive creature. They are alive.

Then, feeling as if I had just fallen asleep, the alarm jolted me from my dreams. It was time to go.

Our crew of seven raced northward on Interstate 35. The van was eerily quiet. Some of the customers were excited. Many were nervous, anxious, apprehensive. They worried that we might make a mistake and get too close to, or worse yet, be caught in, a tornado. Some were sad, thinking about what might happen should a big tornado actually hit someone's home. Would someone be killed that day?

"This is a day all storm chasers dream about," I said, turning around to face them from the front passenger seat. "It looks like all the ingredients are coming together to produce a significant tornado outbreak. I reviewed the data earlier this morning, and let me tell you, it looks scary."

We reviewed the weather ingredients that together could produce the type of storms we were hoping for. Moisture. Instability. Shear. Lift. As we sped north, the high-risk warning from the Storm Prediction Center was still in place. It called for a 60% chance of hail larger than two inches in diameter and a 25% chance of strong to violent tornadoes. I'd never seen it that high before.

MARCH 28, 2007. Texas panhandle. This large F3 tornado occurred early in the season and was the most photogenic tornado of the year.

MAY 13, 2009. Kay County, Oklahoma. The intense close-up tornado was witnessed by my tour group. We were pummeled by tennis-ball-sized hail during this photo.

JUNE 26, 2008. North Central South Dakota. A gorgeous rotating supercell that produced several tornadoes. The tornado and rotating wall cloud can be seen above a herd of horses.

MAY 29, 2008. Near Elmwood, Nebraska. A violent supercell thunderstorm that produced grapefruit-sized hail and would later drop a tornado that damaged the city of Kearney.

JUNE 16, 2008. Southwest Oklahoma. A photogenic and intense high-precipitation supercell. The storm produced one tornado and lots of hail.

JULY 19, 2008. North Dakota. This was one of the longest-lived supercells I have ever witnessed. It was alive for nearly twelve hours and would travel 400 miles.

JULY 3, 2007. Kit Carson County, Colorado. One of nearly a dozen tornadoes produced from a single storm. I was able to watch the tornado from as near as 300 yards away.

MAY 10, 2009. Davis Mountains, Southwest Texas. An extremely photogenic supercell thunderstorm that produced baseball-sized hail. It forced us to seek shelter with the U.S. Border Patrol south of Marathon.

JUNE 24, 2003. Manchester, South Dakota. This F4 tornado was one of the most violent to occur that year. It destroyed the entire town (which has not been rebuilt) and was the finale to a day in which we saw sixteen tornadoes.

"My job is to get us into position for the first tornadic beast of the day and then chase until we can't chase anymore," I continued. "The storms will only be moving at about 30 mph, so we should be able to stay with the supercells as they develop. We'll be able to get pretty close if we want to."

Colton looked at me. "How close?"

"As close as we want to. Within a few hundred yards."

The van erupted with excitement, laughing, clapping, and cheering. Sensing an underlying nervousness behind everyone's superficial excitement, though, I quickly added: "I promise you we will stay safe and out of harm's way." Previous seasons had yielded their share of very close calls, and I didn't need to get any closer.

Around 9:00 a.m., we crossed into Kansas from Oklahoma and two hours later pulled into Salina, Kansas, roughly eighty miles south of our target chase area. There we stopped to refuel, and everyone used the restrooms and grabbed snacks. From there on out, we'd be in "sipping mode." Care in food and fluid intake are crucial when you're chasing a big storm—you do not want to stop for a bathroom break because someone drank or ate too much. Tornadoes wait for no one. And successfully chasing depends as much on pacing your fluid and food intake as it does anything else.

I looked at the data again. Our plan was still on track. Conditions were intensifying precisely where I thought they would, and it was just approaching noon! How volatile was the atmosphere going to get as the day wore on?

As we got back on the road after our stop, Salina faded from view behind us, and we pushed onward toward Concordia. My cell phone rang; it was David calling from his office in Houston, Texas.

"Roger, I'm fully expecting a significant tornado outbreak," he said. "The atmosphere is getting well focused in your area. I'd look for rapid supercell thunderstorm development just to your west." On this tour David used his considerable meteorological savvy to serve as a nowcaster, someone who stays back in an office, constantly reviewing updated data and calling us with critical information and recommendations.

Around 2:00 p.m. we arrived in Concordia. Based on David's advice and on the updated computer models, I decided to continue north into extreme southern Nebraska and then head west. We followed U.S. Highway 81 to Chester, Nebraska, then turned west on Highway 136 with our sights set on Beaver City, a tiny rural town of six hundred on the border of historic Pawnee and Sioux territory, first settled by pioneers in the late 1860s and early 1870s. Aside from sitting squarely in the heart of tornado country, Beaver City had two modest claims to fame: Dr. Frank A. Brewster, known as the world's first flying doctor, and Edwin Perkins, the creator of Kool-Aid, had both lived there.

As we drove toward Beaver City, David's predictions came true before our eyes. Several thunderstorms developed along the northern edge of the low-pressure system where atmospheric lift was strongest, and some of them quickly became severe. My plan was to target the southernmost storm for our chase.

David rang through on my phone again.

"That southernmost storm is becoming a monster. Get west as quickly as you can, and catch it," he said. "The air surrounding that storm is looking like the most volatile in the country!"

As we crossed into Furnas County, we turned onto a rural road lined with telephone poles and views of farm fields and waves of grain that continued uninterrupted to the horizon. The storm stood before us, its structure by then well formed. My eyes traced a path from earth to sky, taking it all in. Strong winds were screaming into the base of the storm and racing upward in the storm's updraft. A wall cloud—the rotating, localized lowering of the cloud base beneath the rain-free portion of a thunderstorm that often precedes tornado development—was rapidly forming. In the vault region of the storm where updrafts were strongest and the largest hailstones would be falling, intense lightning strafed through the clouds. And in the cloud's uppermost reaches, the anvil—the topmost portion of the storm where the updraft has pushed the cloud into the jet stream—had become crisply defined, extending to the east. The storm had become a full-fledged supercell—a severe thunderstorm with an intense, long-lived, rotating updraft known as a mesocyclone—and it meant business.

Seven miles east of Beaver City, we stopped briefly to watch the storm. To the southeast, the storm was dumping hail, obscuring our view of the ground. We were too far away to see if there was a tornado, and we pressed onward, passing the occasional farmhouse. It was 5:00 p.m., and we were fifteen minutes from reaching Highway 283, where we planned to turn south to get a closer view.

Then, suddenly, a tornado was about to form. On the horizon a finger of cloud descended from the base of the supercell thunderstorm. The van grew quiet as we all waited for the weather to unfold before our very eyes. Then, at 5:09 p.m., with the funnel cloud reaching halfway to the ground, a debris cloud began rising from the earth. "We have a tornado!" I yelled. "Do you see it?"

We sped past silos en route to a closer view of the developing tornado, but it proved short-lived. The touchdown was brief, and the funnel cloud retreated up into the base of the storm minutes later.

Having passed through Beaver City, we stopped again, then on the town's west side. "Oh, my God. What a storm! What structure!" I could hardly contain my excitement. "Let's get up here, stop, and just watch this thing," I told Tim. "It is a freaking beast. Just stop here."

Between the horizon and the base of the storm, the sky glowed a fiery orange. The base of the supercell, silhouetted against the sun, appeared coal black. A dirt plume caused by the rear-flank downdraft cut across the farm fields directly beneath the storm. "Go ahead and get out. Have fun," I told everyone. "But we may get another tornado. Remember that when we yell we gotta go when the times comes."

The seven of us spilled out onto the roadside to photograph the storm again as it churned across the countryside directly toward us. A steady wind blew in our faces. The van's engine continued running, and we left the doors open, ready to jump back in at a moment's notice. Above the sound of the wind in our ears, the dashboard dinged constantly, reminding Tim that the keys were still in the ignition. "What an absolutely monstrous supercell," I offered. "This thing is phenomenal."

Thunder echoed constantly. Suddenly, an intense bolt of lightning struck just a few hundred yards away and sent us scrambling back into the van. Tim moved us a bit farther to the east, keeping us ahead of the storm and in full view of the developing weather. We stopped again, but with fierce lightning flashing all around, only a few of us clambered out of the van. The wall cloud had begun to rotate much more rapidly. Multiple vortices reached down from the base of the cloud and danced around one another. Soon, they merged into a single truncated cone, a funnel cloud extending part way down from the base of the thunderstorm about two miles to our south. It was 5:20 p.m.

"What are we looking at?" Adam asked.

"We've got a funnel cloud about a third of the way down to the ground and getting fatter," I answered. "It's spinning like a top."

We continued east, keeping pace ahead of the storm and the funnel cloud. My gaze was fixed out the window to the south. "This is gonna be a monster tornado," I said to no one in particular. "Here it comes! A tornado!"

The truncated cone, which had been hovering at about one-third height from the ground, suddenly started to descend. Tim pulled over onto the side of the highway so we could watch. "Just look at it, folks," I said. We could clearly see the funnel twisting and rotating fiercely. A pair of birds flew across our view, getting themselves out of harm's way. In the foreground a small patch of trees that obscured our view of the ground started to sway violently in the growing wind.

"We're going to have to move to a place where we can get good visibility of the base of it," I told Tim. "It's coming down." The funnel, meanwhile, continued to descend as if being extruded from a mold, its slender length reaching for the ground like a snake.

"Head down the road a quarter mile, turn around, and let's watch it," I continued. "But be ready to vacate. This thing is only about a mile from us."

The funnel continued to grow thicker, now reaching more than halfway to the ground. The base of the funnel had tendrils of cloud reaching and spiraling toward the ground. A large debris cloud formed at ground level and swirled violently. "Oh, my God. Look at that thing," someone said.

I turned to Tim: "Pull us a little farther forward to get us away from any power lines."

"It's coming right at us," he said as the van crept forward.

"Yeah, it is. Just a couple of minutes. We're fine here for now," I said. "Do not move until I say so, please."

A sliver of funnel cloud reached for the ground, and the main funnel followed quickly behind it, sucking more and more air up into the maelstrom. Finally the funnel cloud touched down, curving to the ground like a giant elephant's trunk, all the while moving closer and closer to our position.

"Back us up carefully," I said hurriedly. "Back us up, please." Then, turning to the five awestruck clients in the back of the van: "You're less than a mile from a very strong tornado, folks."

Tim was quickly growing worried. "Don't go anywhere yet. Not until we see debris in the air," I told him. The tornado continued to approach us, marching east from right to left. "If you want to be close, you're there, buddy," I said to Colton. He responded simply with a maniacal laugh, motivated in part by having faced his weather fears but also, I'm sure, from being scared witless with the tornado bearing down on us.

"Back us up along the side of the road, and be ready to make a getaway," I told Tim. "That thing is about a half a mile from us." Tim gingerly inched us backward down the road but not nearly fast enough for my comfort. "There's nobody behind us. Back us up down this road a ways, please," I said with growing urgency.

Rain started to fall as Tim continued backward down the road. "Keep going! We're not in harm's way here," I said. "The tornado is going to pass south of us."

The debris fan grew to massive proportions, five times the width of the tornado itself. Dirt and trees swirled in the air around the base of the growing beast. "We're going to get pummeled here, but I don't care," I said, more to myself than to anyone riding in the van.

"There's debris in the air, all around the left side of the tornado. It hit some structure over there," someone said. The tornado had slammed into several farmhouses, and pieces of fence, roof, and siding were ripped into the air, hundreds of yards off the ground. Aside from that solitary comment and a couple of oohs and aahs, the van was almost silent, with everyone awed and dumbstruck at what they saw.

The entire base of the supercell thunderstorm wrapped and rotated around the upper reaches of the tornado, which was rapidly growing brown as it steadily sucked up more topsoil and debris, with its bottom quickly becoming black. It no longer narrowed as it reached the ground. It was becoming huge, thickest at the top and bottom, with a slight waist at its middle, like a fattened hourglass. It had become what storm chasers call a stovepipe.

As the tornado churned east at 15 mph, the debris cloud grew so large that it no longer had defined boundaries, completely obscuring the base of the tornado with the earth swirling in the air around it. Even at this massive size, the beast continued to grow before our very eyes. "It doesn't get much better than that," I said.

"No, it doesn't," was all Jacquie could offer from the back seat.

Suddenly we started to hear the deafening thud of hail slamming into the roof of the van. There was so much debris around the base of the tornado, and the twister was so close, it looked like a sandstorm coming at us.

"Go ahead," I said, turning to Tim. "We've got an RFD jet coming at us from the south. We've gotta get moving."

Tim floored it, and the van's engine revved as we accelerated away from the approaching tornado. "Go east three or four miles. We'll get beyond it and then sit and watch it again," I told him. It was 5:35 p.m.

As we sped along the road, the tornado started to weaken and grow smaller, but we weren't out of danger yet. Even as tornadoes weaken in the final moments of their lives, they can still be quite violent. And then there is the debris—trees, fences, pieces of houses—that will come crashing back to earth after their violent ride in the funnel.

The twister roped out—the final stage of a funnel cloud before it disappears, seemingly into thin air—but the debris cloud on the ground remained strong. "Oh, shit! You'd better keep us moving, please," I suddenly said to Tim. "You gotta go quick. We've gotta move, buddy."

The debris cloud tore through a farm field right alongside the road, approaching us fast. It was right on top of us, so close I was forced to crane my neck back just to look at it. Debris filled the roadway and continued to come crashing down around us. Lightning flashed all around. We raced to get in front of the debris cloud, and a huge cloud-to-ground lightning strike rocked the countryside just ahead of us.

Then, as quickly as the violence had borne down on us, it ceased. The wind died down; the dust slowly settled. Mother Nature's blender had stopped, at least for now. But the day was far from over.

We drove east of Beaver City, ahead of the supercell, and regrouped. Conditions looked ripe for more tornadoes to form. We spilled out of the van into an empty school parking lot and looked back at the storm we had just experienced. The group was in disbelief at what they had witnessed. It's not often that you get to view a strong tornado from less than half a mile away. In many ways, it's like observing a grizzly bear in the wild: you can get close, and you can watch it, but if you're not careful, it can kill you.

I looked up at the storm we had just been chasing. It was dying, the victim of its own occlusion. A strongly rotating supercell storm that spawns a big tornado has an incredible amount of rotational wind. When that wind wraps around the backside of the storm, it literally cuts the storm in half. The rear half of the storm—the half that gave birth to the tornado—will slowly fade away, occluded. The forward half of the storm, however, if conditions are right, can recycle into a new supercell thunderstorm capable of producing more tornadoes.

Gazing skyward, I saw a new supercell forming ahead of the dying one. I expected it to take another twenty to thirty minutes for the storm to fully regenerate. We jumped into the van as rain started to fall and headed east toward the tiny town of Orleans. "This thing should recycle and do it again," I said to the group. "And if it's going to produce another tornado, it's going to do it right..."

I was in the midst of finishing my thought when I noticed a short funnel flirting out of the base of the cloud. "It may never touch down, but if it does, it will touch down in those trees in the distance," I said, pointing to a clump of cottonwoods toward the horizon. "Okay, when I tell you to get out of here, do," I told Tim. "It's getting really close. It's trying. Let's not go yet, though."

We waited eagerly to see what would develop. A small debris cloud formed near the clump of trees, but that was all we would see. "I don't think it's going to do it," I said, and we continued east out of the rain toward Orleans.

We stopped along the roadside again, and Jacquie pointed to the sky just to our northwest. Yet another funnel cloud was descending from the storm, and then to my surprise, at 6:11 p.m. a debris swirl formed on the ground just a quarter mile to our north. The funnel cloud soon spanned the distance from cloud to ground, becoming a ghostly white elephant trunk. Its slender length made a kink at midheight, where the tornado's funnel made a hard left turn before spiraling to the ground.

"Wow!" Jacquie mustered. "That is close!"

Just a few hundred yards to our north, on the edge of Orleans, the tornado crossed the road we had just been driving on. I started to get out of the van to video the scene when hail suddenly sent me back inside. "Uh-oh! I'm about to get hammered," I said, to which everyone in the van let out a chuckle.

The hail quickly became extreme, with marble- and golf-ball-size hail falling all around us, and the occasional baseball-size behemoth. Rain and wind lashed at the field of grain next to us. Just to our north the tornado had grown huge and was moving east-southeast on a collision course with downtown Orleans and us.

"All right, Tim. Take us around. We've gotta go! We've gotta go!" I said.

We sped through a residential neighborhood of single-story homes, slab driveways, and cars. "Just keep going!" I implored Tim. "This thing may be hitting the north side of Orleans."

The debris fan now was just a few hundred yards north of the highway. "Look at it! It's very close!" I exclaimed. Tim's window was open so I could film the tornado to our north as we sped east. He kept craning his neck to look out the open window at the storm. "Holy shit!" he said.

"Tim, can you drive?" I chided. Tim refocused on the road ahead and sped us through Orleans and back into open country, where we stopped alongside a wheat field for me to get out and shoot a very quick video.

"We've gotta floor it, Roger!" Tim yelled out to me. The tornado was just two hundred yards away and approaching fast. As I jumped back into the van, I watched a farmhouse get hit and destroyed, its entire roof and other debris hurled into the sky above us in the adjacent wheat field.

"You gotta go! Fast! Or we're gonna die!" I yelled. "I'm not joking!"

"It's floored," Tim said as we peeled away from the tornado. Then suddenly he added: "I can't see! There's all water inside the windshield."

With the driver's window down while we drove and filmed earlier, rain and hail blown in by the wind had obscured Tim's view out the front window. "We gotta keep going," I told him with growing urgency while I searched for a towel to clean off his window.

Once we were half a mile east of the tornado, we stopped briefly to look back. The tornado, still heading east-southeast, crossed the highway—Route 89—just as a car came racing out of a driveway in front of it. I couldn't believe it. How could that driver not have seen the tornado?

We continued east toward the town of Alma but first had to head south for one mile on Highway 183 before we could pick up our next eastbound road, Highway 136. It was an escape route that would keep us moving dangerously close along the tornado's projected path, and we needed to move fast to stay ahead of it.

But as we turned south onto Highway 183, a large group of amateur and professional storm chasers pulled out onto the road ahead of us. The sudden mess of cars on the road caused the traffic to come to a complete stop. We were stuck, and the tornado was only a quarter mile away and closing in. A rush of panic and adrenaline filled my brain. We had no way to escape the destructive tornado.

A million ideas raced through my mind in a matter of seconds as I debated our plan of action. Were we going to die? Should we get out of the van and run into a ditch? Should we try to run to shelter in someone's farmhouse? Before I had a chance to make a decision, traffic started to move again, just as the tornado roped out above our heads, less than a hundred yards out the front window of the van. It was a narrow and lucky escape, and we stopped for a moment in the rain and hail to watch the tornado breathe its last breath in the sky above.

"It's gone. It's gone, folks," I said through a heavy sigh of relief. We picked up our eastbound road—Highway 136—and drove to Alma as debris fell from the sky around us. At last out of danger, I sat back and gazed out the window at the quaint town. First settled by a group of forty pioneers in 1870, Alma "exploded" in growth in 1880 with the construction of the Burlington and Missouri Railroad, ballooning the town's population to three hundred. Not long after, the first school was organized in a sod house, and the town continued to grow slowly but surely. Today, the community of twelve hundred is a picturesque image of quality of life in small-town America and for us a safe haven from the danger we had just left behind.

Then, passing through the oasis of town and heading again into the wide-open spaces of the Great Plains, we left the storm behind us as it weakened.

Farther to the east, I spied another storm that looked very explosive. David called again from Houston. The storm to our east was quickly becoming a monster supercell, he said. We should race to catch it. Tim took us east to Chester, Nebraska, but we couldn't stay with the storm, and we had to abandon it as our chase target. Only later would we learn what that storm became and what we missed.

We paused in Chester and watched the skies to our south, over north-central Kansas. Thunderstorms were rapidly forming there, and soon enough, at 7:50 p.m., my weather radar picked up a severe-thunderstorm warning for Republic County, Kansas, just twenty miles away. The storm was tracking northeast at 40 mph, headed straight for our location.

We cruised south from Chester on U.S. Highway 81 and crossed into Kansas, then turned west toward the town of Republic. The storm, clearly visible ahead of us, looked like a classic "mothership" supercell, an indication that the storm was rotating rapidly. Lightning streaked through the clouds almost continuously, and the clouds themselves looked like a stack of plates ascending to the heavens.

I had Tim pull over on the side of the road, long before we reached the rain, so we could sit and simply admire the storm. The supercell hovered ahead of us, its clouds colored a deep slate blue. Around the base of the rotation, cauliflower-like white puffs of cloud masked the setting sun somewhere behind. It was calm—there was almost no wind where we stood. While we saw intense lightning, we heard no thunder. The storm itself seemed distant, though in fact it loomed not far off.

A dog ran up alongside the van from a nearby farmhouse and started yelping and crying. He seemed to sense that something bad was about to happen and didn't want to be there when it did. "Go home, buddy," one of the men called out from inside the van.

A tornado suddenly appeared from the supercell. It was shaped like a pencil and stabbed at the ground hard when it descended. "Get up on the hill, and just stop and watch it," I told Tim. "It'll come right at us." Two short minutes later, however, it was gone.

The storm continued its march out of the southwest, and soon, at 8:15 p.m., as the sun was beginning to set in earnest with the sky turning a dark pink, it gave birth to another tornado. A debris cloud swirled up from beneath the wall cloud. "It's trying hard," Richard called out. "Come on. Here it comes!"

One vortex formed, followed by another and then another. Wisps of funnel cloud reached for the ground as the three small vortices revolved around one another. It was a spectacular sight. The debris cloud and the funnels flirted with one another, glancing their tendrils of cloud off one another in a midair dance. Then the trio of funnels merged into a single tornado, churning across the countryside for eight long minutes as we watched in awe, with our cameras recording it all from their homes atop a forest of tripods. "This thing's not done yet," I told everyone, referring to the supercell.

When the tornado finally roped out, lingering in the sky beneath the old wall cloud, we headed east and north, reversing our course back to Chester, in order to stay with the storm. As we reached Chester the radar image on a dashboard-mounted computer screen between the driver and passenger seats showed a strong signature. A supercell thunderstorm had exploded in the last fifteen to twenty minutes, and we weren't far behind.

As we raced along the highway, another elephant-trunk tornado touched down, but we couldn't afford to give it notice. If we didn't keep moving, the chase would be over as the supercell raced away from us to the northeast.

Night had fallen, and we drove through the darkness beneath the base of a huge supercell, illuminated only by the streaks of lightning that ripped through the cloud. "The show's probably over by this time," I told the van. "But you never know."

We turned east onto Highway 136 to stay with the storm, losing ground on the supercell as we ran out of good roads. As the storm moved off into the distance, it gave us one last tornado, the ominous silhouette visible to us only when lightning flashed far behind it. It was a sort of farewell at the end of an incredible day.

It was 9:00 p.m., and we were all tired and completely drained from a day none of us would soon forget.

In all, seventy tornadoes were confirmed that day, with reports suggesting as many as eighty-three, leaving a swath of destruction that stretched from far eastern Wyoming all the way into Michigan. The biggest tornadoes and the most intense destruction, by far, however, were concentrated in southern Nebraska and central Iowa. Hail as large as grapefruits and softballs fell in many areas. Trees were stripped of their bark and limbs. Another storm chaser near the Fillmore-Thayer County line reported seeing cows flying through the air—the next morning a farm four miles north of Alexandria reported their herd of twenty to twenty-five cattle missing.

But worst of all was the tornado that decimated the town of Hallam, Nebraska. It was born from the supercell we chased toward Chester but weren't able to catch. The twister descended from the sky and quickly grew to proportions seldom seen before or since. The funnel cloud at times was an unimaginable two-and-a-half miles wide—a new record for the largest known tornado—and the tornado was rated an F4 on the Fujita Scale of Tornado Intensity, with winds estimated between 207 and 260 mph. Houses were ripped from their foundations or plucked from the face of the earth entirely, leaving only a set of concrete stairs that led to the front door on a plot of land that once held a home. One person was killed. Ninety-five percent of the homes in Hallam were seriously damaged. Fifty-five railroad cars were derailed. The tornado stayed on the ground for an amazing fifty-four miles, completely leveling 158 homes and causing $160 million in damage, including $60 million in crop damage. One hundred cattle and fifty hogs were lost, and 150,000 acres of cropland sustained significant damage. The Hallam twister was one of twenty deadly tornadoes in 2004. Of the twenty-eight significant twisters that year, the May 22 Hallam monster was the most violent.

Reports of such damage trickled in as we drove south and east toward Olathe, Kansas, south-southwest of Kansas City, where we planned to meet up with a second van carrying the rest of the tour group who couldn't make it for May 22. Along the way we stopped at a drive-in for dinner, at Richard's request, in downtown Marysville, Kansas. After a long day of chasing, it was finally time to eat some real food and digest what we had experienced that day. For hours we'd been running on little more than our adrenaline and excitement, and as we all came off our storm-chasing highs, we suddenly realized how starved we actually were.

"Wow! What a day! I can't believe the luck we had," I said as we walked up to the window to place our orders.

A local walked over, curious about our incessant jabbering.

"We saw at least five tornadoes today!" Adam told the man. "Want to see the video of it?" He pulled his camcorder out and cued up the video. "Look how big that tornado is!" he said, with his excitement boiling over. "Wow! We were really close!"

Richard looked at me. "Was that the best day you've ever had on a tour?"

"It's in the top ten; that's for sure!" I responded. "For sheer numbers other days rank top. But for intensity it's right up there."

"I loved it," he said through a wide grin. "I had been waiting for years to see that." A compliment, to be sure.

Late that night we trickled into Olathe, and Caryn and I finally reunited after the long day. The customers in her van were understandably disappointed, but the next day looked to be a high-tornado-potential day for Illinois, just to our east. Even so, it would be difficult to top the day we had just experienced.

Exhausted, we checked in to our respective hotel rooms. Caryn and I settled in and caught up on the day's events. Then I set my computer on the hotel-room desk and logged on to the Internet. I pulled up a new set of weather data from the Storm Prediction Center and reviewed the computer models. I made my predictions for the next day and sometime late that night fell into a fitful sleep of tornado dreams.

CHAPTER NINE

Probe Launch

The end of the 2004 chase season came all too soon, and before I knew it it was the middle of winter. While other people brighten up with holiday cheer, storm chasers fall into a fit of depression. Winter is the saddest time of year. There are no storms to chase, no distant sounds of rumbling thunder, no towering cumulus clouds or lightning knifing across the skies. There are only short days with cold, gray, dreary skies. From a storm chaser's perspective, it doesn't get much gloomier than that.

Many times, chasers fall victim to what is known as SDS or Supercell Deprivation Syndrome. It typically sets in sometime early in the winter and by the New Year has dragged a storm chaser into a bottomless pit of despair. Knowing that months may pass before the next storm to chase, your inner being withers to a sad, lonely version of its former self.

The treatment is universal. Storm chasers spend countless hours in front of the television, watching DVDs from other chasers and of their own past chases. Each video provides a temporary "fix." But it's just that: temporary. Inevitably, you need another and then another.

Chasers reminisce, drifting back into their own memories. Or they watch the skies, searching in vain for any sign that the weather pattern may be shifting. They prowl the Internet, looking for new gadgets to buy. They do anything they can to pass the time until storm-chasing season returns. Anything, that is, except fix their vehicles. A broken windshield, sure. But hail dents and other body damage? Never. Each chase vehicle's dimpled paint job is like a personal signature that tells the story of a chaser's past seasons: Nebraska 2004, Iowa 2002, South Dakota 2000.

But if one single event provides a better fix than any other, it's the National Storm Chasers Convention, held in Denver, Colorado. By February 2005 it had become the most popular event of its kind in the country. Dr. Greg Forbes of The Weather Channel was the keynote speaker. Forbes had studied under Dr. Ted Fujita, developer of the Fujita Scale of Tornado Intensity. The three-day weekend included social events, breakfasts, dinners, and one-and-a-half days of renowned speakers.

The convention's beginnings, however, were much more humble. Perhaps it's because misery loves company. Or because storm chasers could use a support group. Or because storm chasers feed off one another's anticipation and excitement and motivation. Whatever the reason, we started getting together informally in 1998.

In January of that year Tim Samaras invited a small group of fellow storm-chasing friends to come to his house in Lakewood, a suburb of Denver. Only six to ten people showed up. My son, Adam, and I, were two of those people, invited by a friend of a friend. Tim and I immediately hit it off with our mutual interest in storm chasing. Videos on a big-screen television in the living room, appetizers in the kitchen, and beer and pizza that night rounded out that first year's "convention."

In 1999 Tim decided to do it again. Only this time he cast a wider net. We sent invitations to email listservs and posted notices on Internet bulletin boards. Some thirty-five people RSVP'd, and nearly sixty showed up at Tim's house. Amazingly, they came not only from Colorado but from Nebraska, Kansas, Oklahoma. Tim set up multiple TVs and VCRs, and we printed T-shirts for everyone who attended.

By 2000 we realized that the informal get-together had grown too big for Tim's house. "This is starting to get crazy," Tim told me.

"Why not have it at an area hotel?" I suggested. We did exactly that. Storm chasers are a unique group, and expanding the convention to foster greater camaraderie within the small, tight-knit community seemed the way to go.

I pestered The Weather Channel to sponsor the event. They finally offered a one-time $2000 sponsorship, more to get me out of their hair than anything else. But the money helped. We rented a large room at a hotel near Denver International Airport, set up screens for videos and DVDs, catered food, and asked the hotel to open a cash bar. Having done no formal advertising, Tim and I were overjoyed when nearly one hundred people showed up!

Year by year the Denver Storm Chasers Convention grew. It wasn't all smooth sailing, of course. During one comical year, subzero temperatures and roving power outages caused a blackout in the middle of the convention. Ironically, weather had interrupted a conference about weather. But Tim came to the rescue. He had one of the most sophisticated and well-equipped chase vehicles of any chaser in the country, so we found the longest extension cord we could get our hands on and ran it out from the convention ballroom and to a power inverter on Tim's vehicle. It powered all the equipment until the electricity returned. Nothing could stop a group of storm chasers from getting their fix.

By early 2005 more than two hundred people attended. KMGH, a Denver-area television station, was the primary sponsor. In addition to Dr. Greg Forbes as the keynote, speakers included Mike Nelson, a television personality and meteorologist, and Dr. Eric Rasmussen, the director of VORTEX, a tornado-research project. The winter all of a sudden didn't look quite as gloomy as it once had. Chasers had something to look forward to. But of course nothing was a substitute for the real thing, and as spring 2005 approached, I was ready to hit the road again, destined for the Great Plains.

By early May 2005 I had gotten my wish. I was out on the plains once again with Tour 1 of the Silver Lining season. It felt good—actually, great—to be back out. Nothing came as naturally to me as life on the plains, hunting the winds.

May 11 found us in southwest Nebraska. It was the last day of the tour, and we generally didn't venture more than six hours' driving time from our home base in Oklahoma City on those days. People had to get back to catch flights home, and I had to do a quick "turnaround" before the next tour started.

After a successful tornado intercept near Benkelman, Nebraska, we turned and made a beeline for Oklahoma City. By 9:00 p.m. we were only in western Kansas, and I knew it'd be a long night. Little did I know that it was just the beginning of a string of sleep-deprived days.

We arrived in Oklahoma City sometime during the wee hours of the morning on May 12. I was looking forward to a break, even if only for a day. You don't chase on the rest day between tours unless conditions looked utterly fantastic. Luckily or unluckily for me, depending on your perspective, they were.

The forecast models for May 12 hinted at a forming dryline in the Texas panhandle along Interstate 27. There was good moisture, good instability, and thanks to a low-pressure system moving through, good wind shear as well. Things looked so good, in fact, that David Gold and I decided to run an impromptu "on call" tour for May 12. Anyone from Tour 1 who could stay and anyone from Tour 2 who arrived early was welcome to come along. David organized a group of his own in Texas and set off north for the chase target area.

I said goodbye to my day of rest, left a message at the hotel's front desk letting folks know we'd be out chasing and would return later that night, and set out to service the van. When I returned shortly before 1:00 p.m., two people from Tour 1—George and Lisa—and two people from Tour 2—Marie and Sue—were ready to go. Alister Chapman, who filmed *Twister Tours* and the Winn couple from England back in 2000 for National Geographic, was there, too. In the years since his success with *Twister Tours,* Alister had come on board with Silver Lining Tours as a driver and a consultant on all things electronic- and video-related. He would be my driver in the lead van, and his past experience as a rally driver would be invaluable on more than one occasion.

Aside from the last-minute notice, this tour was different for quite another reason. Also standing in the lobby of the hotel was a five-person film crew from Cosmospace, a production company filming a tornado documentary that would appear on Japan's Nippon Television. Their goal—and thus my goal—was to drop a custom-designed probe directly in the path of a twister. Like Tim Samaras in Manchester, South Dakota, in 2003, we'd purposely position ourselves in a tornado's path; only this time, instead of taking scientific measurements, we hoped to capture video footage from the inside of a twister.

Months earlier, in December 2004, I had received an email from Kaori Mayama, a producer for Cosmospace. "I'm looking for someone who can assist with a television program we're filming to develop a probe that will get footage of the inside of a tornado," she wrote. "I think you may be able to help me."

"This is a difficult project," I responded, explaining the challenges. "The likelihood of success is very small. Many chasers have tried, but few have actually succeeded." In fact, Tim was the *only* storm chaser I knew of who *had* succeeded. Kaori was undeterred.

Over the next several months we developed the probe. Based on my knowledge and Tim's experience with his Turtles, we settled on a simple design—a flat, circular base, topped with a short cone, similar in size and shape to the hats worn by the Vietnamese in the rice fields. We'd cut holes in the shell of the probe, and fit those holes with watertight Plexiglas inserts both to permit filming and to protect the cameras housed within. Five cameras were squeezed inside—four pointing in the cardinal directions, and one pointed straight up at the apex of the cone.

The probe had to be heavy in order to prevent it from getting sucked up into a tornado's winds, so we had it built out of heavy sheet metal by a guy in Denver I knew only as "Joey." Fifteen hundred dollars in materials and fabrication costs and $2000 in camera equipment later, we had a probe. It weighed a whopping 130 pounds. We retrofitted it with two handles welded to the sides, so that a pair of strong people could quickly deploy the probe. With the unit's aerodynamic design and heavy weight, we felt confident that if we could place it in front of a tornado, we'd get the footage we were after.

Kaori and her crew—two men to deploy the probe and three women, including Kaori, to film the sequences—would come to the United States for two attempts at deployment: once in May and again in June. Standing in the lobby of the hotel in Oklahoma City on May 12, they were ready to go, one day earlier than expected. Out front their rental van—with the back seat removed so they could fit the probe—sat waiting.

We prepared to rush out the door and into the vans at 1:00 p.m. sharp. I looked at Kaori. "Is your team ready to go?" She smiled and eagerly nodded yes. Kaori was fluent in English, and Sam, one of the Japanese men, was, too. The rest of their crew spoke little English. We understood one another nonetheless—we all knew what we were there to do and what had to be done. It was already relatively late in the day, and cumulus towers were rising along the dryline that ran from Amarillo to Lubbock. It looked like Plainview, Texas, was quickly becoming the focal point of the action to be, and we did everything we could to get there as quickly and safely as possible.

As we blasted down Interstate 44 to Lawton and then west through Altus, Oklahoma, into the Texas panhandle north of Childress, conditions only improved. Earlier that day the Storm Prediction Center had placed the highest probability of severe-thunderstorm development—a moderate risk that day—over western Kansas and the Kansas-Nebraska border. But David Gold's uncanny forecasting sense proved prophetic. The SPC shifted its forecast, placing the highest probability over the Texas panhandle and the Oklahoma-Texas border. "This is an extremely dangerous situation," the SPC warned. Large, damaging hail, supercell thunderstorms, and tornadoes were not only possible but likely.

Near Plainview the first storm of the day fired up. It took only an hour for it to become severe, and not long after, the National Weather Service issued a tornado warning because of strong rotation in the storm that was picked up by radar. We soon heard reports that a tornado had touched down near the Plainview airport. We were too late! David's team hadn't quite reached the target area, either.

But while we were too late for that storm, it was only the beginning. We had some time yet, and atmospheric conditions were ripe for the show to continue. I fully expected more storms to form. I just hoped we'd chase them before *too many* storms formed and they choked one another out, producing heavy rain but no tornadoes.

I saw a large severe storm directly ahead of us, with more developing behind it to the southwest. David and his team were on the southwestern-most storm, which was showing signs of rotation. We were on the northeastern-most storm. That wasn't my preference. Generally, you'd want to chase the newest storms, developing the farthest upwind, which on that day was to the southwest. The farther downwind you "play," the more chance there is for the storm to be affected by the ones behind it. Typically, that means that the anvil from one storm "seeds" the next one in front of it. That seeding has the net effect of weakening a storm and producing heavy rain, thus squashing the potential for tornadoes or large hail.

I would have liked to have been farther west, but time was not on our side, and the northeastern storm was showing signs of rotation, too. We parked our caravan of chase vans east of Turkey, Texas, and watched. The storm had a good updraft and a low-hanging wall cloud. Lightning streaked through the anvil, and thunder echoed constantly.

"Is this where we should deploy the probe?" Kaori asked.

"Not yet," I told her. "There's nothing tornadic about this storm. At least not right now. Just be ready." She and her crew looked nervously excited.

Something wasn't quite right about the storm, however. Within a span of just minutes, it stretched out and weakened. Cold air raced downward and outward from under the storm, developing a gust front, strong surface winds that indicated the storm's downdraft was strong than its updraft. Such a scenario usually signals the demise of a storm, and in this case, it was. We loaded into the vans and drove west of Turkey to watch supercell number two get its act together as it approached our position.

We stopped our armada along the side of Highway 86 on a dirt side road, and by then, we weren't alone. A Doppler-on-Wheels truck was there—mobile radar—and so were several storm chasers. We were all watching and hoping, waiting for something to happen, waiting for a tornado to form before our eyes.

My cell phone rang. It was David. "We just watched a couple of weak tornadic circulations under the base of the storm to the southwest, which is just south of Plainview right now," he told me. I hung up the phone. Should we pick up anchor and race to meet David? I agonized over the decision. Both the Plainview storm and our storm were under tornado warnings, and several storms in between were under severe-thunderstorm warnings.

Before I had a chance to make a final decision, something started happening with our storm. A wall cloud formed and began to rotate. More and more chasers crowded onto the tiny dirt side road as minute by minute it appeared that the storm just might produce a tornado. The wall cloud chiseled down to a defined point, where a fat cone-shaped funnel cloud slowly rotated. The Japanese stood nearby, anticipating my command to deploy the probe. The funnel cloud descended halfway to the ground, but still no debris cloud had formed. To the west I could see the strong RFD winds wrapping around the storm's updraft base. Normally, this would accelerate tornado formation. But for some reason the entire storm died a surprising and disappointingly quick death.

What to do then? I could see David's storm not far to the west. We decided to race west to the town of Silverton and reevaluate. As we neared Silverton, golf-ball-size hail rained down. We quickly turned south onto Highway 207 and raced past the storm's hail core before any damage could occur to the vans. As we emerged from the precipitation, I saw a large updraft directly to our southwest. Rain and hail wrapped around the southern edge of the storm, obscuring the view for David and his team. From our vantage, however, we had clear sight of the storm.

David rang through on my cell phone again with another update. A new supercell had formed to their west, and it was looking great. I felt like my team couldn't catch a break! We tried and tried to get west and south from Oklahoma City, to be able to chase the best storms of the day. But just as we reached the best storm, another would form even farther south and west.

We continued slowly south, when to my surprise a funnel started to form at our two o'clock over a tan field of cropland. A gray funnel cloud descended out of the dark blue base of the storm. First one-quarter of the way to the ground, then halfway to the ground. Could we finally be catching a break? Three-quarters of the way to the ground. Within seconds, a debris cloud kicked up, and we had an official tornado only two miles to our southwest, moving east.

"Thank you, Jesus!" one of the women in back cried out. "I just can't believe this!"

We crept south toward the tornado as it grew larger and larger, until it almost looked like an extension of the supercell above it. "We're fine," I told the van, trying to calm the fears of another woman in back who had become mildly frantic.

Cars from other chasers were stopped in the middle of the road, blocking traffic. "Come on, chaser," I said in frustration. "Get the hell out of the way."

We stopped the vans and jumped out to take pictures. The film crew was similarly glued to the tornado. Suddenly, Sam's voice yelled out. "Should we deploy the probe?"

I watched the tornado for a few moments, gauging its speed and direction of travel. "Drive two miles south on this road and deploy it," I yelled back. If the tornado continued to intensify, it should cross the road at that exact location. "When you get there, watch the tornado and make sure you're directly in its path," I added.

They scrambled into the truck and quickly sped off, with one man in back turning on the cameras and securing the probe cover, Sam driving, and the three ladies filming the whole scene. They had less than five minutes to reach the location, deploy the probe, and race out of harm's way. I hoped they would make it.

The rest of us stood on the roadside, mesmerized by what was unfolding before our eyes. The tornado's debris cloud had grown truly massive, and you could see power lines and transformers explode. The twister was headed directly for Highway 207, the road that we and the Japanese were on.

I ran back to the van and checked my map for potential eastbound road options. There weren't many. Only one road—County Road 60—looked like a viable option. But it was two miles to our south, which would bring us dangerously close to, or possibly on a direct collision course with, the tornado.

As we neared the Highway 207–County Road 60 intersection, the tornado bore down just a few hundred yards west of the road. "Where are the Japanese?" someone asked.

"Up there," I said, pointing to a vehicle on the highway ahead, nearly directly beneath the leading edge of the tornado. Was it really them? I couldn't be sure.

"Well, they'd better get out of the way," a women yelled.

David called again. "No, I don't have time!" I hollered into my phone. "There's a big tornado on the ground in front of me. Call me back later!" With that I flipped the phone shut, never taking my eyes off the twister, which was only a quarter mile away.

Alister crept the van forward. "What a monster!" I blurted out, unable to contain my excitement. "Keep driving."

We stopped three hundred yards north of the tornado and watched it cross the road and head into open fields east of the highway. The debris cloud and tornado appeared to blot out the entire sky. Minutes after it entered the open field, the twister weakened and roped out. For a few precious moments, the funnel hung in midair, disconnected from the cloud above and ground below. Then it was gone, and the thick, brown debris cloud slowly spread out along the ground, sinking back to earth.

Suddenly, I heard a loud thud on the ground, followed by another, and then another. Baseball- to softball-size hail was crashing to the ground! "Drive, Alister!" I yelled out. "We're going to knock out windows! We're going to lose every window. I'm serious!"

We had to get east ahead of the approaching hailstorm. Alister turned onto County Road 60, while a poor jackrabbit frantically darted back and forth in the road, searching in vain for an escape from the hail. A large hailstone found its mark, giving the jackrabbit a sad but mercifully quick death. The hailstones were big enough to kill us, too, if we weren't inside the van. But we were still in danger, and we needed to get out of the onslaught.

As we raced to escape the hail, a second tornado formed right in front of us. There was no funnel cloud at first, but a pronounced debris cloud built from the ground up, until a funnel cloud descended and the tornado was fully formed.

Just then, an immense hailstone slammed into Alister's driver-side door. "I can feel the concussion from the stones, Roger!" he screamed. Every time the largest hailstones hit the top and sides of the van, we felt instant shock waves rock the vehicle. When the stones hit the asphalt in front of us, they shattered into big pieces.

All of a sudden, a softball-size hailstone hit the back left window of the van, shattering it, and sending shards of glass all over the back two seats. Marie and Sue, in the rearmost seat, started screaming, then covered themselves with jackets and towels to protect themselves. We had to either find shelter or get out of the hail. But getting out of the hail required driving directly through the second tornado that raged in front of us.

Within a minute or two, we drove past a farmhouse with an aluminum carport attached to the side. I didn't know if anyone was home or not, but it didn't matter. We pulled off the highway and up to the carport. Everyone stayed in the van while I ran to the front door to see if anyone was home. No one was, or at least they didn't hear me knocking over the sound of the hail on the rooftop.

I turned around and watched the second tornado dissipate, but the most intense hail was about to arrive. We didn't have time to ponder another move. Alister opened the door of the van and told everyone to run under the carport. Staying in the van would have been too dangerous. Everyone piled out, and as Marie and Sue leapt from the van and ran under the refuge of the carport, glass fell from their laps.

The wind and rain and especially hail on the aluminum roof were deafening. The mammoth hailstones stripped the leaves and branches off trees in the front yard of the farmhouse. The ground was littered with hail. Windows on the house were knocked out, and the siding took a mighty beating.

The storm raged on for half an hour before the hail subsided and we could emerge from the protection of the carport. With a light rain falling and thunder still rumbling, we clambered back into the van and drove west, away from the hailstorm that had just passed. When we looked back to the east, the upper reaches of the storm looked green, colored from all the ice—hailstones—that hung suspended in the updraft.

Another storm was developing to our west, but we were safe, at least for now. But where were the Japanese? Were they okay? Were they even alive? With most of the power lines, and many of the cell towers, in the area toppled by the tornado and the storm, we had no cell-phone service. Alister took us back to Highway 207, where we hoped to locate the Japanese film crew. We turned south onto 207, toward the town of South Plains, but power lines, trees, and fencing blocked our path. Horses ran around the highway, dazed and scared, covered in mud. Cattle from a nearby ranch were scattered across the countryside, wandering free. Many storm chasers were parked along the roadside there as well. Most of their vehicles had no windows, no headlights, no side-view mirrors. The roof-mounted weather instruments of some of the storm chasers were demolished, too. We got out and walked around, marveling at the "ice rocks" that covered the ground. The largest hailstones were embedded in the ground, cratered into the muddy earth like meteorites that had fallen from space.

My cell phone suddenly and unexpectedly rang back in the van. I ran to answer it. It was the Japanese. "Roger, I am so glad to hear your voice!" Sam said. "We are in South Plains, just on the other side of some downed power lines."

Everyone was okay, he told me. "We were able to deploy the probe! Near the junction of Highway 207 and County Road 60," he continued. "After the tornado passed, we had to crawl over fallen power lines to retrieve it. The probe was covered in mud, but the cameras inside seem fine and completely dry. We think it survived, and we're hopeful that it took a direct hit!"

Sam recounted how the women filmed as he carried the 130-pound probe—by himself—and set it down in the road. When he looked up, the tornado was a little over a hundred yards away. Red dirt, pieces of trees, wood and insulation from houses swirled in the air above. He ran back to the van and jumped in, where the other man was waiting in the driver's seat, ready to hit the accelerator. I marveled at what Sam was able to do with the adrenaline rushing.

I was glad they were all safe, but next we had to figure out how to meet up again. Downed power lines blocked the only improved road between us and them. There seemed to be only one possible route—an unimproved dirt road that connected County Road 60 with an east-west road near South Plains. But after all the rain and hail, would the road even be passable?

A new supercell was approaching from the southwest, and getting stuck in the mud was a bad idea. Alister turned onto the unimproved road, and immediately the van began to slide and fishtail. Alister drove superbly, calling upon every ounce of his skill as a former rally driver, to maintain the van's forward momentum and keep us from drifting off the road.

Happily back on pavement, we turned west and headed for South Plains, where Kaori, Sam, and the rest of the rattled crew waited. We pulled into the parking lot at a gas station, and Sam came running over, embracing me with a big hug. "It's good to see you again," he said.

The final storm of the day signaled its approach with rain and lightning. Our team piled into the vehicles and drove south and east, out of the path of the storm. We had had enough for one day. As darkness fell, we stopped east of Floydada, where it was dry, to film the storm and its lightning from a distance. The storm tried more than once to form a tornado but never did. The lightning was so constant that the thunder never seemed to subside. David and his team arrived later in the evening, and we all shared stories.

Two very weak tornadoes hit Plainview, where David's crew chased. But the best "show" had been in South Plains, and as any storm chaser would be, they were disappointed to have missed it. The tornado that bore down on us and the Japanese as they deployed their probe on Highway 207 was a relatively powerful F2. At least two cars were flipped over by the strength of its winds. At times the tornado was more than half a mile wide, and it was its strongest precisely when it crossed the highway. In all, nine tornadoes hit the United States that day. Every one of them occurred in the Texas panhandle.

We bid adieu to David and his team, who returned to Dallas that night. Late that evening, we rolled wearily back into Oklahoma City. The Japanese crew stayed with Tour 2 for another week and then returned to Japan. Ultimately, they discovered that the tornado from May 12, 2005, had given them the footage they were after:

"Go, go, go, go!" the women yelled, filming Sam as he deployed the probe. "Okay, okay," he responded, struggling with the 130-pound behemoth. Suddenly, the conversation switched to their native language, Japanese, but the frantic urgency in their voices was unmistakable. Then a simple English phrase: "Let's go!" They jumped into the van, only seconds before the tornado hit the road. As they sped away, filming out the back windows of the van, the tornado steamrolled across the highway, appearing to hit the probe directly.

The probe's version: With the cameras rolling, the probe peered up at Sam, who carried it into the road. The probe clunked down onto the pavement and then rotated as Sam positioned one of the cameras to face the twister directly. The tornado bore down, growing closer and closer. The winds and precipitation picked up, and a tumbleweed blew across the scene. Power lines alongside the road began to sway, and as the tornado marched ever closer, they were ripped from the poles, some falling to the ground in a shower of sparks. A barn with a lime pit was the next victim. As the tornado crashed into the barn, the roof ripped off, and streaks of white mixed in with the red funnel as the lime was sucked up into the maelstrom. The sky grew dark, with the tornado directly overhead. Hailstones bounced off the ground and the probe's body, while debris swirled more and more violently all around. Then everything went black as the debris cloud passed directly over the probe. The tornado's edge skirted past, and the winds changed direction. Little by little, the skies grew lighter, the winds decreased, and the precipitation increased with the arrival of the rain and hail core of the storm. The road flooded. Within minutes a cow wandered across the highway all by its lonesome, loose on the plains after the fences on its ranch were destroyed.

Such is the rhythm of life on the Great Plains. All is quiet and calm. Then, for a few minutes or perhaps a few hours, violence and destruction and maybe death literally blow through town. But the interruption in the pace of daily life is just that, an interruption. In the wake of a tornado, life returns to its casual, relaxed pace. Cattle still graze in their fields. Farmers still tend to their crops. Buildings are rebuilt, and life determinedly marches on.

Storm chasers, though, follow the action. When the slow pace of life resumes in one place, storm chasers look skyward and follow their instincts and their forecasts to the next "hot spot," the next place where the action will be. It isn't always an easy life, spending long hours on the road and away from family, but it's the only life we know and the only one we want.

CHAPTER TEN

The Streak

S treaks. They're the way we measure ultimate achievement in a given discipline—2,632: consecutive Major League Baseball games played by Cal Ripken Jr.; 229: straight games with at least one reception by Jerry Rice in the National Football League; 122: consecutive winning streak in the 400-meter hurdles by Edwin Moses; 56: consecutive-game hitting streak by Joe DiMaggio; 51: consecutive games scoring at least one point by Wayne Gretzky in the National Hockey League; 47: straight games with a touchdown pass by Johnny Unitas; 4: consecutive major pro golf titles won by Tiger Woods.

In storm chasing the Holy Grail, the ultimate streak, is a simple, humble number—2: consecutive days successfully chasing a tornado. Making such a streak happen is like aligning the planets. So many factors must come into harmonious synchronicity: weather, your forecasts, your decisions about chase target areas, time. They all must be on your side. Mother Nature may offer up tornadoes on consecutive days, but that doesn't mean you'll be there to see them. In early June 2005, however, we achieved the storm-chasing equivalent of finding the Holy Grail *and* Noah's Ark.

On the afternoon of June 5, two vanloads of clients arrived in Denver for the start of a six-day tour. That night we drove to Gillette, Wyoming, in the northeastern corner of the state just west of Devil's Tower National Monument. By the morning of June 6, weather analysis showed a surface low-pressure system developing directly north of us, in southeastern Montana. Surface winds had shifted to the southeast, pumping in warm, humid air. In the atmosphere above, winds at midlevels were out of the southwest, thanks to another system moving eastward from the northern Rockies out over the northern High Plains.

Overall, there didn't seem to be an atmospheric focus for storms, although conditions held some promise. However, the mountains of northeastern Wyoming and southeastern Montana just might provide the focus—like the heat of the sun's rays, which causes heating that in turn causes updrafts, mountains can provide orographic lift, by forcing the air up and over their summits and ridges. That lifting could be the trigger we needed for thunderstorm formation. The Storm Prediction Center weighed in with a slight risk for severe thunderstorms in our area and a small threat for tornadoes. Still, the SPC figured that large hail was more of a worry than anything else.

Without a clear sense of exactly where storms might pop up, we stayed put in the hotel while I monitored the constantly updating weather info from my laptop. At 10:30 a.m. the SPC upgraded the area over southeastern Montana and the western Dakotas to a moderate risk, with an increase in the probability for hail and tornadoes. The concern was specifically for isolated supercells capable of producing hail that was baseball size and larger and also tornadoes. I perked up like a puppy being offered a treat.

Our group ate at a local Chinese restaurant for lunch and then watched the sky, satellite, and radar for the first sign of what was to come. By early afternoon a warm front developed with backing winds that shifted out of the east to the north of the front. Combined with the midlevel winds out of the southwest, it created an atmospheric environment with tremendous amounts of wind shear. Any storm that could form and sustain itself would likely rotate. It was time to move.

We left Gillette and ventured east toward Devil's Tower before turning north into Alzada, Montana, just across the state line, where we parked and waited, watched, and waited some more. By 4:00 p.m. weather conditions pulled us north to Ekalaka, where we stationed ourselves on a hill east of town with a good view of the surrounding area. Soon a low-precipitation supercell formed, complete with "mothership" structure. Dew points were in the mid-50s, which, for that elevation and latitude, were shifting into an acceptable range conducive to severe storms. As we watched, though, the supercell tracked northeast across the warm front and into cooler air and quickly died. The trick would be for forming storms to mature before they crossed the front line.

Around 4:30 p.m. another storm formed far to our southwest. I was afraid we were too far away to watch it develop and mature, but it tracked northeast, directly toward us. There weren't many roads to choose from—the routes were a sparse network of gravel and dirt roads scattered about the hills and dry creek beds. We didn't have much choice but to sit and watch the storm intensify as it bore down on us.

Within twenty minutes, the storm was close enough for us to see the updraft base churning away, with rear-flank downdraft winds eroding its southwest side as the rotation intensified. Lightning strafed across the sky in the storm's anvil, while thunder echoed in the hills and valleys that separated us from the supercell. The storm's updraft morphed into a "stack of plates," a look indicating strong rotation. Moisture, in the visible form of low clouds, streamed in from the east, along the warm frontal boundary. All the makings of a tornado-ripe environment were coming into play.

Moments later a wall cloud started to form—an immediate precursor to a tornado. A National Geographic crew along for the ride focused their cameras on the wall-cloud area. To everyone's surprise a funnel cloud formed away from the wall cloud, farther downwind. That funnel dissipated almost as soon as it formed, but the wall cloud grew in size and depth. Then at 5:40 p.m. the storm produced a tornado before our very eyes.

A long, snaking funnel touched down some three or four miles to our southwest, with a few buttes and pine trees framing the stunning view. The tornado danced around, changing shapes and sizes, all the while remaining in firm contact with the ground. Five minutes later, though, and it was gone.

The large, block-shaped wall cloud, on the other hand, remained intact. We could see strong rotation within the wall cloud and a rapid rising motion on its east side. Clearly it was still very capable of producing tornadoes.

Soon the wall cloud and updraft base were only a few miles from our location. Lightning flashed overhead, and an instant crash of thunder let us all know that the storm was quite alive, still active, and very close. Suddenly a tapered elephant trunk funnel descended from the wall cloud. Its sides were ragged—a sign that winds were rushing around it, helping to tighten its core and increase its rotational speed. Seconds later, it touched down as our second official tornado of the day.

The twister spun over and across ridges to our west and southwest, while the storm's tilted updraft loomed overhead. Quarter-size hail sporadically fell around us as the most dangerous part of the storm approached. The tornado took the shape of a drill press, appearing to dig into the ground near the buttes west of us.

Within minutes it lifted back into the sky and vanished, but simultaneously a third and much larger funnel formed. It was a large, wide cone that descended to the ground just behind the buttes two miles to our west. The twelve tour clients were ecstatic. After ten minutes the large tornado weakened, its funnel shrank, and it roped out before vanishing.

By then the hailstones had grown larger—golf-ball size—and were falling ever harder. Not wanting to get caught on our gravel road, we climbed into the vans shortly after 7:00 p.m. and blasted northeast on Route 7 through Baker, Montana, then turned east into far western North Dakota, just south of Interstate 94. There we stopped and watch as our supercell merged with a complex of large and dangerous storms, forming a squall line that constantly spat out lightning that illuminated the sky and struck a little too close to our location for comfort.

I moved our tour group and film crew farther east, to a safer location from which we would be out of the lightning hazard and be able to watch the squall line form a shelf cloud that yielded 60-mph straight-line winds that flipped over semi trucks on the interstate. We stayed ahead of the squall line until we reached Dickenson, North Dakota, where we'd stay for the night. Shortly after we arrived in town, so did the squall line, with its 60- to 70-mph winds, torrential rain, small hail, and copious lightning. That night we went to bed having successfully chased tornadoes on a day when twisters cropped up in only four isolated and distant parts of the country: California, Texas, Nebraska, and southeastern Montana.

When I awoke in our Dickenson hotel the next morning, June 7, I couldn't believe what I saw on my computer. The SPC had issued another moderate-risk outlook, focused on western and central South Dakota, just to our south! Things seemed too good to be true. All the ingredients for a severe-weather outbreak were coming together just a few hundred miles to our south. We would have a short drive to get into position for the day's chase.

My initial target was Wall, South Dakota, a stop on Interstate 90 surrounded by the Buffalo Gap National Grasslands and sitting at the gateway to Badlands National Park. The town of Wall was first established as a stop on the C&NW Railroad in the summer of 1907 and was named for a nearby geologic feature that served as a barrier to traffic. In the years since, Wall has become most famous as the birthplace of the Wall Drug Store, home of "free ice water."

It was December 1931, and the Hustead family bought the only drug store in town. Business was bad, not just for the store but for the entire community of 326 residents, most of whom were farmers wiped out by the Depression, the drought, or both. It was a godforsaken place filled with God-loving people, and the Husteads kept the faith that they'd find a way to make their store profitable. Some might say it was divine inspiration. Others would say it was the rush of traffic to Mount Rushmore to the west and Yellowstone even farther west. But the idea came nonetheless: Offer free ice water to travelers as a way to bring them out of the heat and into the store.

It worked. On a busy summer day, the home of "free ice water" may see upward of twenty thousand tourists. Add one storm chaser, twelve tour clients, and a National Geographic film crew to that list.

As late morning moved into early afternoon, we moved south toward the Pine Ridge Indian Reservation, where we could sit and watch storms ride the boundary line of two weather systems. By early afternoon warm, moist air lifting over the Black Hills to our west coalesced into storms that quickly became severe under the influence of strong wind shear and good instability. The storms raced away from our location to the northeast, but I made the difficult decision to stay put, confident that patience would pay off and yield better storms later in the day.

Finally around 4:00 p.m. storms began to form over the southern Black Hills. One lone cell formed near the Nebraska border and tracked northeast into Badlands National Park. It had a beautiful liberty-bell shape—very photogenic, but its base was fairly high off the ground for tornadoes to form. We drove southeast to the town of Interior, which sits squeezed between the eastern edge of Badlands and the northern edge of Pine Ridge. Soon the National Weather Service issued a severe-thunderstorm warning for the cell.

We stayed put, watching in awe as the storm spun rapidly, eventually developing a wall cloud at its base. Expecting something to happen soon, we inched southward toward the town of Wanblee to get closer to the storm. We weren't five miles south of Interior when a funnel cloud descended from the wall cloud. It began innocently as a small nub but then stretched out into a snaking funnel that reached halfway to the ground. From our vantage atop a high hill, we watched a debris swirl rise up seven to ten miles to our southwest. The funnel was officially a tornado. We could see the entire tornado and storm structure in view, looking very much like *The Wizard of Oz*.

"We're going to get closer so we can have a better view of the tornado," I told everyone. With the Badlands network of roads that duck in and out of hills and valleys, however, I couldn't find a good place for us to watch, and to my dismay the tornado roped out some two to four miles from us. We arrived in Wanblee just as baseball-size hail started falling. It was time to get out of town and head farther east, hoping the storm would recycle and offer up another tornado.

It wasn't to be. The storm's downdraft had become too strong, compromising the integrity of the updraft and shifting the storm's primary mode of action from tornadoes and hail to rain and wind. Ten miles east of Wanblee, we looked back to see other thunderstorms merging into a single, long squall line that would soon overtake our cell.

We snaked our way along gravel and dirt roads to Interstate 94 east of Wall. Our supercell was directly over the highway and spinning like a top! The circular base and striated updraft was a sight to behold. Best of all, a massive wall cloud seemed to be hugging the interstate, prompting the National Weather Service to issue a tornado warning. Twenty miles to our west, though, I could see the squall line with its shelf cloud and lightning flashes closing rapidly on our supercell. Time was not on our side. If our storm was to produce another tornado, it had to do so soon, before it was swallowed up into the advancing squall line.

We blasted east on I-94, busting through the storm's mesocyclone and emerging into clear territory east of the storm. A long, snaking funnel descended from the storm's southern edge, but I knew it wouldn't last. The squall line was on the heels of the supercell, and within minutes it had been engulfed into the complex.

Our priority became to stay out ahead of the squall line and its 60-plus-mph winds. Wind-damage reports were coming in fast and furiously, and we wanted to seek shelter before we became a part of that tally. Our vans raced east on I-94, eventually pulling into a hotel in Chamberlain along the Missouri River. Around 1:00 a.m. the squall line raced through town, producing 80-mph winds and heavy rain and causing downed trees and power lines. A few hearty souls stayed up to watch the display, but I had long since fallen asleep in a warm cocoon of bed sheets. I would need my energy for the next day. Besides, it was our second day of tornadoes in a row. We had caught the Holy Grail.

The morning of June 8 dawned calm and dry. The front that had passed overnight took with it all the moisture and instability. If we were going to catch tornadoes for an unbelievable third day in a row, it was looking like we would either need to make a long drive well into Minnesota or head south for what looked like a marginal weather setup in southeastern Nebraska and eastern Kansas. I was torn between the choices. A third choice seemed more inviting—make it a "down" day, during which we could rest and leisurely make our way to western Kansas, where the setup for June 9 was looking a whole lot better.

But when the Storm Prediction Center issued its 10:30 a.m. outlook, eastern Kansas had been upgraded to moderate risk. Talk about a surprise! The wind shear wasn't great—weaker wind shear favored high-precipitation supercells that might form weak tornadoes but nothing extreme. On the other hand instability was forecast to be extreme, and oftentimes very strong instability can compensate for weaker wind shear. Heading to eastern Kansas was a chance we had to take. It was already 11:00 a.m., though, and we had several hundred miles to cover before the storms formed. If we could make it to the Kansas-Nebraska border by 4:00 p.m., I figured, we'd be in good shape.

We raced down Interstate 29 through Sioux Falls, then Sioux City and Omaha, Nebraska. From Omaha we jogged west onto Route 75 and followed it south into northeastern Kansas. Around 4:00 p.m. we rolled into Holton, north of Topeka, just as cumulus towers started forming. From Holton I directed us southeast to the tiny town of Oskaloosa, where I had spent one of my high school years and where my wife, Caryn, grew up.

As we arrived in Oskaloosa, one cumulus tower in particular sparked into a thunderstorm, its cloud top shooting from thirty thousand feet to sixty thousand feet in less than twenty minutes. Sometime near 5:00 p.m. a wall cloud started to form and quickly began rotating. Moments later— seemingly over the town of Oskaloosa—an ominous, large, dark, cone-shaped funnel formed. I feared it would touch down in town and cause significant damage to my wife's hometown. A debris cloud rose up from the earth beneath the funnel, thankfully appearing to be west of town.

The storm tracked almost due north, sparing Oskaloosa. The supercell was quickly becoming obscured in rain and hail, and we drove through town to try to get closer to it. As we emerged out the west side of town, golf-ball-size hail pelted the vans but soon subsided, sparing our windshields.

Northeastern Kansas is hilly, treed country, which didn't help our view of the storm and its updraft base. It was hard to tell if there was a tornado or not, between the trees and the precipitation obscuring our view. Soon, though, we arrived alongside a clearing and could see a long, slender tornado on the ground about two miles ahead of us. Trees were being ripped from the ground and thrown like matchsticks. The sun shone on the western side of the tornado, casting it a ghostly white. It was absolutely beautiful, and I was reminded of a quote from Tom Grazulis, founder of The Tornado Project: "Few other phenomena can form and vanish so quickly, leave behind such misery, and still be seen as beautiful."

Not long after we caught the tornado, it roped out and became disjointed as pieces of funnel hung in the air and the entire storm collapsed. We had found the needle in the haystack today, and no one on tour could have been happier. Just eight tornado reports were submitted for the entire country, one of which was in northeastern Kansas, just outside the town of Oskaloosa.

As dusk fell storms built along the boundary line to our southwest, forming a chain of storms that stretched from Topeka almost all the way to Wichita, roughly along the path of Interstate 35. We grabbed dinner in Lawrence, Kansas—the unlikely home of the Golf Course Superintendents Association of America—and then headed west, planning to spend the night in Hays, Kansas. Northwest Kansas was still looking like the hot spot for June 9, and we wanted to preposition ourselves for the next day as best we could.

During the drive west to Hays, we stopped outside Topeka on the western outskirts of the city, to watch some of the most incredible lightning I have ever witnessed. A large supercell was in its decaying stage, during which such storms often have lightning that crawls through the anvil like a spider. We parked near a cluster of radio-tower antennas that stood several hundred feet tall. As we sat and watched, lightning would arc up from the radio towers and into the anvil of the supercell. The spectacular sight—which repeated itself a dozen times or so—elicited screams of joy and excitement from our entire group.

Then, realizing that it was close to 11:00 p.m. and we still had 150 miles to drive until Hays, we climbed back into the vans to resume our journey. Far from being tired, both vans seemed supercharged by the lighting we had just witnessed, and chatter of the day's tornado carried us through the night. Finally, we settled into our hotel in Hays around 1:00 a.m. and collapsed into a deep sleep.

Before I at last turned in for the night, though, I couldn't resist one peek at the weather data for the next day. The SPC was forecasting yet another moderate risk, this time for western Kansas. It was the fourth day in a row of moderate-risk outlooks, in itself quite a rare feat. As tired as I was from the endless days of chasing, I could barely sleep through my excitement and anticipation for June 9, which promised to be not just icing on the cake. It might very well be the best day of the quartet for tornadoes.

Early the next morning I shook off the cobwebs from a fitful night of sleep. The National Geographic film crew, after filming with us on June 6, had taken a two-day respite and was back with us to film on June 9. I rallied the troops for an earlier-than-usual departure. Too many key ingredients were in place—heating, strong shear, extreme instability, an intersection of boundary lines—and I expected the show to commence sooner in the afternoon than on previous days.

In the lobby of the hotel, I briefed both vans like a captain psyching up his football team. "There will be huge hailstorms today," I told them. "That's certain. More importantly, the possibility of a tornado outbreak is definitely there."

An old outflow boundary from previous thunderstorms lay west to east across northern Kansas. The dryline—the boundary separating hot, dry desert air to the west from warm, moist air to the east—ran north to south, intersecting the outflow boundary west of Hill City, Kansas. That was our chase target.

Thanks to the long drive west the night before, Hill City was only an hour from Hays, affording us time to stop for a leisurely lunch in WaKeeney along Interstate 70 before heading north to Hill City. After lunch weather maps showed that the east-west boundary had drifted south. The north-south dryline, meanwhile, had stayed stationary about seventy-five miles east of the Colorado border in western Kansas. My strategy was for us to drift slowly northwest toward the boundary intersection and wait for storms to form.

By 2:00 p.m. large cumulus towers were developing along the boundaries. Many quickly became severe and raced off into southern Nebraska. "Are we going to chase them?" the film crew asked, eager to get in on some action.

"My plan is to sit tight, right here," I told them. "We're going to wait for the real show."

The storms racing off into Nebraska were moving north of the east-west boundary into colder air, where they'd become hailstorms but probably wouldn't produce tornadoes. We needed to stay where we were and watched as storms formed along the boundary intersection. Official storm reports would later vindicate my decision—not a single tornado was reported in Nebraska on June 9.

At 2:30 p.m. we had our first storm. It formed directly south of us and slowly moved to the northeast. Thunder echoed across the plains as large raindrops pelted us. I was intimately familiar with this part of the country and wanted no part of getting mired in the mud on a potentially big tornado day, so we moved east a few miles so that the storm was then to our southwest.

We watched the explosion of the updraft in real time as it rocketed upward, rolling and boiling up like the cloud of an atomic bomb. Visibility was superb, and we all stood in awe as the scene unfolded. Within thirty short minutes, the National Weather Service issued a severe-thunderstorm warning for our cell.

Around 4:00 p.m. the storm was directly to our west, continuing its northeastward advance. We were in the perfect position. . . . Then a small, new updraft developed almost overhead, dropping quarter-size hail on us and, more importantly, heavy rain. My worst nightmare was realized. The road turned into one long puddle of mud. It took us nearly half an hour to cover just two miles, struggling to get the vans east of the precipitation. We got lucky.

But we needed more than luck. We needed speed. The storm by then was well north of us, and we had ground to make up, quickly. The vans jumped onto Route 283 and headed north and east on gravel roads that hadn't yet seen the rain and hail and were dry. At last we caught the storm, pulling up beneath the base of a large, block-shaped wall cloud spinning rapidly below the supercell's base. Almost on the heels of our arrival, the National Weather Service issued a tornado warning for the storm, centered precisely at our location.

We stair-stepped east and north into Graham County as the wall cloud descended. A tornado seemed imminent. Then a dirt plume kicked up on the western and southern sides of the wall cloud at ground level. It was the rear-flank downdraft. The only thing yet to develop was the tornado itself. We parked at a gravel road and watched as a pencil-shaped tornado descended to the ground from the wall cloud, just one mile north of us. It quickly grew into a drill-press type tornado, tapered from top to bottom, and lit ghostly white by the sun's rays.

The tornado crossed the road directly in front of us. Just then, my good friend and tornado researcher Tim Samaras sped past, attempting to drop his probe in front of the twister. The tornado proved too fast, and Tim wasn't able to catch it. At least not on that day.

We all jumped back into the vans, and I vectored us east and north again through the prairie lands. Within ten minutes we were directly in the tornado's path as it grew to enormous proportions, possibly as much as one mile in width. It was truly a monster. Dirt, rain, and hail partially obscured the base of the tornado, but the storm's structure above—the tilted updraft—was awesome.

Encroaching rain and hail, and the tornado itself bearing down on our position, forced us to relocate once again. Then the unthinkable happened. The film crew lost control of their vehicle on the slick roads, sliding off the road and into a ditch, where they broke the steering column of the truck. They were disabled.

With a vanload of people and the supercell's intense precipitation core on our heels, I couldn't risk endangering the lives of the dozen tour clients and made the agonizingly difficult decision to leave the film crew behind, stranded for now. It was a split-second decision made in the face of real danger, a decision no storm chaser ever wants to make.

Thankfully, the tornado passed a few miles north of the film crew, and they were later able to get a new vehicle and meet up with us to resume the chase.

Meanwhile, safely beyond the reach of the storm's precipitation core, we pulled the two vans over in the town of Damar, about five miles ahead of the then-dying tornado. With a cyclic supercell like the one we were chasing, however, oftentimes a new mesocyclone will form east of the old one. From our position five miles east of the old meso, that meant the new mesocyclone would form almost over our heads. Looking up in the sky above, I could see a merry-go-round of rotation and was worried that a new tornado might spawn on top of us at any time.

Suddenly, a client yelled, "Tornado!"

I looked to the west to see a twister make contact with the ground a mile away.

"There's another one!" someone else hollered.

To the south, on the outer periphery of the mesocyclone, a second tornado stabbed at the ground. I spun around, trying to survey all directions to take measure of the situation. To my amazement another large tornado formed just north of us. In total three tornadoes hemmed us in from three compass points—the north, west, and south. If we didn't leave for safer skies to the east, we'd be in serious trouble.

The vans blasted toward the towns of Palco and Zurich. We pulled over at the intersection with a dirt road and spilled out of the vans to watch the beastly sight. Storm chasers were everywhere. Everyone had cameras and camcorders capturing the entire spectacle. The smaller of the tornadoes withered, while a single larger tornado strengthened to our north. A bolt of lightning cut straight through the tornado, striking the earth in the foreground.

"Back into the vans!" I ordered. "Let's move north to get closer."

I drove north as quickly as I could while the tornado bore down on the same road, on course to cross our path ahead. All of a sudden we hit mud again. My lead van slid sideways, nearly careening into a ditch as the National Geographic crew had. I turned the steering wheel into the skid, hoping to recover. Our momentum kept us moving forward, and as I straightened out the van, we rumbled past a creek and up a small hill. At the top of the hill we passed a small grove of trees, and there it was: the tornado churning across the road a quarter mile ahead. Farther to the northeast yet another tornado was growing in size and stature.

Then, the rear-flank downdraft winds slammed into the van at 80 mph. We were going nowhere. We unloaded onto the muddy road and soaked up the scene from our vantage point, watching as the white tornado in the foreground roped out, leaving a dark brown tornado in the background, spinning away until it disappeared behind a veil of rain and hail.

We needed to get back to pavement. The vans spun around and backtracked on the muddy road, finally reaching the asphalt of Route 18. We turned east and drove into Plainville, where I refueled the vans and looked at the latest radar. Another tornadic supercell—a tail-end Charlie—had developed southwest of WaKeeney, only forty miles away. Reports started coming in of significant tornado damage to farms south of town.

Our caravan drove south to Hays and then west onto Interstate 70. We could plainly see the menacing supercell to our southwest, approaching the highway. As we continued slowly west on I-70, additional reports came in of overturned semi trucks on the interstate ahead. Within minutes I could make out the faint outline of a poorly contrasted tornado southwest of Ellis, halfway between Hays and WaKeeney.

With the tornado three miles to our south, and with a large rotating wall cloud directly over the interstate, we exited to watch and then prepared to turn back east, to escape the oncoming supercell. As the storm approached, it lost its supercell structure and shifted into a raging squall line. We stayed ahead of the storm, filming and admiring its lightning displays, before finally ending up in Hays at the same hotel from the night before. We were tired, hungry, thirsty, and absolutely thrilled.

By the end of the day, the official count for tornado reports numbered forty-five, with the most intense cluster of reported twisters in northwestern Kansas. As for us, our day ended with the number four. Four consecutive days of tornadoes. It was an accomplishment born of opportunity. Never before or since have I witnessed tornadoes on so many days in a row. It is a record for Silver Lining Tours that will in all likelihood stand for a very long time. Such an accomplishment required good forecasting, a healthy dose of luck, and, of course, the cooperation of Mother Nature. For those four days in June 2005, she took us on a wild ride circling the High Plains, beginning in Denver, journeying north through Wyoming to Montana, east into the Dakotas, south through Nebraska to Kansas, and finally west through Kansas back to Denver. It was a streak to be remembered. But as with all streaks—storm chasing, sporting, or otherwise—they are made to be broken, and someday Mother Nature may provide another such opportunity . . . whether next year, next decade, or next century.

CHAPTER ELEVEN

Katrina

Storm chasing is a last great frontier, an unconquerable endeavor. And as I evolved as a storm chaser, I sought new and bigger challenges. Could I make a better forecast? Hunt larger supercells? Get even closer to a tornado? Maybe inevitably, I broadened my horizons and set my sights on an entirely different beast: hurricanes. Tornadoes took Mother Nature's fury and focused it like a laser beam. Hurricanes, on the other hand, were a sledgehammer.

Chasing them was a fundamentally different proposition from speeding around the Great Plains in pursuit of supercells. With tornadoes the goal was to safely observe from a distance—even if a close distance—without directly experiencing the wrath of the storm. With hurricanes the opposite was true. If you chased a hurricane well, you'd position yourself squarely in the path of the storm, sit and wait, and then let it hit you with its full force.

Hurricanes also provided a welcome extension to the storm-chasing season. Primary tornado season began in spring and lasted through summer. Hurricane season, by comparison, began in summer, and lasted through fall. Officially, it started June 1 and ended November 30. But if I'd learned one thing in my decades of storm chasing, it's that Mother Nature doesn't always like to play by the rules. Hurricanes, for their part, have occurred as early March and as late as December. But the important thing for me was that as tornado season peaked and then faded, hurricane season was just reaching its prime.

I dabbled with hurricane chasing during the 2004 season, when I chased hurricanes Jeanne and Charley. Jeanne hit Vero Beach, Florida, as a Category Three storm. On the Saffir/Simpson Hurricane Scale, Category Three storms pack sustained winds of 111 to 130 mph, and damage is described as "extensive." Jeanne lived up to the category rating. She came ashore with 120-mph winds. Buildings collapsed. Trees toppled. Waves destroyed beachfronts. The storm's nine-to-twelve-foot storm surge filled shopping malls with seawater.

As the 2005 tornado season wound down, I scanned the Atlantic for hurricanes. Many had already barreled through the Caribbean Sea, the Gulf of Mexico, and the Atlantic Ocean, and 2005 was quickly shaping up to be a record-breaking year for sheer number of hurricanes. I sat home on August 26, having completed the last Silver Lining tour of the season, reviewing reports from the National Hurricane Center in Miami. It looked like my first hurricane-chasing opportunity of the year was on its way: a storm named Katrina.

Katrina had begun humbly, and namelessly, more than two weeks earlier—on August 11—off the west coast of Africa. By August 19 she was north of Puerto Rico, where she produced a large area of showers and thunderstorms. She slowly consolidated, moving northwestward just east of the Turks and Caicos on August 22. Then she turned west, setting her sights on southern Florida. As she crossed the southeastern Bahamas one day later, the storm system developed into a tropical depression, officially named Tropical Depression Twelve. By that night Tropical Depression Twelve sat over the central Bahamas, and the next day—August 24—the cyclone became Katrina, the eleventh tropical storm of the 2005 Atlantic hurricane season. On August 25 Katrina turned directly west, heading for Florida, and later that day, she reached hurricane status just two hours before her center made landfall. She hit Florida as a Category One storm, centered almost directly over the Miami-Dade and Broward County line.

By then Katrina had a well-formed eye, and she tracked straight across the Florida peninsula, spending just six hours over land. During that time she weakened slightly, but after emerging into the Gulf of Mexico early on the 26th, she quickly regained strength.

Sitting at home in Bennett, Colorado, I contemplated whether I should chase Katrina or not. Category Three Jeanne had done extensive damage in Florida. Forecasters were anticipating that Katrina would strengthen into a Category Four or Five storm. Did I even want to know what that would be like? And did I want to be there when it happened?

After waffling back and forth, I finally decided that it was a "go." If I stayed inland a few miles, I figured, then I would be safe from the impending storm surge that would swamp the low-lying coastline of the Gulf states. My chase target—or, perhaps more accurately, my "get there, sit, and wait" target—was Diamond Head, Mississippi. I called the local Comfort Inn and made reservations for August 28 through 31, unsure of how long I'd need to stay if I got stuck because of Katrina's effects on the area.

I also posted a message to my email listserv. Did anyone want to come along? One person said yes, North Carolina businessman Ed Schoenborn. Ed had chased with me many times on the Great Plains. In fact, during one season with Silver Lining Tours he booked every tour. Some sixty-five years old, standing just five feet six inches tall, with virtually no hair and thick, black-rimmed eyeglasses, Ed's diminutive frame balanced out his larger-than-life thirst for adventure. He had been to every continent and to both the North and South poles. Chasing Hurricane Katrina fit right in with his adventurous exploits.

Our plan was to fly into Houston, Texas, well removed from Katrina's path. I would arrive first, pick up a rental SUV, buy and fill gas cans, strap them to the roof, and purchase one week's worth of groceries—food and water—at a local supermarket. We had no idea how much flooding or damage or blocked roads we'd encounter. Best to be fully prepared for the worst.

The morning of August 28 I headed to Denver International Airport. Forecasters' predictions about Katrina strengthening were right. As she moved west over the Gulf of Mexico between August 26 and August 28, she went through two periods of rapid intensification. On August 27, she grew from a relatively weak Category One hurricane to a Category Three storm. In just that day Katrina nearly doubled in size; she was huge. Katrina fully spanned the Gulf of Mexico from north to south, extending from Mississippi all the way to Mexico's Yucatan Peninsula. In the east-west direction, she was more than half the width of the Gulf. One day later the second and more rapid intensification occurred. She "blew up" from a low-end Category Three storm to a devastating Category Five hurricane in fewer than twelve hours. Just 170 nautical miles southeast of the mouth of the Mississippi River, Katrina's sustained winds exceeded 155 mph and peaked at 175 mph. If she made landfall at that strength, the damage would be catastrophic.

I arrived in Houston under partly cloudy skies and warm, humid conditions. In the three hours before Ed arrived, I stocked the SUV and then returned to the airport to pick him up. "Roger!" he yelled out across the terminal's baggage claim area, slightly embarrassing me. He ran up to me, dropped his bag, and gave me a big hug. "What do you think we'll see? What's going to happen?" His questions came nonstop. Hurricane Katrina was bigger than any storm I'd ever chased. Ed had never chased a hurricane at all. For both of us there was a fear of the unknown. But we were excited, too.

It didn't take long for us to reach Interstate 10, and we headed directly east, destined for the Louisiana-Mississippi border 360 miles away. Our timing was lucky. Earlier in the day both the eastbound and westbound lanes of Interstate 10 had been converted to westbound only, to accommodate the massive numbers of people evacuating Louisiana. By the time we pulled onto the interstate, normal traffic patterns had resumed.

The Louisiana border, though, was a sight to behold. Bumper-to-bumper traffic in the westbound lanes stretched as far as the eye could see. In the eastbound lanes we were virtually the only traffic. It was sobering—to see all the traffic, people doing whatever they could to get out of harm's way. And here we were, racing east directly into the path of what so many people wanted desperately to avoid.

Approaching Baton Rouge, I found a radio station that was broadcasting regular updates of the hurricane's status. Then NOAA weather radio broke into the transmission with an announcement: *Hurricane Katrina is a very dangerous Category Five storm heading for the Louisiana coastline. Sustained winds are now 175 mph, with gusts over 200 mph.*

I looked at Ed. Winds that strong would destroy anything in their path. Should we just turn around? How would we find a structure strong enough to withstand the force and keep us safe? Would the storm surge be too deep, even miles inland? Most of the coastal communities have elevations of just ten to twenty feet, even inland away from the shoreline. A Category Five storm brings storm surges greater than eighteen feet. Would we be able to survive?

As we passed Baton Rouge, I turned onto Interstate 12 east, keeping us north of New Orleans and still en route to Diamond Head. Not long after merging onto Interstate 12, my cell phone rang; it was the Comfort Inn. "The eastern eye wall is forecast to pass very close to here. The whole town is shutting down and vacating," the hotel's manager told me. "We're closing down. Don't come." Then she hung up.

What to do? Where could we go? The latest forecast called for the eye of the hurricane to make landfall between Slidell, Louisiana, and Diamond Head, Mississippi. Our goal was to experience the eye, but we also didn't want to get demolished by the strongest winds and greatest storm surge, both of which would be directly to the east of the eye. We set our sights on Slidell, on the northeastern shore of Lake Pontchartrain.

It was close enough to ground zero to get hit by the eye but was far enough west to avoid the strongest part of the storm. A five-level parking garage attached to Slidell Memorial Hospital could provide refuge for us, and we knew the hospital would have emergency services and power around the clock.

Soon the outermost rain bands from Katrina arrived, and the winds began to pick up. It was 7:00 p.m., and we were starting to lose daylight. By 8:00 p.m. we were nearly in Slidell. Still the roads were choked with cars, their headlights shining through the rain and darkness as people fled New Orleans. Traffic was so bad that cars were running out of gas and people were simply abandoning them in the middle of the road. We exited the interstate, turned onto Gause Boulevard in downtown Slidell, and drove west seven blocks to Slidell Memorial.

Pulling into the hospital's parking garage, we found one other storm chaser already there, Tim Marshall. Tim was an editor of *Storm Track,* an online magazine, and a well-known storm-damage-analysis expert. We parked near Tim on the lowest level of the garage and got out to talk. Though we were both normally excited and confident when chasing storms, I think each of us was concerned about Katrina's power, and we secretly hoped that her winds would actually diminish a bit before she made landfall. We also worried about the storm surge. With Katrina's counterclockwise rotation, areas east of the eye would get the worst of it, as the incredible winds essentially pushed the ocean into the coastline there. In Slidell, to the west of the eye, winds would come out of the north, holding back the storm surge somewhat. But as Katrina moved north of town, the winds in Slidell would shift out of the west. That wind direction would take the waters of Lake Pontchartrain and push them directly into Slidell.

I fired up my laptop. Based on radar and satellite imagery, I estimated that Katrina's eye would hit us sometime early on August 29. That night, as Ed and I stood in the garage talking, the wind and rain grew steadily stronger. Soon it was midnight, but neither of us could fall asleep. A transformer adjacent to the garage exploded, and everything went black. Then the power turned back on as the hospital's backup generator came to life.

Sometime in the wee hours of the morning, Ed and I finally fell asleep. Bands of wind and rain would pass, each more intense than the last. The cracking and breaking of trees and the sound of metal being ripped from the exterior of the garage repeatedly jolted me awake. Around 6:00 a.m. I woke for good.

At that same time the National Weather Service issued an updated hurricane warning: *Extremely dangerous Category Four Hurricane Katrina preparing to move onshore. . . . Hurricane-force wind gusts occurring over most of southeastern Louisiana, including the City of New Orleans and Lake Pontchartrain. . . . Preparations to protect life and property should have been completed. . . . The center of major hurricane Katrina is about 70 miles south-southeast of New Orleans . . . moving toward the north near 15 mph. . . . Maximum sustained winds are near 145 mph, with higher gusts. . . . Hurricane-force winds extend outward up to 120 miles from the center, and tropical storm-force winds extend outward up to 230 miles. . . . Coastal storm-surge flooding of eighteen to twenty-two feet above normal tide levels… along with large and dangerous battering waves. . . . Rainfall totals of five to ten inches, with isolated maximum amounts of fifteen inches. . . . Scattered tornadoes will be possible.*

The warning posed an almost-worst-case scenario; Katrina had suddenly weakened. She was still ferocious and deadly, to be sure, but no longer the catastrophic Category Five she was just hours earlier.

With Ed still asleep in the passenger seat, I quietly opened the driver-side door and slipped out. My back ached, and my left arm was asleep after using it as a pillow. I quickly overlooked the pain, though, as the scene outside the garage captured my attention. The roads were flooded under a foot of water. Streets were littered with debris. The rain fell horizontally, whipped sideways by the strengthening winds. Traffic lights flashed. Power lines and poles were toppled. The roof was torn off a gas station on the corner across the street.

I walked upstairs to a higher level of the garage and found Tim awake, too. A few other chasers had arrived in the middle of the night to experience the wrath of Katrina as well. Ed appeared minutes later as we all stood, chatting. I took refuge in a stairwell on the perimeter of the garage. With cinder-block walls on three sides, and an open side that faced west, away from the prevailing winds, it offered an excellent vantage point.

Ed and I retreated to the SUV, where we ate a breakfast smorgasbord: Pop-Tarts, cookies, beef jerky, bottled orange juice. It was hardly satisfying, but we didn't care; we just needed food in our stomachs. When we finished breakfast at about 8:00 a.m., Katrina's eye was just east of New Orleans and about twenty miles to our south. The eye wall is an exercise in contrasts— just outside the eye wall a hurricane unleashes its worst rain, its worst wind; just inside the eye wall, a hurricane is at its calmest. We had about one hour before it would arrive, and I wanted to survey the neighborhood before things got any worse.

As we pulled out of the garage and onto Gause Boulevard, water came up to the bottom of the SUV's doors. The truck created a wake in the road, like a boat, as we drove. The winds—nearing 100 mph—lashed at a strip mall, tearing off the stores' signs. Plumes of water sprayed off the rooftops.

Gas-station canopies were toppled over. Trees were fallen everywhere—on cars, on houses, on power lines, in the streets. Shingles were being plucked from the roofs of the ranch-style brick homes in the neighborhood.

We returned to the parking garage and parked on the second level, escaping the rising waters. I backed the SUV up against the hospital wall, where it would be protected from the worst winds. Tim was still there in the garage and so were several police officers monitoring the storm for the town. The wind screamed through the levels of the garage, whistling and howling over the clamor of metal and wood crashing and breaking outside. The wind and rain grew so intense that at times the gas station across the street disappeared from view. Water poured out of each garage level and into the stairwell, which had become something of a waterfall.

I scrambled up to level three but quickly retreated—signs that hung from the ceiling of the garage were being ripped off and hurled through the air like missiles.

Katrina slammed into Slidell as a strong Category Three–borderline Category Four hurricane. Her maximum sustained winds reached 125 mph, and as they slammed into Slidell, the parking garage rumbled and shook, as if an earthquake were shaking its foundation.

Then, as quickly as the winds roared up, they nearly ceased. The eye had arrived. The sun poked out between the chaos of clouds overhead. It was a moment of peace and quiet. Ed and I jumped into the truck and set out to explore, but we didn't make it far. Either the streets were blocked with debris or the flood waters were too deep. Duplex homes and condominiums were stripped of their walls and roofs, reduced to bare studs. A Best Western was completely caved in; its roof was gone. The windows were gone. Doors to the motel rooms swung open. Beds and other furniture were overturned and tossed everywhere. Gas-station pumps were ripped right off their concrete slabs. Roof metal was wrapped around telephone poles like twist ties on a bag of bread.

With the southern eye wall approaching and with conditions about to deteriorate, we returned to the garage. But someone had left a car parked at the entrance to the second level. I was forced to leave the SUV on the ramp. As long as the waters remained below ten feet, we'd be fine. The hurricane-force winds returned, battering us for nearly an hour. Then, slowly, things started to subside.

It was then that I noticed the flood waters rapidly rising. I estimated they were two to three feet deep immediately outside the garage, deeper in some areas. Tim, who had brought along waders, walked out into the street, and the water immediately rose over his waist belt. Our fears were being realized. Katrina had caused Lake Pontchartrain to rise and then pushed those waters eastward into Slidell, where the storm surge reached twelve to sixteen feet. Then the levees and floodwalls were overtopped or breached, and the real flooding began.

If we didn't get out soon, we'd be stranded. Other chasers, who had arrived in low-clearance sedans, already were. I didn't want the same fate for us. We had to make a break for it. If we could drive east on Gause and reach the Interstate, we'd be home free. It was only a quarter mile away, but it looked rough.

We decided to try to find another way. I drove in a circle around the outside of the parking garage, looking for an alternate route; there wasn't one. Every road looked too flooded to drive on. We sat for a moment, thinking. As we contemplated our options, a piece of tin flew through the air and slammed into the back of the truck. We retreated to the parking garage, but the lower level was filling with water. I decided to try to get out before I knew that I couldn't.

I turned onto Gause, determined to reach the interstate. Water came nearly to the handles of the SUV's doors. I prayed that the engine stayed running. Tim, who had also decided to leave, drove just ahead of us in his large pickup truck. The wake he created allowed us to drive immediately behind in slightly shallower water. As we inched our way eastward, the water withdrew to only one or two feet deep. We were out of the worst of it, and Ed and I both breathed a deep sigh of relief. Tim paused to wave goodbye, and then he turned for home—Dallas, Texas.

Slidell was deserted. The community was a scene of total devastation. After seeing a church in ruins, with the walls of the pastor's office flattened and his paperwork scattered everywhere, we decided we had seen enough.

With no cell phones, no electricity, no telephones, no television, there was no way to know the extent of the damage beyond what we could see with our own eyes. But I was curious about what had happened east of the eye, where the worst winds and worst storm surge would have been. At Interstate 12 we turned east to find out. The interstate was green, covered in debris and leaves and fallen trees. It looked like a war zone. Then, as we came up over a hill, I slammed on my brakes. The highway disappeared completely beneath what looked like a lake. Not a single car was visible, and a doe and fawn waded through the edge of the water just ahead of us. Animals emerged from the forest, escaping the flooded lowlands.

I turned around and drove west in the eastbound lanes, with no other option. When we came to the Interstate 10–Interstate 12 junction north of Slidell, I turned south on 10, wanting to see how New Orleans had faired. About one mile down the road, three cars heading north flashed their lights and honked their horns at us. They were trying to warn us. As we neared the bridge over Lake Pontchartrain, I saw that sections of the bridge were simply gone, collapsed into the lake. With no other choice, we returned to Interstate 12 and headed west, away from the storm's destructive path and toward Texas.

Too much debris on the interstate forced us onto side roads for a while. By 6:00 p.m. we had reached Baton Rouge. Power was out, and no businesses were open. I poured the last of our gas into the tank and gave the empty cans to a local resident. We continued westward, the destruction quickly becoming less and less as we left the storm's track. By midevening, we were at the Texas line. We tried to find a hotel room, but there were none available. My cell phone worked again, though, and I called all over the Houston area looking for a hotel with a vacancy. Finally, I found two rooms available in Galveston, which had been hit by the deadliest hurricane in United States history—a 1900 cyclone that killed eight thousand people.

Before Ed and I retired for the night, we gave each other a strong hug, realizing that we had witnessed history and—maybe more so—realizing that we were alive.

That night, August 29, as Katrina moved over central Mississippi, she quickly weakened, becoming a Category One storm. Just six hours later she had weakened to a tropical storm, and by August 30 she was over the

Tennessee Valley as a tropical depression. Sometime around August 31, Katrina was no more, absorbed into the weather over the eastern Great Lakes.

◉

The rest of Katrina's story—her aftermath—was best told in the popular media in the weeks and months following the storm; best told in the terms of her impact on individual human lives and in the photos and videos that came out of the rescue efforts to follow:

Eighty percent of the City of New Orleans flooded within a day of Katrina's landfall, in many places to depths of twenty feet.

More than fifteen hundred people died as a direct result of the storm, making Katrina the third deadliest hurricane in U.S. history. Only two others—a 1928 hurricane that hit Lake Okeechobee, Florida, and the 1900 hurricane that pummeled Galveston, Texas—killed more people. Of the fifteen deadliest hurricanes in the nation's history, all but two occurred before 1939. One was Hurricane Audrey in 1957; the other was Katrina.

Katrina overnight became the costliest hurricane in U.S. history as well, causing an estimated $81 billion in damage. Even when adjusted for inflation, Katrina was nearly twice as costly as number two, 1992's Hurricane Andrew.

By some measures, Katrina—at least as a weather pattern—was following the rules. August is the second most common month for hurricanes, behind only September. And Louisiana is the third most affected state for hurricanes, behind only Texas and Florida.

By other measures, though, there was something different about Katrina and about the 2005 hurricane season in general. Every year an average of five hurricanes and two major hurricanes—Category Four or Five—hit the United States. In recent years that average has increased to eight and four, respectively. But in 2005 a disproportionate and record fifteen hurricanes hit the United States, with seven of those hurricanes classified as "major," the second most in the country's recorded history. What's more, the scale and scope of the devastation from Katrina was far beyond her Category Three rating. Storms much worse have done much less.

Answering the "why" is a task best left to meteorologists and atmospheric scientists. On that day I was there as a storm chaser, determined to experience the "what." But rather than walk away from Katrina with her being simply another notch in my belt, I felt the experience had a deeper and more profound meaning. As it was for so many Americans, the experience was a humbling reminder of the awesome power of Mother Nature and one that I hope the United States never experiences again.

CHAPTER TWELVE

Close to Home

It was August 20, 2006—almost one year to the day since I had boarded a plane in Denver bound for Hurricane Katrina and the Gulf Coast. The 2006 tornado season was winding down, and I was ready for a break. The tours with Silver Lining were finished, and any chasing I did would be at my own discretion, whenever my motivation or the conditions were good enough to warrant leaving home.

Life on the road as a storm chaser was rewarding and thrilling, but it was also exhausting. Long hours, days, and weeks spent crisscrossing the Great Plains took their toll, and as much fun as it was hunting tornadoes, it was just as nice returning home. Living out of a suitcase had its appeal, but so did a home-cooked meal, a shower in my own home, and a good night's rest in my own bed.

It was warm and humid on August 20, and the sun shone brightly. I wanted to get my yard duties finished by early afternoon, so I wouldn't end up sitting on my riding lawn mower during the hottest part of the day. Caryn was inside working on projects of her own. Her sister, Caryl, was visiting, too.

Around 2:00 p.m. I finished the lawn work and went inside to cool off. But even a day off from chasing wasn't truly a day off, and I couldn't resist sitting down at the computer to glance at the forecast models. The Storm Prediction Center had our area under a risk watch for severe storms. I became cautiously optimistic.

Even on such days at home, severe weather was never far from my mind or far from the house. In 2003 when Caryn and I set out to buy a home in Colorado, we had two major factors to consider: her horses and my storms. She needed enough land to build a barn or two, a pen, and eventually—we hoped—an indoor arena, a place where she could train and show her quarter horses. I needed a place that put me close to the severe-weather and tornado action, a place that put me in or on the doorstep of the Great Plains. Like anyone whose passion centered around landscape—climbers near mountains, fishermen near water, cowboys near ranches—I had to live in a place where I could practice my passion-turned-profession.

In Colorado that place was the Denver Convergence Vorticity Zone—the DCVZ. I had lived there once before, when Allison, Adam, Nikole and I lived in our split-level house in Green Valley Ranch after I transferred to Lowry with the air force in the 1980s.

A ranch-style house on five acres of land just outside rural Bennett, Colorado, became our new home in the DCVZ, the place that Caryn and I would build together, along with her son, Colton.

Living in the DCVZ was and is a blessing. I loved it. During noncommercial-tour times, I still chased. Often it was a family affair, chasing with Caryn or Colton or both. Other times it was with friends. But living in the DCVZ allowed it to happen. I didn't have to board a plane or schedule long trips in advance; I could chase on a moment's notice, literally out my front door.

Other middle-aged men would wake up, drink a morning cup of coffee, read the newspaper. I checked weather-forecasting models from the National Weather Service and the Storm Prediction Center. If it looked like a good day to chase from home, I cleared my schedule, and that was it. I didn't chase every storm—the peak chase season took its toll on my body, and the older I got, the longer it took me to recuperate from a chase. But I did chase the storms that held the most promise, those that looked like they'd become supercellular or would produce tornadoes.

On that hot afternoon in August 2006, it looked like things might do just that. The DCVZ boundary line had set up, running that day from

Castle Rock northward, past our house in Bennett, and up to Fort Morgan. There was good instability and good moisture, and dew points east of the boundary line were rising. By 3:00 p.m. cumulus towers were developing along the boundary, and a thunderstorm was organizing to the north near Fort Morgan.

My chase instinct started to take hold. I positioned my camera on the front deck of the house, set to record a time-lapse video of the developing storms. Half an hour later I came back out and saw several towers developing, while the original thunderstorm to the north threw out lightning bolts frequently.

As I stood on the deck watching, I noticed how each cumulus tower would rise, begin to corkscrew with rotation, and then die. Just as each storm dissipated, though, it would spawn a brief funnel. This process continued, storm by storm, and each time a new storm developed, it was larger and stronger than the last.

Around 5:00 p.m. two significant storms formed—one just southwest of the house and the other nearly overhead. The storm to the southwest spat out rain and lightning and quarter-size hail. The developing storm overhead was different. The base was long and stretched out, hardly the compact updraft base that was conducive to rotation and ultimately tornadoes. Yet, as I gazed up at the base, a slim, gray funnel formed, protruding roughly a thousand feet below the cloud base.

I watched it for a minute before walking through the yard to get into a position where I could see the ground below and determine whether or not it was causing a debris cloud. Sure enough, within minutes a debris swirl formed and grew. The funnel cloud continued its descent, and with the debris cloud already well formed, it was undoubtedly a tornado.

"Caryn!" I yelled from the yard. She came running out to see the twister. The long, dark brown, slender, snaking funnel was fully formed just three miles north of the house. She turned and ran inside to call the National Weather Service to report a tornado, while I grabbed my camcorder to video the twister.

"Jump in the car," she said hurriedly, bursting out the front door of the house. "We'll go chase it."

Chasing like that—impromptu, spur of the moment, from home—was a regular occurrence. A year had yet to pass since we'd lived in Bennett that a tornado hadn't formed within twenty-five miles of the house. In 2004 Colton and I chased a series of twisters that rumbled across Colorado, including several in Elbert County near the communities of Agate and Simla. One year later Caryn and I chased local tornadoes again, those twisters barely requiring us to hit the road since they came almost directly at the house. Now in August 2006 we were at it again.

Chasing from home with Caryn was a true pleasure, one that brought together my two greatest loves. At other times, chasing caused a tension inside me. I wanted to chase; there was never a question about that. But after spending months on the road, sometimes I wanted nothing more than just to spend time with her. I missed her tremendously during those times that we were away from one another. The desire to chase pulled at me just as strongly, however. Chasing together as a couple alleviated both those stresses. It felt like the way things were meant to be.

We jumped in the car, with Caryn's sister, Caryl, along for the ride. Caryn and Caryl grew up in Oskaloosa, Kansas, and though Caryn had seen many tornadoes with me since we'd been married, Caryl hadn't seen a tornado since the 1966 twister leveled Topeka.

We raced northward on Manilla Road, headed straight for the twister. The funnel cloud left the cloud base almost horizontally, parallel to the horizon line, and then made a sharp right turn as it plunged to the ground. It began needle-thin, colored milky white and pink, but grew in width along its length until it reached the wide, black debris cloud at its base. At midheight, we could see a tight vortex confined within a larger, transparent funnel cloud.

We bounced along the road, with the tornado just four or five miles northwest of Bennett and only two or three miles from our house. It was quite a different feeling seeing a tornado so close to my home. When I was out chasing storms on the plains in other states, it was always someone else's home. It was terrible to think that way, but it happened. What if a tornado destroyed our house, though? Where would we go? How long would it take for the insurance company to process a claim and we could start rebuilding?

What would happen if one of us or one of our animals was hurt or killed? They were questions I had never had to ask myself. Yet living on Colorado's High Plains forced me to face the storms and the tornadoes they formed. I couldn't simply chase them as a storm chaser, dancing around their danger, leaving the destruction behind and returning to my safe haven when it was all said and done. The tornadoes followed me home. I had to confront them and their consequences. It gave my chasing a deeper meaning and gave me a unique empathy for the people who lived in Tornado Alley. I wasn't some hack storm chaser who was gawking at their misfortune, making a buck selling videos and taking customers on tours. I was also one of them.

As we continued driving north, the tornado crossed Manilla Road heading west. Soon, a second and then a third tornado formed. What a sight! Three tornadoes in a single camera shot. The third tornado rapidly became the biggest. We crossed Interstate 70, still heading north on Manilla, with the tornado some four hundred yards wide. Yellow, brown, and red dirt was sucked up into the monster as it rolled across the dusty ranch country north of Bennett. I wanted to get closer, but we couldn't. We ran out of roads.

After nearly thirty minutes all three tornadoes dissipated with surprising suddenness. The storm made a last attempt to form another tornado, with a funnel that spun over our heads. But it never formed, and we returned to the house in time for dinner, with the snow-capped Rocky Mountains in the distance.

Such chases close to home were a true luxury. But that luxury came with a price: the risk that our house would be hit. Hopefully, our house will never take a direct hit. But we live on the High Plains, where everyday life and tornadoes exist in an intimate love-hate relationship. And I am afraid that the time will come when we will experience what so many others already have.

CHAPTER THIRTEEN

A Long, Rewarding Journey

Despite the relative success of the close-to-home chase in August, the 2006 storm-chasing season couldn't end soon enough. The heart of the season was frankly dismal from a chaser's perspective. Mother Nature just didn't produce tornadoes the way she normally did. In fact, the severe weather pattern that summer basically flipped the previous two-year trend on its head.

In 2004 and 2005 tornadoes increased in frequency from March onward and peaked in June. But in 2006 March and April proved the biggest tornado producers, coughing up more than twice the number of twisters that formed during those same months in either 2004 or 2005. Then, the atmosphere shut down. A strong cold front from Canada pushed southward deep into the Gulf of Mexico, blocking any of the necessary moisture that would normally feed storms on the Great Plains. It largely spared the United States from Mother Nature's wrath, but it also resulted in a long and frustrating summer. During June and July the 2006 season offered up fewer than half the number of tornadoes that had occurred during those same months in each of the two years prior. After April 7 there wasn't a significant tornado anywhere in the country for a month, until one occurred in Texas on May 9. And after that there wasn't another significant tornado for more than two and a half months. In a word the summer was quiet.

From a storm chaser's perspective, so few tornadoes to intercept meant that spotting twisters was an agonizingly difficult proposition. I saw a tornado on May 5 in the Texas panhandle and didn't see another until June 23 in Nebraska.

Finally in August the atmosphere woke up. Maybe that was one reason I was so eager to chase from home on August 20, even though I had originally planned for it to be a rest day around the house. I felt tornado deprived, and I wasn't going to pass up any opportunity to salvage an otherwise subpar chase season.

Just four days later a second chance at salvation came. The jet stream pulled north over southern Canada and the northern United States—the Gulf of Mexico was open for business, sending its moisture northward into the Plains. A cold front moving east across the Dakotas into Minnesota and a warm front pushing north through South Dakota promised to form a boundary line that would become tornadic. Dew points were forecast to rise into the seventies. The Storm Prediction Center was anticipating a moderate risk for severe storms over the Dakotas and Minnesota, specifically stating the threat for a few strong tornadoes. If the weather unfolded as expected, August 24 would be *the* day. I had to chase.

I notified my on-call tour group—folks who lived locally and were interested in chasing, last minute, for one or two days at a time—that the potential for severe weather looked good. But there was a catch: We were looking at one long drive from Denver to east-central South Dakota and back in two days—fifteen hundred to two thousand miles in forty-eight hours. I was going, whether people wanted to come or not.

Three did. Two customers signed on: Donna Garduno and Jon Callahan. Donna, from the Denver metro area, had chased with me earlier in 2006 but hadn't seen a tornado. Jon, from York, Nebraska, had also chased with me before, but he, too, hadn't seen a tornado. I hoped that August 24 would change that for both of them. We were also joined by my friend, Jon Merage, an up-and-coming storm chaser from Denver.

Late on the afternoon of August 23, I notified the group that we were a "go." The Denver-based contingent would meet at my house, and we'd pick up Jon in Nebraska on our way to South Dakota.

My alarm clock rang loudly at 4:30 a.m. on the morning of August 24.

I reached over, hit the snooze button, and almost fell back to sleep. Then I realized what day it was and bolted out of bed, headed for the shower. I was filled with excitement but dreaded the eleven- to twelve-hour drive we faced to reach the chase target area. I habitually checked the SPC forecast models on the computer, and the atmosphere looked on target for a severe-weather outbreak.

I crept back into the bedroom, leaned over, and kissed Caryn. She stirred ever so slightly. "Be careful," she said wearily from behind closed eyes. "I love you." I smiled, told her that I loved her, too, and quietly closed the bedroom door on my way out.

With my gear already loaded in the van the night before, I grabbed my keys and walked out the front door. Donna was already there, waiting and ready to go. Jon Merage soon showed up, and we climbed into my van and set a course for Nebraska.

By midmorning, we had passed North Platte, heading eastbound on Interstate 80. We arrived in York around noon, where we met a smiling Jon Callahan at a truck stop on the south side of town. In his late forties, Jon was reliably upbeat and a welcome burst of happy energy after our already long drive from Denver. With the van and our stomachs refueled, we merged back onto Interstate 80, destined for Omaha and Interstate 29 north. We passed Omaha around 1:00 p.m. and headed north toward Sioux Falls, South Dakota.

Sioux Falls was our initial target for the day. Forecast models predicted two clusters of intense storms that should be developing by late afternoon. Sioux Falls sat squarely between them.

We arrived around 4:00 p.m. and stopped at a mall in central Sioux Falls to freshen up after the long drive and check the radar data to see how things were developing. Severe storms were growing to our north, along the South Dakota–North Dakota border, while a tongue of moisture fed into a boundary line to the west of Sioux Falls, near Chamberlain, South Dakota. I targeted the area to the west, where the best moisture and atmospheric instability existed.

As we blasted west on Interstate 90, a series of severe storms grew just east of Chamberlain, but their cloud bases were too high off the ground for the storms to produce much more than hail and wind. But to our northwest another cell exploded near Pierre; it had potential. Soon the cell was under a severe-thunderstorm warning, and twenty short minutes later, it was upgraded to a tornado warning. We had to reach the storm!

It was probably some forty-five minutes to our northwest, moving southeast. I estimated that it would pass about thirty miles directly north of our position. We turned off the interstate onto a small road that took us straight north toward the town of Miller, which would be directly in the path of the supercell. Soon reports came over the radio that the storm had already produced a tornado. We were late. We could only hope that the storm wasn't a "one-hit wonder," that it would be cyclic and produce tornado after tornado.

We sped north on Highway 281 toward Wolsey and then turned onto U.S. Highway 14 west toward Miller. Highway 14 was a special highway for me; three years earlier on Highway 14 we had chased the monstrous tornado that destroyed the small town of Manchester. That part of South Dakota, it seemed, got raked with tornadoes all the time. It was a tough place to live, one where residents kept constant vigil, with one eye on their everyday lives and the other eye watching skyward.

As we arrived in Wolsey, the storm was plainly visible. A strong updraft indicated the storm's intensity. The supercell's structure resembled a spiraling barber's pole, only with a flared base. The beast was spinning rapidly, and it meant business. We turned onto Highway 14 and made our way quickly but cautiously toward Miller.

Still some ten miles east of Miller, we encountered a barrage of cloud-to-ground lightning strikes, occurring in fifteen-second intervals. Mile by mile, we got closer to Miller, where we could see dirt being kicked up off the farm fields by the storm's rear-flank downdraft. Suddenly a lowering formed under the storm, like a soup bowl stuck on the underside of the supercell. A tornado would form soon!

When we arrived in Miller, the tornado sirens were blaring. I stopped us on the north side of the highway near a small airport and set up camp. Within two minutes a long, fat, cone-shaped funnel formed to the west, just on the other side of town. A few moments later the tornado touched down.

It was 5:07 p.m.

"Oh, my God," I blurted out, afraid that Miller would suffer a direct hit. "Please do not hit the town."

The dark twister churned toward Miller against an orange and tan sky, with the tornado, by then a relatively powerful F2, just a mile outside of town. The tornado tracked slowly, with great bands of rain sheeting down from the sky around the funnel. A water tower stood in silhouette in the foreground, providing a sense of scale for the twister behind it. Then we heard the urgent call of distant sirens going off in the far part of town—additional warning for the residents of the impending twister.

Thankfully, the tornado edged past the south side of town, and we watched as it fed off the moist, unstable, energetic atmosphere of the plains, sucking up and chewing away at the earth of the nation's breadbasket.

Soon we were in danger, as baseball-size hail approached us. I had been pummeled by such large hail before, and I didn't want to go through that again. We raced east ahead of the storm on Highway 14, watching as the tornado slowly dissipated. Another funnel quickly came down to the east of where the first had faded. We drove past tan fields under dark skies, with the dark gray tornado at our three o'clock. The second tornado danced around to our southwest, but vanished within a mere three minutes. Even so, the storm had established its pattern—it was cyclic.

We stopped near the town of Wessington, where our quartet of chasers unloaded from the van. "Is that a funnel cloud right there?" Jon C. asked. "That is some intense motion."

Jon was right. A funnel was descending. "Let's go down another mile and get a clear view with no trees interfering with us," I suggested.

Having repositioned, we watched as the tornado strengthened, rapidly sucking the scud clouds into the storm's base. The wild and violent motion was at once chaotic and beautifully orchestrated, as if the clouds participated in some elaborate atmospheric dance. Then just a mile to the west of the tornado, a second debris cloud formed, and soon we had two fully formed tornadoes before us.

The western tornado quickly diminished, but the eastern tornado grew to an enormous size. Large debris was suddenly hurled into the air.

The tornado hit a farmstead, and it continued to strengthen as it marched eastward, with more farmsteads in its path. I had seen tornadoes *close* to my home in Bennett, but my house had never been *hit* by a twister. It was hard to know exactly how those people must have felt, as the tornado destroyed in seconds what it took them a lifetime to build, but I had an idea. I thought back to the Manchester twister and the total devastation it caused, and I flashed back to Topeka 1966, when I was nine years old and the monster of my childhood rumbled through the city.

The tornado marched on, fortunately missing both Wessington and nearby Wolsey. I was thankful we didn't have to find out what would have happened if it had directly hit those small country communities.

We repositioned in southwest Wolsey to watch as the tornado waltzed past the town. The storm at that point produced very little lightning, as if the supercell only had so much energy to give and poured itself into the tornado at the expense of the lightning.

As the tornado passed a half mile to our south, the tornado sirens in town were blaring in our ears. Some residents had gone to the local church seeking shelter, but many were standing out in their yards, watching as their town was spared. The twister had grown into a fat stovepipe and was a violent F3. Only thirty minutes had elapsed since the first tornado touched down in Miller.

Golf-ball-size hail began falling as we watched the tornado in awe. Not wanting to break another windshield, we jumped back into the van and raced off. We needed to get to the southeast. The only reasonable road to take us there was familiar Highway 281. The route, however, would require us to punch through the edge of the storm. We waited for the tornado to cross the highway, then raced south through wind-blown rain and hail. Moments later we encountered the damage path from the tornado. Power lines were strewn across the highway, as were highway signs and debris from someone's demolished ranch. The winds howled at 60 to 80 mph as I climbed out of the van to lower my rooftop antennas so we could drive beneath the power lines. I didn't want to drive across the lines that lay in other parts of the road for fear that they were still live and might get tangled in the wheels.

We carefully continued south as the rain and wind slackened. The tornado—my 304th since becoming a storm chaser—had grown to a proportion and scale that almost defied belief. "I'm officially impressed," Donna said. "This is beyond my expectations." There was a rare moment of quiet in the van, as we all just soaked up the scene.

Immediately to our west, just off the highway, was a badly damaged farmstead. "We have to go see if everyone is okay," I told the van. As we drove up the driveway, with a rainbow actually starting to appear—even as the tornado still churned not far away—we saw that the homestead's garage and several small outbuildings were completely destroyed. But the home itself was completely intact, and the family inside was unharmed.

We resumed our journey through the tornado's damage path, coming across a pickup truck that had been tossed fifty feet and flipped over by the winds. A side road was completely blocked by a roof from a barn or house that had been ripped off and deposited in the roadway, completely intact. Cars were stuck on the other side, their drivers scratching their heads at the bizarre sight.

I turned the van east onto Highway 26, speeding past the small village of Virgil. The tornado then was to our northeast, a ghostly gray with a huge reddish brown debris cloud. As we approached a junction with north-south Highway 37—just south of Huron—we heard reports of damage in and around the town. We continued eastbound past the intersection, struggling to get ahead of the tornado and the storm's precipitation. Just as the road turned from pavement to gravel and dirt, we emerged from the rain and hail and were grateful for dry ground to drive on.

We stopped neared the junction with Highway 29 as the tornado at last began to rope out. For a few moments the twister danced across the prairie like the classic twister from *The Wizard of Oz*. The sun poked out, illuminating the tornado with soft pink light. Even as the tornado thinned and roped out, in one last breath of energy it built a renewed debris cloud before vanishing forever. Then, just like that, all was quiet again, save for the hum of the van's engine in the background.

Seventeen tornadoes hit the northern plains that day, the last official twister forming north of us near Iroquois at 6:56 p.m. As many as twenty-six tornadoes were reported, though, and we experienced a total of seven tornadoes in the prairie of South Dakota. The strongest of the day, official or otherwise, was the F3 that rumbled past Wessington and Wolsey and dissipated near Huron.

The trek from Denver to South Dakota that began so much earlier that day had been a long journey but a rewarding one. Though we faced a 750-mile drive back to Denver, the return home was all the more bearable knowing that our trip was not in vain. The weather had held promise, and that promise was kept.

CHAPTER FOURTEEN

March Madness

Late March 2007. The National Storm Chasers Convention in Denver had taken place one-and-a-half short months earlier. Across the High Plains, storm chasers' thoughts were of blizzards and mountain snowstorms. Not severe weather. And certainly not tornadoes. March was one of the rarest months for such weather.

But something about March 2007 was different, more than I had ever seen during my twenty-plus years in Colorado as a storm chaser. Precisely 182 tornadoes erupted across the High Plains that month, when the average was just 87. Seventy-five of those tornadoes exploded in a single day, the biggest tornadic outbreak in all of 2007. It was March 28.

During the days leading up to the 28th, an unusually strong low-pressure system hovered over the western United States, while an abundance of moisture—uncharacteristic of March—swept up from the Gulf. All of the ingredients of a stereotypical severe-weather outbreak were coming together in atypical fashion, centered far to the west over the High Plains of Colorado, western Kansas and Nebraska, and the Texas and Oklahoma panhandles.

As unlikely as it was, the chase was on. I was joined by two people— Cathy Murphy, a Denver local who lived in Arvada, and Gawain Charlton-Perrin, an attorney from the Chicago area. Gawain flew into Denver late on March 27, and early on the morning of the 28th, Cathy and I met him at his airport hotel.

It seemed the whole of the High Plains was ready to burst to life that day. The SPC placed a moderate-risk rating over an enormous swath of tornado country, reaching from Nebraska deep into Texas. Over most of that area, the forecast called for a significant chance of tornadoes—with a 15 percent chance of tornadoes within twenty-five miles of any given point and a 10 percent probability of tornadoes rated EF2 to EF5. (The EF stood for the Enhanced Fujita Scale, a refined version of the F scale that had been in use for so many years.) The 15 percent probability of tornadoes far exceeded the 5 percent chance that had been forecast on other days when I had scored some of my best tornado intercepts. March 28, 2007, promised to be one to remember.

With such a large potential chase area, I focused our hunt over the Texas panhandle, between Amarillo and Lubbock. In May 2005 that area had given us the chase of our lives, when the Japanese scrambled to deploy their probe. In March 2007 I thought that swath of Tornado Alley would do it again. Based on the forecast models, I expected storms to form and then track northeast at a blazing 45 to 60 mph. It would be impossible to catch them from behind. My goal was to get in front of the storms, about one hour downwind, and wait for them to come to us, maturing and producing tornadoes. Then we'd wave good-bye as the storms raced past.

We left Denver heading east and southeast on Interstate 70 and then turned south on Highway 287 through Lamar, making a beeline for the Texas panhandle. Fog and haze grew steadily thicker as we drove south, a good sign of the moisture in the atmosphere. As we entered the Texas panhandle near Stratford, I told Cathy and Gawain about a monster twister I had seen there on May 15, 2003. A mile-wide tornado crossed the road we were on and stayed on the ground for nearly thirty minutes. Would we be that fortunate again? Only time would tell.

By early afternoon we had arrived in Amarillo, where we stopped to gas up and grab a bite to eat. We were famished, having not eaten at all during the six-hour drive from Denver. A corridor running north-south just east of Amarillo and Lubbock seemed to have the most potential, and we turned onto Interstate 40 east toward McLean, where just one month earlier I had seen my first-ever February tornado.

Watching from a gravel road off the highway near McLean, we saw cumulus towers develop to our southeast. After half an hour, one young thunderstorm in particular seemed intent on becoming something much greater. We sped eastbound on Interstate 40, hoping to intercept the fast-moving storm just west of Shamrock. We made it in time, but the storm wasn't yet ready to build into a tornadic supercell. It eventually did, however. As it raced off into Oklahoma, it spawned several tornadoes, including an EF2 that killed two people in Elmwood.

We concentrated our efforts on a new line of storms coming at us from much farther to the southwest, near Plainview, Texas. Over the course of thirty minutes, that line of storms coalesced into two dominant supercell thunderstorms. As we sped toward Silverton hoping to intercept them, my weather radio squealed with the National Weather Service warning tones. The robotic, monotone voice followed with a tornado warning for the area southwest of Silverton. We were still fifty miles away and late! I had been late before, including in August 2006 in South Dakota. I could only hope for a similar scenario—either cyclic storms or new storm formation behind the existing line of supercells.

Weather radar showed one of the two supercells to be absolutely massive. It had a characteristic "hook echo" on the radar image, a sure sign of the storm's strong rotation. Soon reports came in of a tornado from the storm and then a second. All three of us were getting anxious. Had we missed the show? Something deep inside—my storm-chaser's instinct—told me the day had just begun.

We continued south on Highway 256 near the Briscoe-Hall County line. Finally I could see the updraft base of the storm directly to our west. Farther to the southwest an elephant-trunk tornado became visible, but it dissipated before we got much closer. I took us farther south, paralleling Highway 256 on a road farther west.

Another supercell formed just north of the one that dropped the brief elephant trunk. A large lowering of the cloud base formed, and a few moments later fingers of cloud condensation descended to the ground, twirling around one another—a multivortex tornado. The fingers merged into a single large tornado that was so large it appeared the entire thunderstorm was sitting on the ground. But despite its size, the twister was relatively weak and soon fizzled.

Too many storms were popping up along the boundary line, impeding one another's ability to organize into a truly powerful supercell. I pointed the van to the south and southwest. We needed to get into pristine air that hadn't yet been affected by earlier storms. A storm that formed behind all the others—a tail-end Charlie—would be our best bet. With no competition for moisture or energy, it could feed directly off pure south winds that would flow into the updraft, often causing it to become the most intense storm in the line.

Just such a storm was forming, and I immediately sped toward the intersection of Highways 70 and 86. As we approached, the storm had developed a wall cloud. The updraft was clearly defined, and the storm's anvil streamed off to the north. It had that *look,* a look that I had seen dozens if not hundreds of times before. It was a look that told me the storm was ready to produce a significant tornado.

We sat at the highway intersection, waiting for something to happen. Cars occasionally drove by on the wet roads. The supercell sat to our west, a big blue-gray mass of cloud. Hail began to fall while the odd lightning bolt flashed. The winds, at least where we stood, were calm, and a fiery orange sunset glowed in the sliver of sky between cloud base and horizon line.

I took us farther west on Highway 86 to get *really* close to the storm. It was then that a truncated, cone-shaped funnel began to descend. "Here it comes," Gawain observed.

A debris cloud quickly formed, a swirling mess of soil and vegetation at ground level. The black funnel started to descend in earnest, with a smaller nipple of funnel cloud thrusting toward the earth. The funnel paused in its descent, then retreated, then grew again. The tornado-to-be seemed unsure whether it wanted to form or not.

A motorist pulled over next to us, getting out of his car just long enough to snap a photo before driving on. A storm chaser drove by not far behind, plainly identifiable with the vehicle's roof-mounted instrumentation. We retreated back to our intersection, and shortly thereafter several fingers of condensation funnel extended to the ground from the rotating wall cloud.

"This is going to produce a violent tornado," I told Cathy and Gawain.

David Gold called on my cell phone. He had been nowcasting for us from his home office. "I don't have time to talk right now, David," I told him. The funnel was on the verge of becoming an elephant trunk one mile to our west. Once on the ground, the tornado tracked north, still to our west, and then northwest. "My God, look at that," I blurted. "That is incredible."

After what felt like an eternity, a wide debris cloud began to take shape. It was faint, but it was there. The sun peeked out of the clouds to the west and lit the bottom half of the tornado a milky white. Meanwhile, the debris cloud kicked up tons of red west-Texas dirt. It was one of the most beautiful tornadoes I'd ever seen, achingly photogenic. And it was all the more spectacular given the twister's location in an open field, away from homes where it could do damage and mar the otherwise thrilling moment.

With the storm and the tornado speeding north at 50 mph, I realized that if we didn't get moving we'd lose it. We sped north on Highway 70, watching as the tornado churned its way up and over a rise in the distance, steamrolling across the rolling hills, open fields, and trees and shrubs of Texas's panhandle country.

Other storm chasers clogged the two-lane road, making our progress slow. We were falling behind the storm. A sheriff sped past us in a pickup truck, with his lights and sirens blazing. He pulled off on the side of the road, and most of the storm chasers followed suit. We continued north—he apparently wasn't interested in stopping us—and soon neared the town of Brice.

The tornado bent from cloud to ground like a great horn of plenty. As it began to rope out, it stretched to the ground in a taught line at a forty-five-degree angle. The funnel became ghostly white, and as the rope grew thinner and thinner, its cloud-to-ground span was tenuous. "It'll be gone in about thirty seconds," I told Cathy and Gawain. Then it disappeared. "That was a big one," I remarked.

With a moment to catch our breath, I checked the latest weather radar. Numerous supercell thunderstorms were clustered to our north. However, the storm we were chasing turned northeast—into virgin air that would allow its continued development. I had a feeling it would intensify again.

David Gold rang through on my phone, confirming my suspicions. "Stay with that storm, Roger," he told me. "I'm pretty certain it will produce at least one more strong tornado."

Our plan of attack was to get to Clarendon and then speed southeast through Lelia Lake to Hedley. But doing so would take us directly through the storm's rain and hail core. The supercell was virtually on top of us, with the strongest rotation heading for a point between Lelia Lake and Hedley. If the rotation spawned a tornado while we were en route, it'd be on a path to intersect our highway.

We raced out of Clarendon as the rain and hail—then quarter size—caught us. With the torrential precipitation, I could only drive 35 to 40 mph, not nearly fast enough to make it past the approaching storm and out of the danger zone. "Where are you?" David asked, calling again to check on our status. I told him our location and that it was too dangerous to drive any faster. "You're going to have to step on it if you're going to get ahead of the updraft. It looks like the storm is getting ready to spit out a tornado."

I couldn't see anything, let alone a forming tornado, with the rain and hail. The road had become white with a layer of hail. "We may lose a windshield here," I told my passengers. "Oh, well." The tornado was the real prize, and as long as we weren't in mortal danger from the hail, I wasn't going to let it deter me. I'd driven through bad hail before, and the collateral damage it caused to my van was a small price to pay to intercept a tornado's fleeting presence on the plains.

As I grit my teeth with determination, white-knuckle-driving through the hail swath, a baseball-size hailstone slammed into the hood of the van. "Hang on, guys," I said, keeping my eyes trained on the road ahead. "This may get a little wild and scary." Amazingly, all the largest hail-stones managed to miss the front windshield.

As we approached Lelia Lake, the hail slackened, improving my view, but the storm's RFD winds blew across the highway. One semi truck nearly toppled over, and the driver pulled to the side of the road. A pickup truck with a trailer full of all-terrain vehicles swerved from side to side, fighting to maintain control in the winds.

I looked south and was startled to see a tornado on the ground, just several hundred yards away! Trees were being ripped from the ground, and debris was flying all over. The twister was on a collision course with the van. "You guys have to keep your eye on it," I told Cathy and Gawain as I pressed the accelerator to the floor. "It's coming toward the road. It's coming right at us. We're in the path."

The tornado bore down on us as I tried to race past it. "Where is it? Is it behind us?" I asked. When the twister was only a hundred yards away from us, it lifted off the ground and into the sky, crossing the highway in the air above us. "Okay, we've made it," I said through a deep sigh of relief. It was one of the closest calls I had ever had.

I stopped for a moment to calm my nerves, all the while the van rocking in the RFD winds screaming past us. We continued to Hedley and then went north out of town on Highway 273, where it appeared the storm wasn't quite finished. After five minutes we reached a point parallel to the storm, which was just to our west heading north-northeast. "We have a tornado!" I yelled. Soon, however, we lost sight of the twister as it became wrapped in rain and hail from the storm. Continuing to chase such a tornado was a bad idea—it would be nearly impossible to stay out of the path of what we couldn't clearly see in the first place.

I drove us back toward McLean, our original chase target for the day. The storm dropped one last tornado, larger than any we had seen that day. But it quickly disappeared from view, also hidden behind rain and hail. "It's too bad," Cathy said. "It looks like the perfect cone coming down."

With the sky totally dark, we called it a day and turned for home. It was then that the first reports began to trickle in of the fatal twister in Oklahoma and of another in Holly, Colorado. The Holly twister was the first fatal tornado in Colorado in more than forty years, and it hit the small, rural community near the Kansas border by surprise. There wasn't time for the town to activate the warning sirens. When a startled resident saw the twister barreling toward town, he called 911. "Are there any tornadoes around?" he asked. "Because there's one in my backyard, and it's bigger than God." The EF3 tornado slammed into Holly moments later. Gustavo Puga and his wife, Rosemary Rosales, were home with their three-year-old daughter, Noelia. When the tornado smashed into their house, it tore the home from its foundation. The family was sucked up into the twister and thrown from the house. They all landed in a tree in the yard, with Gustavo holding Noelia tight to his chest. She was virtually uninjured, but Gustavo's wife Rosemary later died at the hospital from traumatic injuries.

◉

The year 2007 proved to be a particularly devastating year for tornadoes—twenty-five killer tornadoes caused seventy-nine fatalities. Surprisingly, despite advances in warning systems and a growth in the understanding of tornado formation over the years, tornadoes in the most recent years appeared to be getting more and more deadly. They killed thirty-six people in 2004, thirty-eight in 2005, sixty-seven in 2006, and then seventy-nine in 2007. There's been much speculation about whether or not tornado frequency in the United States, as well as tornado severity, has any link to El Niño or global climate change. In scientific studies focused on the El Niño/Southern Oscillation (ENSO) phenomenon, differences between El Niño and La Niña years have been statistically insignificant. Further, any ENSO-caused fluctuations in tornadoes have been overrun by two other trends—an increase in tornado-reporting efficiency, resulting in a linear increase of about fifteen tornado reports per year, and a seemingly repeating ten-year tornado cycle of highs and lows. As far as global climate change, meteorologists and atmospheric scientists have barely scratched the surface. It's simply too early to draw any reliable conclusions, despite rampant media hype and speculation. One thing is certain, though: As of mid-March 2008, the 2008 tornado year was shaping up to be a record setter. The running total of tornado reports for the year sat at 462, more than four times the count for any of the three previous years for that time of year. If such a trend continues, 2008 will far surpass any year in recorded history for sheer number of tornadoes. Their severity and impact on human life remains to be seen.

Even so, the deadly tornadoes of the 2000s paled in comparison to the worst tornadoes Mother Nature has spawned. The twenty-five deadliest twisters in U.S. history have each individually killed more than 75 people. All of those twisters occurred prior to 1954. The deadliest—the Tri-State tornado of 1925—killed 695 people.

It was a time when tornadoes were little understood and warning systems virtually nonexistent. The United States had come out of its "dark era" of tornado reporting just nine years earlier. On the morning of March 18, 1925, a surface low-pressure system tracked across northwest Arkansas and southwest Missouri heading northeast—as so many storms do—across Missouri, Illinois, and Indiana. A warm front extended east from the low, while a cold front trailed behind to the southwest. Warm, moist air funneled up from the Gulf, and strong wind sheer completed the weather setup.

Then at 1:01 p.m. a tornado touched down north-northwest of Ellington, Missouri. It wasn't much at first, but it stayed on the ground and grew steadily stronger until it reached F5 status. The first person died in Ellington. Ten more died before the twister left the Ozarks and Missouri behind. In Illinois the devastation was magnified many times over. At 2:30 p.m. the entire town of Gorham was wiped from the map, and 34 people died. Over the next forty minutes, 541 more people were killed and another 1,423 seriously injured as the tornado tore a mile-wide swath of destruction through the towns of Murphysboro, De Soto, Hurst-Bush, and West Frankfort. In West Frankfort some 800 miners were five hundred feet below ground when the tornado hit. They lost power and escaped via a shaft. Back on the surface they discovered that most of the destroyed homes were their miners' cottages and that most of the dead were their wives and children. The Great Tri-State Tornado bore down on Indiana next, where more lives were lost and half the town of Princeton was destroyed. Finally, at 4:30 p.m. the twister lifted into the sky just three miles southwest of Petersburg, Indiana, sparing the community.

In its wake of devastation, the twister left behind a smattering of records that more than eighty years later have never been broken. Single deadliest tornado: 695 dead. Longest continuous path on the ground: 219 miles. Longest duration: 3.5 hours.

Other statistics are equally staggering. With an average speed of 62 mph and a peak speed of 73 mph, it was the third fastest tornado in history. More than fifteen thousand homes were destroyed, and 2,027 people were injured. Interestingly, the tornado had an almost arrow-straight track, traveling to the northeast at sixty-nine degrees in a perfect line for 183 of its 219 miles.

The National Weather Service office in Paducah, Kentucky, called it a "once in several hundred years" tornado.

As we drove north into the night, the complex of supercells rumbling through the Texas panhandle had one more blow to deliver. Flashes of lightning occasionally revealed brief glimpses of the countryside. One such glimpse illuminated a fat, ominous wedge tornado crossing the highway north of us. It missed us, as well as the towns of Miami and Canadian, Texas. But the F3 was not completely benign—it killed one person and caused $3 million in damage.

In Elk City, Oklahoma, we found a hotel and crashed for the night. By the next morning, when we completed our return to Denver, the day's final tally had become clear: 75 confirmed tornadoes, distributed evenly throughout the SPC's original forecast area—from Texas to Nebraska. The 182 tornadoes in March 2007 and the 75 tornadoes on March 28 in particular weren't records by any means. The one-month record belonged to May 2003, when a confirmed 543 tornadoes touched down. The one-day record was held by April 3 and 4, 1974, when 147 tornadoes touched down in the United States in a single twenty-four-hour period. But March was memorable nonetheless, not only for the magnitude of the outbreak but for *how early* in the season that outbreak occurred.

As the 2007 chase season continued, the anomaly of March proved to be a precursor to another strange season. As with 2006, the Great Plains saw a large number of tornadoes throughout early spring and then relatively few in the heart of the season, from late spring through the middle of summer.

On July 3, with the Silver Lining tours having finished days earlier, I sat at home for a day of rest. It wasn't just a day that I didn't plan to chase. I didn't even *want* to chase. But as I'd discovered in previous years, rest days had a nasty habit of turning into chase days.

Despite a less-than-promising atmospheric setup that morning, a series of landspouts—nonsupercell tornadoes—formed east of my home in Bennett, Colorado. As I had hundreds or even thousands of times before, I jumped in my van and raced across the High Plains, checking radar data, watching the skies, and filming with my cameras. I was alone on that particular day—chasing by myself and for myself.

I sat in the driver seat of the van, watching as a tornado crossed a dirt road directly ahead of me. It was just two blocks to my north, and I could see each piece of debris clearly. I watched sadly as a farm animal was sucked up into the twister and thrown to the ground. It never moved again. Telephone poles alongside the road snapped like matchsticks. Split-rail fencing flattened under the force of the winds.

At that moment a thought entered my mind. I had always wanted to drive *through* a tornado. Why, I couldn't exactly say. But this seemed like the perfect opportunity. No customers or family in the van, just me. The twister was right there, a few hundred yards away. Why not go for it? I put my video camera on its dashboard mount, shifted into drive, and started toward the tornado. It was just a hundred yards away.

Suddenly, a large piece of wood slammed into the side of the van, jolting me awake. Had I gone mad? Had I become possessed by the tornado, drawing me into its destructive clutches under some hypnotic spell? There was almost no way I would survive driving directly into it. Did I want to become like that innocent farm animal? Tossed aside by the tornado, dead? I regained my wits and drove home.

That final tornado on the afternoon of July 3 turned out to be my last tornado intercept of 2007. It was just as well; I was tired and ready for a break. But I knew that a break wouldn't last long.

CHAPTER FIFTEEN

Supertyphoon

A little over a month after that last tornado of 2007, my phone rang from half a world away. On the other end of the line was Stuart Robinson, a good friend of mine who lives in Leicestershire, England. Stuart and I first met in 2002 when he was a client with Silver Lining Tours. A year later he graduated from SLT's Master Class and went on to become an accomplished and respected storm chaser, particularly in England, where he was in high demand for appearances on television programs produced by the BBC, ITV, Channel 4, and Sky.

"Roger, what do you think about chasing a hurricane together this fall?" Stuart asked.

It was an enticing proposition. Stuart and I had teamed up in 2005 to chase Hurricane Rita and had great fun together. Like me, Stuart is a storm junkie—the bigger, badder, and stronger, the better. As if Stuart's company wasn't enough, he sweetened the deal: North One TV, a London-based production company, wanted to send along a filmmaker to document our chase. All expenses paid. Anywhere in the world. Try to intercept the eye. Saying yes was a no-brainer. I'd never chased outside North America, and the prospect of an international storm-chasing expedition had me ecstatic.

As always, I returned to the most fundamental question for any storm chaser: What storm to chase? Stuart and I agreed that we wanted nothing less than a Category Four storm on the Saffir-Simpson scale, with sustained winds between 131 and 155 mph. Such a storm would make for great television, with intense winds, high waves, pounding rain, and a healthy dose of adrenaline.

August bled into September, and soon October was looming. But still the right storm at the right time hadn't presented itself to us. Then on the morning of October 1 a tropical depression formed in the Pacific Ocean between Guam and Taiwan. It wasn't much, but it held promise.

The Joint Typhoon Warning Center (JTWC) was the first to track it. The JTWC is a U.S. Department of Defense agency responsible for issuing tropical cyclone (also known as hurricanes or typhoons) warnings for the Pacific and Indian oceans. The agency was formed in 1959 and was located at Nimitz Hill, Guam, for its first forty years, before Nimitz Hill closed and JTWC relocated to its present-day location at Naval Base Pearl Harbor, Hawaii. It's staffed by twenty-six U.S. Air Force and Navy personnel that monitor the weather 24 hours a day, 365 days per year, focused on an immense 110-million-square-mile area of the Pacific and Indian oceans, stretching from the west coast of the Americas all the way to the east coast of Africa.

One day later, on October 2, the JTWC upgraded the depression to a tropical storm and named her Krosa, the Cambodian word for "crane." Computer models predicted that Krosa would soon strengthen and become a typhoon.

For tropical storms to upgrade to hurricane (typhoon) status requires a delicate balance of atmospheric conditions. Too much wind shear, not enough heat and moisture, or other low-pressure systems can disrupt a storm's formation and strength. That's one major reason hurricanes so often die rapidly over land—their balance has been disrupted; they've been cut off from the warm ocean influence they desperately need to survive. Krosa, for her part, formed under almost ideal conditions in a region of ocean containing some of the warmest waters anywhere in the world—ocean temperatures hovering in the upper 80s Fahrenheit. Almost like bath water. Such warm water gives off vast amounts of energy for a typhoon to feed on, like pouring gasoline onto a fire.

And feed Krosa did. By the morning of October 3, Krosa had been upgraded again, this time to a full-fledged typhoon with sustained winds of 80 mph and wind gusts near 100 mph. The JTWC warned that Krosa would rapidly intensify as she churned toward the northwest, with her sights set on Taiwan.

I emailed Stuart immediately. *Do you think it's possible for us to fly to Taipei, Taiwan, to intercept this beast? Can the film crew obtain their work visas in time for the trip?* We had hard questions to answer and very little time to answer them. On October 4 Stuart, the filmmaker—Olly Lambert—and I got on the phone. Krosa was already a Category Three storm, with sustained winds between 111 and 130 mph.

"We need to decide soon so we can arrange flights, hotels, rental car," I said. "If we wait a moment too long, flights will be cancelled and the Taipei airport will close. Do we want to pull the trigger and make a run for it before we don't have the option?"

Late that afternoon it was decided—we would go for it. All indications were that Krosa would soon reach Category Five strength. She'd become a supertyphoon, with winds greater than 155 mph, a massive storm surge, and inevitable and widespread structural damage to buildings.

A worry lingered in the back of my mind, though. Would the buildings in Taiwan be strong enough to withstand the onslaught of the storm? I assumed so. I hoped so. Taiwan was a mature and developed country, I reasoned, located in a part of the world that sees its share of cyclones. The integrity of the buildings ought to reflect that. The island's topography put me further at ease. Much of the coast and areas immediately inland are at an elevation of at least forty feet above sea level, putting them out of reach of the storm surge. And a large north-south mountain range that spans the eastern half of the island would provide shelter if needed and serve as a kind of fortress wall to fend off the batterings of Krosa.

I boarded a plane in Denver the night of October 4 and connected through Los Angeles on a fourteen-hour Air China flight that carried me over the Pacific Ocean, across the International Date Line, over Krosa herself, and into Taipei, Taiwan, where I arrived at 6:00 a.m. on October 6. By the time I landed, the JTWC had officially conferred Krosa with supertyphoon status. Her sustained winds were 170 mph, with gusts to 210 mph. A lump grew in my throat. What had I gotten myself into? A storm this strong could level everything in its path, including me. Katrina had been a harsh learning experience, but did the lessons learned there sink in? Here I was again, facing a storm of unimaginable strength, planning to let it hit me squarely in the jaw.

I gathered my bags, cleared customs, and flopped into a seat at a café at the airport where I could wait for Stuart and Olly to arrive at 10:00 a.m., after they flew from London to Shanghai to Taipei. Stuart and Olly emerged from customs together, looking ready to start the adventure. It was the first time I had met Olly face to face. He stood about five foot nine, weighed some 180 pounds, and gazed through confident eyes set behind a pair of thin-rimmed eyeglasses. Olly, I learned, was born in London and studied English literature at Durham University before shifting into documentary filmmaking. Since then he'd worked extensively for Channel 4 and the BBC, holding several titles: producer, director, videographer, often on the same project.

With our rental car in hand—a shiny, new Toyota van—we jumped onto the expressway and charted a course for the Holiday Inn Taipei on the eastern side of the metropolitan area on the northern end of the island. It was tucked up in the hills, where a light rain was already falling, and the winds were blowing, if only gently at that hour.

After encountering a difficult language barrier at the car-rental counter, we were pleasantly surprised to find that everyone at the hotel with whom we came into contact spoke fluent English. The Holiday Inn was unlike any I'd seen in the United States. The lobby was magnificently decorated in marble and elaborate chandeliers. It looked much more the part of a high-end Hilton or Ritz Carlton.

Stuart, Olly, and I agreed to rest in our rooms for a few minutes before we got down to work—outfitting the rental van with our weather equipment and cameras. When I opened the door to my room, I was as surprised as I'd been when we first walked into the lobby. Flat-screen television. WiFi Internet. Pillow-top bed. A well-stocked refrigerator with water, soda, and Taiwanese beer. A basket of goodies, including some very welcome American delicacies—Snickers and Hershey's bars—as well as some not-so-welcome Taiwanese favorites—peanuts with dried fish. As hungry as I was, I couldn't bring myself to try them.

Our chase was to begin later that afternoon and continue overnight, so we didn't have much time to rest. A few hours at most . . . not nearly enough after my exhaustingly long trans-Pacific flight. We convened in the lobby, ready to outfit the van. Stuart clambered on top of the roof, where he affixed an anemometer (to measure wind speed), as well as a thermometer and barometer (to measure temperature and air pressure). Meanwhile, Olly wired the interior of the van with a network of bullet cameras, tiny cylindrical surveillance cameras just 2.5 inches long, meant to capture the action inside the van, including our conversations and facial expressions during the chase.

By early afternoon we were ready. Just before we set off, the hotel manager caught up with us and handed me a sign, printed in Taiwanese. "If you meet the police, this may help you," he said through a smile.

"What does it say?" I asked.

"Typhoon Research Team."

We thanked him and then sped north toward the coast, where we'd intercept a highway we could follow east to the northeast corner of the island. All indications were that this would be ground zero for the typhoon's eye to make landfall. The eye wall contains the fiercest winds of the storm, and that, after all, is what we were after.

As we drove through the small towns that dot the northern coast, we passed a rare sign in English advertising a beverage called "Twister." We just smiled at one another and laughed. Perhaps it was an auspicious sign.

Every street corner seemed to have a 7-Eleven convenience store, well stocked with American snack food, as well as a greater assortment of local treats—rice crackers, dried squid, and many more flavors I can't and don't care to remember.

We reached the coastal city of Chilung, where the winds were beginning to gust to 70 mph, and the Pacific Ocean was a turbulent mess of thirty-foot waves and blowing sea foam. Waves crashed into the rocky shoreline with a thunderous boom, while Stuart leaned into the wind, clad in a head-to-toe rain suit and goggles.

Continuing eastward, we rounded a point of land and pulled into a small town with a deserted gas station. Within minutes, a police officer pulled up. For a moment we worried he would force us to seek shelter, but as he read the Typhoon Research Team sign taped to the inside of our window, he simply waved at us and then drove on. We tinkered with our gear for a few moments to make sure everything was working properly. All the while, the rain grew heavier and heavier as each rain band approached. Winds were beginning to pick up, too, and we agreed it best to find suitable shelter in a coastal town that could withstand a significant storm surge.

Looking at our map, we elected a small town and harbor named Fu-lung as our target. It sits on the northeast coast, directly east of Taipei. When we arrived in town, however, it was abundantly clear that Fu-lung was little more than a small fishing village. There were no sturdy buildings, and the elevation was near sea level, making it susceptible to both storm surge and flooding. We continued onward, rounding the point and turning south toward Ta-li, a much larger city.

At the apex of the point, we were exposed to the full force of Krosa. Pulling off the side of the road, we clambered out of the van to admire nature in reverse. Normally, a stream ran off a seaside cliff and plunged into the sea as a picturesque waterfall. But the water wasn't flowing off the cliff at all. It was flowing *uphill*, turned back by the force of the now 100-mph winds. In the ocean directly to our east, the waves hammered the coast with such strength it sounded like an earthquake, with all the attendant rumbling, smashing, and roaring.

With each mile south that we journeyed, we grew closer to the approaching eye wall, as evidenced by the strengthening wind and rain. As the wind speed surpassed 125 mph, visibility was reduced to almost nil. The force of the wind was ripping the rain into small particles that resembled a fine mist. While we sat on the side of the road, admiring the spectacle, a semi truck and a passenger car drove past us. What was the truck doing out in the middle of the typhoon?

A strong gust of wind hit us, and a moment later hit the truck broadside. I watched in disbelief as the truck tilted and then disappeared behind the lashing rain. When the wind gust subsided and visibility improved, I saw the truck turned over on its side, the driver frantically climbing out of the cab. Almost without missing a beat, he hopped into the passenger car that had been following behind, and the car drove off into the storm, once again leaving us on our own.

As we continued toward Ta-li, Krosa's winds grew quite intense. At 4:00 p.m. she officially made landfall as a Category Four storm, with wind gusts to 160 mph. Tons of plant material flew through the air, as did tree limbs, pebbles plucked from the beaches, and building debris. Occasionally, debris would slam into the side of our van and the windshield with a surprisingly loud thud.

When we arrived in Ta-li, we met a second police officer. "You have to leave," he told us in broken English. "Go find shelter."

We explained what we were doing, and to our astonishment he sped off and left us to the storm. We drove downtown, in hopes of finding a strong building to protect us from the tin and sheet metal that was flying through the air after being stripped off more poorly constructed buildings. Right off the highway, we found what we were looking for—a large metal structure that wasn't going anywhere. Stuart parked the van on the building's south side, to keep us shielded from the predominantly northeast winds.

All three of us spilled out of the van to experience Krosa's fury firsthand. Mixed in with the dominating roar of the wind, I could hear glass shattering, wood splintering, the scrape of debris sliding across the roads, and the high-pitched whistle of the wind screaming through power lines overhead. Olly ran out into the middle of the street to film Stuart and me from a distance.

"Come back, Olly!" we yelled out to him. "It's too dangerous out there!"

A 100-plus-mph wind gust knocked him off his feet, but he regained his footing and returned to the relatively safety in the wind shadow of the structure. Reunited, our trio was puzzled by one aspect of the storm—the winds remained out of the northeast and didn't intensify further. However, had the eye made landfall in Ta-li, as we expected it to, the winds should have increased further and should have shifted out of the southwest. Maybe the eye was passing farther to our south. If it was, how so? Our latest radar and satellite images showed Ta-li as the epicenter of activity.

Stuart fired up the laptop and, incredibly, was able to get a WiFi Internet signal. We soon discovered that the eye, as it approached Taiwan's eastern coastline, had moved sharply south toward I-lan and was now moving back out to sea! The mountains, it turned out, proved an effective repellent to the eye of a typhoon.

Over the course of the next hour, the winds in Ta-li slowly subsided. We piled back into the van and drove south toward the rice paddies of Suao. From there, we'd be able to return to Taipei via a major highway.

As we neared Suao, we encountered extensive damage. Buildings were toppled. Trees were uprooted. Power lines dangled in the winds. Many side roads were impassable, and significant flooding was getting worse. People ran around in the streets, desperately trying to gather whatever of their belongings they could find that hadn't been blown away completely by Krosa. Soon, winds decreased to 50 mph, with 70-mph gusts. Taiwan had dodged a major bullet, and we were all disappointed that we had, too.

As we were driving around Suao, the clouds lifted enough for us to see some of the mountains directly to the west. Most of the vegetation was either completely stripped or flattened to the ground. I later learned that, according to Taiwan's Central Weather Bureau, some locations received more than forty inches of rain in a two-day period. At FengQi Lake in Jiayi County, a staggering 111.2 cm of rain was measured—nearly 3.5 feet.

All that rain caused, in addition to the expected flooding, numerous mud and rock slides on the steep mountain slopes. One of those landslides killed two people in a mountainous area of Taipei. Isolated accidents caused by the high winds claimed two more lives; a traffic accident claimed a fifth life. In total, the death toll from Krosa was mercifully low. But 2.2 million homes were left without power, and Krosa caused more than $1 billion in damage.

While we turned onto the highway to head north to Taipei, Krosa circled around in the Pacific and set her sights on Taiwan once more, this time crossing the northern tip of the island six hours after she first slammed into I-lan, between Ta-li and Suao. She crossed the South China Sea, significantly weakened, and then grazed the edge of mainland China, where more than 1.4 million people were evacuated from the coast. Then, as steadily as she had churned toward Taiwan and then China, she marched back out to sea, crossing just south of Japan and dying somewhere in the north Pacific.

Stuart drove us back to Taipei, where we were amazed to find our hotel nearly unfazed by the storm that had just passed. We flopped into chairs in the lobby and knocked back a few Taiwanese beers, utterly exhausted. "You are the craziest two people I have ever met," Olly said to Stuart and me between swigs of beer. This coming from a documentary filmmaker who'd spent time in war-torn regions such as Afghanistan and the Gaza Strip on video projects.

That night I crawled into bed for a good night's rest but couldn't resist turning on the television to catch up on the Major League Baseball playoffs—a delayed broadcast of the game between the Boston Red Sox and the Cleveland Indians. By the next morning Taipei International Airport had reopened, and Stuart and Olly were on their way back to England. I took off in the early afternoon and, thanks to recrossing the International Date Line, was back in Denver before I even left Taiwan. I hugged and kissed Caryn. It was good to be home. I flipped on the television, grateful to watch the next game of the series live, in real time.

The 2007 season was definitively over. It began with an explosive tornado outbreak in March and was capped off with a supertyphoon in a far-off land. But soon there'd be another chance to chase, whether the next day, the next month, or the next year with the start of the 2008 chase season. Chasing tornadoes was a calling I couldn't deny. I measured my life in miles and storms and twisters and the comings and goings of each storm-chasing season. That wasn't bound to change, not anytime soon. A tornado came close to killing me as a child, and tornadoes had come close to killing me since. But I couldn't walk away from them. Hunting nature's fury was in my blood. It was a part of me.

Epilogue

Despite the tales of destruction within this book's pages, Mother Nature isn't an inherently angry woman. Many of her meteorological processes are in fact meant to calm the weather, to dissipate energy and restore balance. Winds blow from areas of high pressure to areas of low pressure, rushing to even out an imbalance in the pressure gradient. Rains fall from the sky in order to help the atmosphere maintain its balance of moisture, bringing temperature and humidity back into harmonious sync. Lightning streaks from cloud to ground when the difference in charge becomes too great. Yes, Mother Nature likes balance.

Yet there are times when she seemingly rears up in anger. She unleashes tornadoes or hurricanes or other forms of severe weather. Tornadoes, with their compact and awesomely devastating intensity, may be the worst. But for many reasons they shouldn't exist. They are counterintuitive freaks of nature. Tornadoes violate Mother Nature's attempt to restore and maintain balance; they are an intensification of imbalance almost beyond comprehension. Winds concentrate until they blow at hundreds of miles per hour, achieving speeds seen in nothing else on earth.

The conditions that give rise to tornadoes form over a matter of just hours. The tornadoes themselves form in only minutes, exist for a few moments of time, and then disappear. There is little trace of them before their existence and little trace of them after. Like an elusive predator, they may leave signs of their passing, but catching one in the act proves an exceedingly difficult proposition.

Even so, there are hunters who catch these monsters. They do so with skill and precision, with knowledge and a bit of luck. They do it like Roger Hill.

As of this writing, Roger has personally witnessed more than 400 tornadoes, a feat that ranks him in an exclusive pantheon of the world's best storm chasers. And yet, as I chase with Roger and listen to his stories and watch his videos, I'm struck by his overwhelming enthusiasm for each tornado intercept. Each one is as exciting as if it were the first of his life.

Early on, the skeptic in me wondered if the excitement was feigned and if the close calls really brought him as near to death as he claimed. Was it a show for the clients on the tours, to ensure that they all felt that they got their money's worth? Was it melodrama? As I spent more and more time with Roger, over a period of months and then years, I realized that every part of him is genuine. No man would give up a job and a marriage to pursue something about which he wasn't authentically passionate. His enthusiasm is real, the outward evidence of a man living his dream. The danger, too, is real. To get as close to tornadoes as Roger does can be literally life threatening, and only his knowledge and insight keep him and his passengers safe.

But beyond taking my word for it, consider that more than half of Silver Lining Tours' customers are repeat clients. People don't come back for a melodramatic charlatan. They come back because of Roger. His genuine enthusiasm is infectious, chasing with him is fun, and frankly, the man knows how to find tornadoes. He is a master hunter.

From the outside looking in, it would be easy to call Roger—or storm chasers more generally—a selfish breed. They chase for personal reasons, deriving pleasure from something that causes pain for so many people. But that's not entirely accurate. Storm chasers are also driven by a moral and ethical responsibility to help those in need—to warn a town when the tornado they're chasing approaches a community or to help a family when they see a house get hit. That much is obvious.

With Roger, though, there's also a deep desire to find a greater good in his storm chasing. To that end he has worked tirelessly to make life safer for the people living in the heart of Tornado Alley. Some of that work is aimed at improving science's understanding of severe weather and in so doing helping to improve forecasting for tornadoes. This happens through Roger's work as a probe driver for research projects of the National Severe Storms Laboratory.

The large balance of Roger's "giving back" is composed of education. He regularly conducts SKYWARN training sessions. SKYWARN was born in the early 1970s as a way to train storm spotters—individuals who take a position near their community and report wind gusts, hail size, rainfall, and cloud formations that could signal a developing tornado. Roger also speaks for free, conducting presentations and seminars at colleges and universities and at National Weather Service meetings and seminars. And he sends a complimentary copy of his annual-highlights DVD to every National Weather Service office across the plains, so they are able to use his footage during their training classes.

During the writing of this book, a friend of mine—an elementary school teacher in a Denver suburb—asked if "that storm chaser guy" with whom I was writing the book would give a talk for her class of students; they were studying a chapter on weather. "He has a pretty busy schedule coming up, but I can ask," I told her. Roger responded to my email almost immediately: "No problem." It was the best evidence of his commitment to education, to "giving back," and to sharing with others that which has given him so much personal joy.

Hunting Nature's Fury is the story of a man doing what he loves. There are few things more rewarding in life, I think, than following one's true passion. Oftentimes following that passion requires a leap of faith away from the old and familiar. Roger took that leap. He followed his passion and embraced it boldly. We should all have such courage to find what we love and then pursue it relentlessly.

— *Peter Bronski, 2009*

Glossary of Weather Terms

accessory cloud. A cloud that is dependent on a larger cloud system for its development and continuation. Shelf clouds and walls clouds are examples.

advection. The transport of an atmospheric property (cold, heat, moisture) by the wind.

anticyclonic rotation. Rotation opposite that of the earth's rotation (clockwise in the Northern Hemisphere). The opposite of cyclonic rotation.

anvil. The flat, spreading top of a cumulonimbus cloud. Thunderstorm anvils can extend hundreds of miles downwind of the thunderstorm itself and can also spread upwind (a back-sheared anvil).

anvil crawler. A lightning discharge occurring within the anvil of a thunderstorm and appearing to "crawl" along the underside of the anvil.

anvil dome. A large, overshooting top or penetrating top.

arcus. A low, horizontal cloud formation associated with the leading edge of thunderstorm outflow (the gust front). Roll clouds and shelf clouds are examples.

back-building thunderstorm. A thunderstorm in which new development takes place on the upwind side (typically the west or southwest side). Such storms seem to remain stationary or even propagate backwards.

backing winds. Winds that either (a) shift in a counterclockwise direction at a given location over time (from southwesterly to southeasterly) or (b) shift in a counterclockwise direction with height (westerly at the surface, becoming more southerly aloft). Backing of the surface wind can increase the potential for tornado development by increasing directional shear.

back-sheared anvil. A thunderstorm anvil that spreads upwind, against the flow aloft. Such anvils imply a very strong updraft and a high severe-weather potential.

barber pole. A thunderstorm with a visual appearance that resembles curving cloud striations, like the stripes of a barber pole. The barber pole structure is usually most pronounced on the leading edge of the updraft, while the storm's rear-flank downdraft usually erodes the clouds on the trailing side of the updraft.

bear's cage. A region of storm-scale rotation in a thunderstorm that is wrapped in heavy precipitation. The bear's cage often coincides with a radar hook echo and/or the storm's mesocyclone. The term refers to the danger involved in observing such an area visually, which would be done at close range in poor visibility.

beaver tail. A particular type of inflow band with a broad, flat appearance reminiscent of a beaver's tail. It is attached to a supercell's updraft.

bounded weak echo region (BWER). A.k.a. vault. A radar signature within a thunderstorm characterized by a localized minimum in radar reflectivity at low levels and that extends upward into the storm. It is surrounded by higher reflectivity aloft. The BWER is associated with a strong updraft.

bow echo. A linear radar echo that is bent outward into a bow shape. Damaging straight-line winds often occur near the center of the bow echo.

box. A.k.a. watch box. A severe thunderstorm or tornado watch.

bust. An inaccurate forecast or unsuccessful storm chase. Usually a situation in which severe weather is expected but does not occur.

BWER. See bounded weak echo region.

CA. Cloud-to-air lightning.

cap. A.k.a. capping inversion. A layer of relatively warm air aloft—usually several thousand feet above ground level—that suppresses or delays thunderstorm development. Air parcels rising into this layer become cooler than the surrounding air, inhibiting their ability to rise farther. However, while the cap can suppress thunderstorm development, it can also be an ingredient in *severe* thunderstorm outbreaks by separating warm, moist air below from cooler, dry air above. That separation allows atmospheric instability to build, such that when the cap does erode, explosive storms can result.

CAPE. See convective available potential energy (CAPE).

Cb. See cumulonimbus cloud.

CC. Cloud-to-cloud lightning.

cell. Convection in the form of a single updraft, downdraft, or updraft/downdraft pair and evidenced by a dome or tower. A typical thunderstorm consists of several cells (a multicellular thunderstorm).

CG. Cloud-to-ground lightning.

cirrus. High-level clouds (sixteen thousand feet or more) composed of ice crystals. They appear in the form of white, delicate filaments or white patches or bands.

clear slot. A local region of clearing skies or reduced cloud cover indicating an intrusion of drier air. Often believed to be a visual indication of a rear-flank downdraft.

cloud tags. A.k.a. scud. Ragged, detached cloud fragments.

condensation funnel. A funnel-shaped cloud associated with rotation and consisting of condensed water droplets (as opposed to smoke, dust, debris), in contrast to a debris cloud.

convection. The transport of heat and moisture by the movement of a fluid (air). In meteorology, specifically describes the vertical transport of heat moisture, particularly by updrafts and downdrafts in an unstable atmosphere. "Convection" and "thunderstorms" are often used interchangeably, although thunderstorms are only one form of convection. Convection that occurs without cloud formation is known as dry convection, while visible convection is known as moist convection.

convective available potential energy (CAPE). A measure of the amount of energy available for convection. Directly related to the maximum potential vertical speed within an updraft. Higher values indicate greater potential for severe weather.

convective outlook. A forecast containing the area or areas of expected thunderstorm development and severity over the contiguous United States, issued several times daily by the Storm Prediction Center. The terms "approaching," "slight risk," "moderate risk," and "high risk" are used to describe severe thunderstorm potential.

core punch. A penetration by a vehicle into the heavy precipitation core of a thunderstorm.

cumulonimbus cloud. A.k.a. Cb, thunderhead. A cloud characterized by strong vertical development in the form of a huge tower topped by a smooth, flat anvil.

cumulus. Detached clouds, generally dense with sharp outlines, showing vertical development in the form of domes, mounds or towers. Usually tops are rounded, while bases are horizontal.

cyclic storm. A thunderstorm that undergoes cycles of intensification and weakening (pulses) while maintaining its individuality. Cyclic supercells are capable of producing multiple tornadoes (a tornado family).

cyclonic circulation. A.k.a. cyclonic rotation. Circulation or rotation in the same sense as the earth's rotation (counterclockwise in the Northern Hemisphere). Nearly all mesocyclones and strong or violent tornadoes exhibit cyclonic rotation.

debris cloud. A rotating "cloud" of dust or debris near or on the ground, often appearing beneath a condensation funnel and surrounding the base of a tornado. A debris cloud appearing beneath a thunderstorm confirms the presence of a tornado, even in the absence of a condensation funnel.

delta T. The difference in temperature between the top and bottom of an atmospheric layer. Higher values indicate greater instability and potential for severe-thunderstorm development.

dew point. A measure of atmospheric moisture. The temperature to which air must be cooled in order to reach saturation.

directional shear. The component of wind shear due to change in wind direction with height.

diurnal. Daily. Actions completed within the course of a single calendar day.

Doppler radar. Radar that can measure radial velocity (the instantaneous component of motion parallel to the beam, toward or away from the radar antenna).

downburst. A strong downdraft resulting in an outward burst of damaging winds on or near the ground. Can produce damage similar to a strong tornado. Usually associated with thunderstorms.

downdraft. A small-scale column of air that rapidly sinks toward the ground, usually accompanied by precipitation.

dryline. A boundary separating moist and dry air masses. An important factor in severe weather on the Great Plains. Typically lies north-south across the central and southern plains during spring and early summer, separating moist air from the Gulf of Mexico (to the east) and dry desert air from the southwestern states (to the west). Usually advances eastward in the afternoon and retreats westward at night. Crossing the dryline from east to west results in a strong drop in humidity, clearing skies, and a wind shift from south or southeasterly to west or southwesterly. Severe and tornadic storms often form at or just east of the dryline.

dust devil. A small, atmospheric vortex not associated with a thunderstorm.

eye wall. An organized band of clouds immediately surrounding the center (eye) of a hurricane. The strongest winds and most intense rainfall typically occur here.

feeder bands. Lines or bands of low-level clouds that move (feed) into the updraft region of a thunderstorm, usually from the east through the south. Also known as inflow bands.

FFD. See forward-flank downdraft.

forward-flank downdraft (FFD). The main region of downdraft in the forward (leading) part of a supercell. Most of the heavy precipitation is here.

front. A boundary or transition zone between two air masses of different density and temperature. A moving front is named according to the advancing air mass.

Fujita scale. A scale of wind-damage intensity in which wind speeds are inferred from analysis of wind damage.

funnel cloud. A condensation funnel extending from the base of a towering cumulus or Cb cloud. Associated with a rotating column of air that is *not* in contact with the ground, and hence is different from a tornado. A condensation funnel is a tornado and *not* a funnel cloud if either (a) it is in contact with the ground or (b) a debris cloud is visible beneath it.

gust front. The leading edge of gusty surface winds from thunderstorm downdrafts. Sometimes associated with a shelf cloud or roll cloud.

gustnado. Slang term for a gust-front tornado. A small tornado, usually weak and short-lived, along the gust front of a tornado.

high risk. Of severe thunderstorms. Severe weather is expected to affect more than 10 percent of the area.

hook echo. A radar reflectivity pattern characterized by a hook-shaped extension of a thunderstorm, usually in the right-rear portion of the storm (relative to its direction of motion). Often associated with a mesocyclone and indicates favorable conditions for tornado development.

HP supercell. High-precipitation storm. A supercell thunderstorm in which heavy precipitation (including hail) falls on the trailing side of the mesocyclone. Precipitation often completely envelops the area of rotation, making visual identification of any tornadoes difficult and dangerous.

humidity. A measure of the water-vapor content of the air.

inflow bands. See feeder bands.

inflow jets. Local jets of air near the ground flowing inward toward the base of a tornado.

instability. The tendency for air parcels to accelerate upward after being lifted. A prerequisite for severe weather.

inversion. A departure from the usual increase or decrease in an atmospheric property with altitude. Almost always refers to a temperature inversion (an increase in temperature with height, for example, in the lower portion of a cap).

isobar. A line connecting points of equal pressure.

isotherm. A line connecting points of equal temperature.

jet stream. Relatively strong winds concentrated in a narrow stream in the atmosphere, usually referring to horizontal, high-altitude winds. The position and orientation of a jet stream can vary from day to day.

laminar. Smooth flowing. Nonturbulent.

landspout. A tornado that does not arise from organized, storm-scale rotation and is not associated with a wall cloud visually or a mesocyclone on radar. Typically observed beneath Cb clouds or towering cumulus clouds.

lapse rate. The rate of change of an atmospheric variable—usually temperature—with height. Steep lapse rates indicate a rapid decrease in temperature with height and are a sign of instability.

left mover. A thunderstorm that moves to the left relative to the steering winds and to other nearby storms. Often the northern part of a splitting storm.

loaded gun. A situation in which extreme instability is contained by a cap. Explosive thunderstorm development could be expected if the cap weakens or if the air below is heated sufficiently to overcome it.

LP supercell. Low-precipitation supercell. A supercell thunderstorm characterized by a relative lack of visible precipitation. Capable of producing tornadoes and very large hail. Looks like a classic supercell but without the heavy precipitation core.

mammatus clouds. Rounded, smooth, sacklike protrusions hanging from the underside of a cloud.

MCS. See mesoscale convective system.

medium range. In forecasting, three to seven days in advance.

mesocyclone. A storm-scale region of rotation, typically two to six miles in diameter and often found in the rear flank of a supercell (or on the eastern, front, flank of an HP storm). The circulation of a mesocyclone covers an area much larger than the tornado that may develop within it.

mesoscale. Size scale referring to weather systems smaller than synoptic-scale systems but larger than storm-scale systems. Horizontal dimensions generally range from fifty miles to several hundred miles. A squall line is an example.

mesoscale convective system (MCS). A complex of thunderstorms that becomes organized on a scale larger than individual storms. Normally persists for several hours or more. May be round or linear and can include tropical cyclones, squall lines, and others.

microburst. A small, concentrated downburst affecting an area less than 2.5 miles across. Most are short-lived (five minutes).

moderate risk. Of severe thunderstorms. Expected to affect between 5 and 10 percent of an area. Indicates the possibility of a significant severe-weather episode.

moisture advection. The transport of moisture by horizontal winds.

moisture convergence. The degree to which moisture is converging in a given area, based on the effect of converging winds and moisture advection. Areas of persistent moisture convergence are often regions for thunderstorm development, if instability and other factors are favorable.

morning glory. An elongated cloud band, similar in appearance to a roll cloud, usually appearing in the morning when the atmosphere is stable. Similar to ripples on the surface of the water. Several parallel morning glories can often be seen propagating in the same direction.

multicell thunderstorm. A thunderstorm consisting of two or more cells. Most or all are often visible simultaneously, as evidenced by distinct domes or towers in various stages of development. Nearly all thunderstorms, including supercells, are multicellular, although the term is usually used to denote a storm that does not fit the definition of a supercell.

multivortex tornado. A tornado in which two or more condensation funnels or debris clouds are present at the same time, often rotating about a common center or each other. Can be especially damaging.

NEXRAD. See Next Generation Weather Radar.

Next Generation Weather Radar. High-resolution Doppler radar, with an increased emphasis on automation, including the use of algorithms.

NOAA. National Oceanic and Atmospheric Administration.

nocturnal. Related to nighttime. Occurring at night.

nowcast. A short-term weather forecast, generally out to six hours or fewer.

NSSFC. National Severe Storms Forecast Center. Now known as the SPC (Storm Prediction Center).

NSSL. National Severe Storms Laboratory.

NWS. National Weather Service.

occluded mesocyclone. A mesocyclone in which air from the rear-flank downdraft has completely enveloped circulation at low levels, cutting off the inflow of warm, unstable low-level air.

orographic. Related to or caused by physical geography (for example, mountains).

orographic lift. Lifting of air caused by its passing up and over mountains or other landscape features.

orphan anvil. An anvil from a dissipated thunderstorm, below which no other clouds remain.

outflow boundary. A storm-scale or mesoscale boundary separating thunderstorm-cooled air (the outflow) from surrounding air. Similar in effect to a cold front, marked by a wind shift and a drop in temperature. May persist for twenty-four hours or more after the thunderstorm that generated it dissipates. May travel hundreds of miles from its area of origin. New thunderstorms often develop along an outflow boundary, especially near its intersection with another boundary (cold front, dryline, etc.).

overshooting top. A.k.a. penetrating top. A domelike protrusion above a thunderstorm anvil, representing a strong updraft and a higher potential for severe weather with that storm. Often present on a supercell.

PDS watch. A tornado watch with enhanced wording to indicate a Particularly Dangerous Situation.

penetrating top. See overshooting top.

popcorn convection. Showers and thunderstorms that form on a scattered basis with little or no apparent organization, usually in the afternoon in response to diurnal heating. Small, short-lived, very rarely severe; almost always dissipate near or just after sunset.

positive CG. A CG flash that delivers a positive charge to the ground, as opposed to the more common negative charge. Positive CGs occur more frequently in severe thunderstorms, and their presence is detectable by lightning detection networks, although it is not possible to distinguish between positive and negative CG flashes visually.

pseudo cold front. A boundary between a supercell's inflow region and its rear-flank downdraft. Extends outward from the mesocyclone center, usually to the south or southwest. Characterized by the advancing of the downdraft air toward the inflow region. A particular form of gust front.

pseudo warm front. A boundary between a supercell's inflow region and its forward-flank downdraft. Extends outward from the mesocyclone center, usually to the east or southeast.

pulse storm. A thunderstorm within which a brief period (pulse) of strong updraft occurs, generating a short episode of severe weather (large hail, damaging winds) but rarely a tornado.

radial velocity. The component of motion toward or away from a given location (as "seen" by Doppler radar, it is the component of motion parallel to the radar beam). Strong winds blowing perpendicular to the radar beam (left or right or vice versa) cannot be detected.

rain-free base. A dark, horizontal cloud base with no visible precipitation beneath it. Typically marks the location of a thunderstorm's updraft. Tornadoes may develop from a wall cloud attached to the rain-free base or from the rain-free base itself. The rain-free base isn't necessarily rain free—it may contain hail or large raindrops.

rear-flank downdraft (RFD). A region of dry air subsiding on the back side of, and wrapping around, a mesocyclone. Often visible as a clear slot wrapping around the wall cloud. Scattered large precipitation (rain and hail) at the interface between the clear slot and the wall cloud may show up on radar as a hook echo—the presence of a hook echo is strongly indicative of an RFD.

red watch. A.k.a. red box. A tornado watch.

RFD. See rear-flank downdraft (RFD).

right mover. A thunderstorm that moves appreciably to the right relative to the main steering winds and to nearby thunderstorms. Typically associated with a high potential for severe weather. Supercells are often right movers.

roll cloud. A low, horizontal tube-shaped arcus cloud associated with a thunderstorm gust front. Relatively rare. Is completely detached from the thunderstorm base and other cloud features, distinguishing it from shelf clouds.

rope. A narrow, often-contorted condensation funnel usually associated with the decaying stage of a tornado.

rope stage. The dissipating stage of a tornado, characterized by the thinning and shrinking of the condensation funnel into a rope.

scud. Small, ragged, low cloud fragments that are unattached to a larger cloud base and often seen behind cold fronts and thunderstorm gust fronts. Generally associated with cool, moist air from the thunderstorm outflow.

severe thunderstorm. A thunderstorm that produces tornadoes, hail 0.75 inch or more in diameter, or winds of fifty knots (58 mph) or more.

shear. Variation in wind speed and/or direction over a short distance.

shelf cloud. A low, horizontal wedge-shaped arcus cloud, associated with a thunderstorm gust front. Is attached to the base of the parent cloud above it (usually a thunderstorm).

slight risk. Of severe thunderstorms. Severe thunderstorms are expected to affect between 2 and 5 percent of an area. Implies that severe weather events are expected to be isolated.

SPC. See Storm Prediction Center.

speed shear. The component of wind shear due to a change in wind speed with height (for example, south winds of 20 mph at ten thousand feet, increasing to 50 mph at twenty thousand feet).

splitting storm. A thunderstorm that splits into two storms that follow diverging paths (left and right movers). The left typically moves faster, the right slower, than the original storm. The right is most likely to reach supercell status. The left most often weakens and dissipates but in rare instances can become a very severe anticyclonic rotating storm.

squall line. A solid or nearly solid line or band of active thunderstorms.

staccato lightning. A CG lightning discharge that appears as a single, very bright, short-duration stroke, often with considerable branching.

steering winds. A prevailing synoptic scale flow that governs the movement of smaller features embedded within it.

Storm Prediction Center (SPC). A national forecast center in Norman, Oklahoma. Responsible for providing short-term forecast guidance for severe convection, excessive rainfall, and severe winter weather over the contiguous United States.

storm scale. Referring to weather systems with sizes on the order of individual storms.

straight-line winds. Generally, any wind not associated with rotation. As differentiated from tornadic winds.

stratiform. Having extensive horizontal development, as opposed to the more vertical development of convection. Stratiform clouds cover large areas. Their precipitation is relatively continuous and uniform in intensity (steady rain versus showers).

stratus. A low, generally gray cloud layer with a fairly uniform base.

striations. Grooves or channels in cloud formations, arranged parallel to the flow of air. Often reveal the presence of rotation, as in the barber pole *(which see)*.

suction vortex. A small but very intense vortex within a tornadic circulation.

supercell. A thunderstorm with a persistent rotating updraft. Supercells are rare but are responsible for a very high percentage of severe-weather events, including tornadoes, extremely large hail, and damaging straight-line winds. Frequently are right movers. Radar characteristics usually include a hook echo, bounded weak echo region, and mesocyclone. Visual characteristics usually include a rain-free base (with or without a wall cloud), tail cloud, overshooting top, and back-sheared anvil.

synoptic scale. Size scale referring to weather systems with horizontal dimensions of several hundred miles or more. Most high- and low-pressure areas seen on weather maps are synoptic-scale systems. Contrasted with mesoscale and storm scale.

tail cloud. A horizontal, tail-shaped cloud at low levels extending from the precipitation region of the supercell toward the wall cloud. Base of the tail cloud is about the same as that of the wall cloud. Cloud motion in the tail cloud is away from the precipitation and toward the wall cloud. Contrast with a beaver tail, an inflow band that is attached to the storm's updraft (not the wall cloud) and has a base about the same level as the updraft base (again, not the wall cloud).

tail-end Charlie. The thunderstorm at the southernmost end of a squall line or other line or band of thunderstorms. Since low-level southerly inflow of warm, moist air is relatively unimpeded into this storm, it has a higher probability of strengthening to severe levels than other storms in the line.

tilted storm. A.k.a. tilted updraft. A thunderstorm or cloud tower that is not purely vertical and instead shows a slanted or tilted character. A sign of vertical wind shear, a favorable condition for severe-thunderstorm development.

tornadic vortex signature (TVS). Doppler radar signature indicating intense, concentrated rotation (more so than in a mesocyclone). Strongly increases the probability of a tornado occurrence but does not guarantee it. Not visually observable.

tornado. A violently rotating column of air in contact with the ground and extending from the base of a thunderstorm. A condensation funnel does not need to reach the ground for a tornado to be present. A debris cloud beneath a thunderstorm is all that is needed to confirm the presence of a tornado, even in the total absence of a condensation funnel.

tornado family. A series of tornadoes produced by a single supercell, resulting in damage-path segments along the same general line.

tower. A cloud element showing appreciable upward vertical development. Short for towering cumulus.

triple point. The intersection point between two boundaries (for example, a dryline, outflow boundary, cold front). Often the focus for thunderstorm development. Can also refer to a point on the gust front of a supercell where the warm moist inflow, the forward-flank downdraft, and rear-flank downdraft all intersect. This location is favorable for tornado development.

troposphere. The layer of the atmosphere from the earth's surface up to the tropopause. Characterized by decreasing temperature with height (except in thin layers, such as an inversion or cap), vertical wind motion, appreciable vapor content, and "sensible weather" (rain, clouds, etc.).

TVS. See tornadic vortex signature.

updraft. A small-scale current of rising air. If the air is sufficiently moist, the moisture condenses to become a cumulus cloud, individual tower of a towering cumulus, or Cb.

updraft base. See rain-free base.

veering winds. Winds that shift in a clockwise direction over time at a given location (for example, from southerly to westerly). Or a similar change in direction with height (directional shear, which is important for tornado formation). Contrast with backing winds.

vertically stacked system. A low-pressure system that is not tilted with height. Such systems are typically weakening and slow moving and are less likely to produce severe weather.

virga. Streaks or wisps of precipitation falling from a cloud but evaporating before reaching the ground.

wall cloud. A localized, persistent, often abrupt lowering from a rain-free base. Can range from a fraction of a mile to nearly five miles in diameter. Normally found on the south or southwest (inflow) side of a thunderstorm. Can exhibit rapid upward motion and cyclonic rotation. Not all wall clouds rotate, but rotating wall clouds usually develop before strong or violent tornadoes. Not to be confused with the "eye wall," also sometimes erroneously called a wall cloud, on a tropical cyclone.

warm advection. Transport of warm air into an area by horizontal winds.

warning. A product issued by NWS local offices indicating that a particular weather hazard is either imminent or has been reported. Indicates a need to take action to protect life and property.

watch. An NWS product indicating that a particular hazard is possible, that conditions are favorable for its occurrence; a recommendation for planning, preparation, and increased awareness.

watch box. A severe-thunderstorm or tornado watch.

waterspout. A tornado occurring over water. Normally refers to a small, relatively weak, rotating column of air over water and beneath a Cb or towering cumulus cloud. Most common over tropical or subtropical waters.

wedge. A.k.a. wedge tornado. A large tornado with a condensation funnel that is at least as wide at the ground as it is tall from ground to cloud base. Many large tornadoes are called wedges, but true wedge tornadoes are very rare. Often appear with violent tornadoes (F4 or F5 on the Fujita scale).

wind shear. See shear.

wrapping gust front. A gust front that wraps around a mesocyclone, cutting off the inflow of warm moist air into the mesocyclone circulation and resulting in an occluded mesocyclone.

Bibliography

*H*unting *Nature's Fury* draws heavily upon the personal experience and videography of Roger Hill. However, the authors also consulted the following sources:

Advance Security Products. "Bullet Cameras." http://www.surveillance-spy-cameras.com/bullet-cameras.htm (March 17, 2008).

Alma is for You. "More About Alma." http://www.almaisforyou.com/more/default.asp (November 10, 2006).

Alma, Nebraska. "General Information." http://www.ci.alma.ne.us/general.htm (November 10, 2006).

April 3, 1974. "How the Storm of April 3, 1974 formed." http://www.april31974.com/The_storm.html (March 7, 2008).

Blake, Eric S., Edward N. Rappaport, and Christopher W. Landsea. "NOAA Technical Memorandum NWS TPC-5: The Deadliest, Costliest, and Most Intense United States Tropical Cyclones From 1851 to 2006 (And Other Frequently Requested Hurricane Facts." National Weather Service, National Hurricane Center, Miami, Florida. April 2007.

Branick, Michael. "NOAA Technical Memorandum NWS SR-145: A Comprehensive Glossary of Weather Terms for Storm Spotters." http://www.srh.noaa.gov/oun/severewx/glossary.php (November 21, 2007).

Chicago International Documentary Festival. "Olly Lambert. The Tea Boy of Gaza." http://www.chicagodocfestival.org/07_the%20tea%20boy%20of%20gaza.htm (March 17, 2008).

City Data. "Chester, Nebraska." http://www.city-data.com/city/Chester-Nebraska.html (November 10, 2006).

City of Slidell, Louisiana. "History." http://www.slidell.la.us/history.php (November 27, 2007).

Cloud 9 Tours. "About Us." http://www.cloud9tours.com/aboutus.html (November 19, 2007).

Cloud 9 Tours. "Charles Edwards." http://www.cloud9tours.com/charles.html (November 19, 2007).

Cloud 9 Tours. "Cloud 9 Tours." http://www.cloud9tours.com/ (November 19, 2007).

Denver Channel, The. "Tornado Rips Through Small Colorado Town, Killing Woman." http://www.thedenverchannel.com/print/11425548/detail.html (November 29, 2007).

Digital Typhoon. "Typhoon 200715 (KROSA)—Pressure and Track Charts." http://agora.ex.nii.ac.jp/digital-typhoon/summary/wnp/s/200715.html.en (March 17, 2008).

Earth & Sky. "Will global warming cause more tornadoes?" http://www.earthsky.org/blog/50991 (March 16, 2008).

ESPN. "Page 2's List: Greatest individual streaks." http://espn.go.com/page2/s/list/greatest/records/streaks/individual.html (March 17, 2008).

Felknor, Peter. *The Tri-State Tornado: The Story of America's Greatest Tornado Disaster.* iUniverse, 2004.

Grazulis, Thomas P. *The Tornado: Nature's Ultimate Windstorm.* Norman: University of Oklahoma Press, 2001.

High Plains Regional Climate Center, University of Nebraska–Lincoln. "Tornadoes in the Heartland—May 22, 2004." http://www.hprcc.unl.edu/nebraska/may22-2004tornado-report.html (November 10, 2006).

Joint Typhoon Warning Center. "Joint Typhoon Warning Center Mission Statement." http://metocph.nmci.navy.mil/jtwc/menu/JTWC_mission.html (March 17, 2008).

Knabb, Richard D., Jamie R. Rhome, and Daniel P. Brown. "Tropical Cyclone Report: Hurricane Katrina, 23–30 August 2005 (Updated 10 August 2006)." National Hurricane Center.

Leisure and Sport Review. "Beaver City, Nebraska." http://www.lasr.net/pages/city.php?City_ID=NE0408003 (November 10, 2006).

Levine, Mark. *F5: Devastation, Survival, and the Most Violent Tornado Outbreak of the 20th Century.* New York: Miramax, 2007.

Lightning Eliminators & Consultants, "Lightning 101." http://lecglobal.com/learn/lightning-101/ (March 20, 2008).

McCaul Jr., Eugene W., Dennis E. Buechler, Steven J. Goodman, and Stephen Hodanish. "The Almena, Kansas, Tornado Storm of 3 June 1999: A Long-Lived Supercell with Very Little Cloud-to-Ground Lightning." American Meteorological Society. February 2002, pages 407–415.

National Climatic Data Center. "Event Record Details—Hail, 22 Jun 2003, 06:05:00 PM CST, Aurora, Nebraska." http://www4.ncdc.noaa.gov/cgi-win/wwcgi.dll?wwevent~ShowEvent~505723 (November 25, 2007).

National Climatic Data Center. "Event Record Details—Hurricane/typhoon, 28 August 2005, 11:00:00 AM CST, Louisiana." http://www4.ncdc.noaa.gov/cgi-win/wwcgi.dll?wwevent~ShowEvent~577616 (November 27, 2007).

National Climatic Data Center. "Event Record Details—Tornado, 11 May 2000, 06:03:00 PM CST, Cedar Falls, Iowa." http://www4.ncdc.noaa.gov/cgi-win/wwcgi.dll?wwevent~ShowEvent~387388 (November 21, 2007).

National Climatic Data Center. "Event Record Details—Tornado, 11 May 2000, 06:55:00 PM CST, 3 Miles West of Dunkerton, Iowa." http://www4.ncdc.noaa.gov/cgi-win/wwcgi.dll?wwevent~ShowEvent~387394 (November 21, 2007).

National Climatic Data Center. "Event Record Details—Tornado, 11 May 2000, 07:20:00 PM CST, Dunkerton, Iowa." http://www4.ncdc.noaa.gov/cgi-win/wwcgi.dll?wwevent~ShowEvent~387403 (November 21, 2007).

National Climatic Data Center. "Event Record Details—Tornado, 23 June 2002, 06:34:00 PM CST, 9 Miles North East of Leola, South Dakota." http://www4.ncdc.noaa.gov/cgi-win/wwcgi.dll?wwevent~ShowEvent~475474 (November 23, 2007).

National Climatic Data Center. "Event Record Details—Tornado, 23 June 2002, 07:24:00 PM CST, 5 Miles South East of Barnard, South Dakota." http://www4.ncdc.noaa.gov/cgi-win/wwcgi.dll?wwevent~ShowEvent~475482 (November 23, 2007).

National Climatic Data Center. "Event Record Details—Tornado, 22 May 2004, 07:30:00 PM CST, 1 Mile South of Hallam, Nebraska." http://www4.ncdc.noaa.gov/cgi-win/wwcgi.dll?wwevent~ShowEvent~545045 (November 26, 2007).

National Climatic Data Center. "Event Record Details—Tornado, 12 May 2005, 05:13:00 PM CST, South Plains, Texas." http://www4.ncdc.noaa.gov/cgi-win/wwcgi.dll?wwevent~ShowEvent~596684 (November 26, 2007).

National Climatic Data Center. "Event Record Details—Tornado, 24 Aug 2006, 05:37:00 PM CST, 2 Miles South of Wessington, South Dakota." http://www4.ncdc.noaa.gov/cgi-win/wwcgi.dll?wwevent~ShowEvent~634461 (November 28, 2007).

National Climatic Data Center. "Event Record Details—Tornado, 28 Mar 2007, 06:54:00 PM MST, 2 Miles South of Holly, Colorado." http://www4.ncdc.noaa.gov/cgi-win/wwcgi.dll?wwevent~ShowEvent~646634 (November 29, 2007).

National Climatic Data Center. "Query Results—Tornadoes reported in the U.S. between 05/11/2000 and 05/11/2000." http://www4.ncdc.noaa.gov/cgi-win/wwcgi.dll?wwevent~storms (November 23, 2007).

National Climatic Data Center. "Query Results—Tornadoes reported in the U.S. between 05/12/2000 and 05/12/2000." http://www4.ncdc.noaa.gov/cgi-win/wwcgi.dll?wwevent~storms (November 23, 2007).

National Climatic Data Center. "Query Results—Tornadoes reported in the U.S. between 05/17/2000 and 05/17/2000." http://www4.ncdc.noaa.gov/cgi-win/wwcgi.dll?wwevent~storms (November 23, 2007).

National Climatic Data Center. "Query Results—Tornadoes reported in the U.S. between 06/23/2002 and 06/23/2002." http://www4.ncdc.noaa.gov/cgi-win/wwcgi.dll?wwevent~storms (November 23, 2007).

National Climatic Data Center. "Query Results—Tornadoes reported in the U.S. between 06/24/2003 and 06/24/2003." http://www4.ncdc.noaa.gov/cgi-win/wwcgi.dll?wwevent~storms (November 25, 2007).

National Climatic Data Center. "Query Results—Tornadoes reported in the U.S. between 05/22/2004 and 05/22/2004." http://www4.ncdc.noaa.gov/cgi-win/wwcgi.dll?wwevent~storms (November 26, 2007).

National Climatic Data Center. "Query Results—Tornadoes reported in the U.S. between 08/09/2004 and 08/09/2004." http://www4.ncdc.noaa.gov/cgi-win/wwcgi.dll?wwevent~storms (November 28, 2007).

National Climatic Data Center. "Query Results—Tornadoes reported in the U.S. between 05/12/2005 and 05/12/2005." http://www4.ncdc.noaa.gov/cgi-win/wwcgi.dll?wwevent~storms (November 26, 2007).

National Climatic Data Center. "Query Results—Tornadoes reported in the U.S. between 07/03/2005 and 07/03/2005." http://www4.ncdc.noaa.gov/cgi-win/wwcgi.dll?wwevent~storms (November 28, 2007).

National Climatic Data Center. "Query Results—Tornadoes reported in the U.S. between 08/20/2006 and 08/20/2006." http://www4.ncdc.noaa.gov/cgi-win/wwcgi.dll?wwevent~storms (November 28, 2007).

National Climatic Data Center. "Query Results—Tornadoes reported in the U.S. between 08/24/2006 and 08/24/2006." http://www4.ncdc.noaa.gov/cgi-win/wwcgi.dll?wwevent~storms (November 28, 2007).

National Climatic Data Center. "Query Results—Tornadoes reported in the U.S. between 03/28/2007 and 03/28/2007." http://www4.ncdc.noaa.gov/cgi-win/wwcgi.dll?wwevent~storms (November 29, 2007).

National Climatic Data Center. "U.S. Tornado Climatology." http://www.ncdc.noaa.gov/oa/climate/severeweather/tornadoes.html (March 7, 2008).

National Geographic. "Chasing Tornadoes." http://magma.nationalgeographic.com/ngm/0404/feature1/fulltext.html (November 25, 2007).

National Hurricane Center. "Hurricane Katrina Advisory Number 27." http://www.nhc.noaa.gov/archive/2005/pub/al122005.public.027.shtml? (November 27, 2007).

National Hurricane Center. "Hurricane Katrina Intermediate Advisory Number 26A." http://www.nhc.noaa.gov/archive/2005/pub/al122005.public.a.26.shtml? (November 27, 2007).

National Oceanic and Atmospheric Administration. "The 1966 Topeka Tornado—37th Anniversary." http://www.crh.noaa.gov/top/toptor/66toptor.html (May 16, 2005).

National Oceanic and Atmospheric Administration. "NOAA and the 1974 Tornado Outbreak—Description of Outbreak." http://www.publicaffairs.noaa.gov/storms/description.html (March 7, 2008).

National Oceanic and Atmospheric Administration. "Skywarn Hail Comparison Chart." http://www.srh.noaa.gov/tbw/html/tbw/skywarn/hail.htm (November 18, 2007).

National Oceanic and Atmospheric Administration. "The Topeka Tornado—June 8, 1966." http://www.crh.noaa.gov/top/events/66tornado.php (May 16, 2005).

National Oceanic and Atmospheric Administration. "Tornado Outbreak Across South Central Nebraska." http://www.crh.noaa.gov/gid/Web_Stories/2004/weather/05-22/05_22_04_Tornado.php (November 10, 2006).

National Weather Service Forecast Office—Aberdeen, SD. "The McPherson/Brown County Tornado—June 23rd, 2002." http://www.crh.noaa.gov/abr/?n=BrownMcPhersonTornado.php (November 23, 2007).

National Weather Service Forecast Office—Melbourne, FL. "Lightning Information Center—Interesting facts, myths, trivia and general information about lightning." http://www.srh.noaa.gov/mlb/ltgcenter/ltg_facts.html (March 20, 2008).

National Weather Service Forecast Office—Norman, OK. "NOAA Technical Memorandum NWS SR-145: A Comprehensive Glossary of Weather Terms for Storm Spotters." http://www.srh.noaa.gov/oun/severewx/glossary.php (November 21, 2007).

National Weather Service Forecast Office—Norman, OK. "Storm Summary for the Carrier Tornado of April 21, 1999." http://www.srh.noaa.gov/oun/storms/19990421/ (November 18, 2007).

National Weather Service Forecast Office—Paducah, KY. "NOAA/NWS 1925 Tri-State Tornado Web Site—Startling Statistics." http://www.crh.noaa.gov/pah/1925/ss_body.php (March 7, 2008).

National Weather Service Forecast Office—Paducah, KY. "NOAA/NWS 1925 Tri-State Tornado Web Site—Tornado Track." http://www.crh.noaa.gov/pah/1925/tt_body.php (March 7, 2008).

National Weather Service Forecast Office—Paducah, KY. "NOAA/NWS 1925 Tri-State Tornado Web Site—Weather Ingredients." http://www.crh.noaa.gov/pah/1925/wi_body.php (March 7, 2008).

Nebraska Fast Facts. "Community Profile—Beaver City." http://sites.nppd.com/aedc/fastfacts.asp?form=CP&city=Beaver+City&submit=Run+Report (November 10, 2006).

Nilknarf. "The Great Topeka Tornado of 1966." http://nilknarf.net/stuff/toptornado66.htm (May 16, 2005).

NowPublic. "Powerful Typhoon Krosa Makes Landfall on Taiwan—Twice." http://www.nowpublic.com/weather/powerful-typhoon-krosa-makes-landfall-taiwan-twice (March 17, 2008).

Pateman, Michael, and Drew Vankat. "The Effect of Climate Change on Tornado Frequency and Magnitude." http://jrscience.wcp.muohio.edu/studentresearch/climatechange02/tornado/website/tornado.html (March 16, 2008).

Reuters. "Typhoon hits China, then weakens to storm." http://www.reuters.com/articlePrint?articleId=USPEK205775._CH_.2400 (March 17, 2008).

Risk Management Solutions. "Analysis and Reconstruction of the 1974 Tornado Super Outbreak, RMS Special Report," April 2, 2004.

Schaefer, Joseph T. "The Relationship between El Nino, La Nina, and United States Tornado Activity." http://www.spc.noaa.gov/publications/schaefer/el_nino.htm (March 16, 2008).

Silver Lining Tours. "About—Alister Chapman." http://www.silverliningtours.com/Default.aspx?tabid=74 (November 21, 2007).

Silver Lining Tours. "About—Dr. David Gold." http://www.silverliningtours.com/Default.aspx?tabid=62 (November 19, 2007).

Silver Lining Tours. "About—Stuart Robinson." http://www.silverliningtours.com/AboutUs/StuartRobinson/tabid/205/Default.aspx (March 17, 2008).

Silver Lining Tours. "About Us." http://www.silverliningtours.com/Default.aspx?tabid=55/Default.aspx (November 19, 2007).

Skyways. "Marysville, KS." http://www.skyways.org/kansas/towns/Marysville/index.html (November 10, 2006).

South Dakota's Glacial Lakes & Prairies Tourism Region. "Explore Our Glacial Lakes & Prairies." http://www.sdglaciallakes.com (November 23, 2007).

Storm Prediction Center, NOAA. "The 25 Deadliest U.S. Tornadoes." http://spc.noaa.gov/faq/tornado/killers.html (November 29, 2007).

Storm Prediction Center, NOAA. "2000 Tornado Fatality Information." http://spc.noaa.gov/climo/torn/2000deadlytorn.html (November 21, 2007).

Storm Prediction Center, NOAA. "2002 Tornado Fatality Information." http://spc.noaa.gov/climo/torn/2002deadlytorn.html (November 23, 2007).

Storm Prediction Center, NOAA. "2003 Tornado Fatality Information." http://spc.noaa.gov/climo/torn/2003deadlytorn.html (November 25, 2007).

Storm Prediction Center, NOAA. "2004 Tornado Fatality Information." http://spc.noaa.gov/climo/torn/2004deadlytorn.html (November 26, 2007).

Storm Prediction Center, NOAA. "2005 Tornado Fatality Information." http://spc.noaa.gov/climo/torn/2005deadlytorn.html (November 26, 2007).

Storm Prediction Center, NOAA. "2006 Tornado Fatality Information." http://spc.noaa.gov/climo/torn/2006deadlytorn.html (November 28, 2007).

Storm Prediction Center, NOAA. "2007 Tornado Fatality Information."
http://spc.noaa.gov/climo/torn/2007deadlytorn.html (November 29, 2007).

Storm Prediction Center, NOAA. "20030624's Storm Reports."
http://spc.noaa.gov/climo/reports/030624_rpts.html (November 25, 2007).

Storm Prediction Center, NOAA. "20040809's Storm Reports."
http://spc.noaa.gov/climo/reports/040809_rpts.html (November 26, 2007).

Storm Prediction Center, NOAA. "20050512's Storm Reports."
http://spc.noaa.gov/climo/reports/050512_rpts.html (November 26, 2007).

Storm Prediction Center, NOAA. "20050606's Storm Reports."
http://spc.noaa.gov/climo/reports/050606_rpts.html (March 17, 2008).

Storm Prediction Center, NOAA. "20050607's Storm Reports."
http://spc.noaa.gov/climo/reports/050607_rpts.html (March 17, 2008).

Storm Prediction Center, NOAA. "20050608's Storm Reports."
http://spc.noaa.gov/climo/reports/050608_rpts.html (March 17, 2008).

Storm Prediction Center, NOAA. "20050609's Storm Reports."
http://spc.noaa.gov/climo/reports/050609_rpts.html (March 17, 2008).

Storm Prediction Center, NOAA. "20050703's Storm Reports."
http://spc.noaa.gov/climo/reports/050703_rpts.html (November 28, 2007).

Storm Prediction Center, NOAA. "20060820's Storm Reports."
http://spc.noaa.gov/climo/reports/060820_rpts.html (November 28, 2007).

Storm Prediction Center, NOAA. "20060824's Storm Reports."
http://spc.noaa.gov/climo/reports/060824_rpts.html (November 28, 2007).

Storm Prediction Center, NOAA. "20070328's Storm Reports."
http://spc.noaa.gov/climo/reports/070328_rpts.html (November 29, 2007).

Storm Prediction Center, NOAA. "March 28, 2007, 2000 UTC Day 1
Convective Outlook." http://spc.noaa.gov/products/outlook/archive/2007/
day1otlk_20070328_2000.html (November 29, 2007).

Storm Prediction Center, NOAA. "May 12, 2005 0100 UTC Day 1 Convective
Outlook." http://spc.noaa.gov/products/outlook/archive/2005/
day1otlk_20050512_0100.html (November 26, 2007).

Storm Prediction Center, NOAA. "May 12, 2005 1630 UTC Day 1 Convective
Outlook." http://spc.noaa.gov/products/outlook/archive/2005/
day1otlk_20050512_1630.html (November 26, 2007).

Storm Prediction Center, NOAA. "Monthly Tornado Statistics."
http://spc.noaa.gov/climo/torn/monthlytornstats.html (November 28, 2007).

Storm Prediction Center, NOAA. "The Online Tornado FAQ."
http://spc.noaa.gov/faq/tornado (November 29, 2007).

Storm Prediction Center, NOAA. "Severe Thunderstorm Watch 261."
http://spc.noaa.gov/products/watch/2005/ww0261.html (November 26, 2007).

Storm Prediction Center, NOAA. "Severe Thunderstorm Watch 263."
http://spc.noaa.gov/products/watch/2005/ww0263.html (November 26, 2007).

Storm Prediction Center, NOAA. "Severe Weather Report Archive—
06/09/1987." http://spc.noaa.gov/cgi-bin-spc/getsevereplotpl?Month=
06&Day=09&Year=1987 (November 5, 2007).

Storm Prediction Center, NOAA. "Severe Weather Report Archive—
05/25/1997." http://spc.noaa.gov/cgi-bin-spc/getsevereplot.pl?Month=
05&Day=25&Year=1997 (November 5, 2007).

Storm Prediction Center, NOAA. "Severe Weather Report Archive—
04/02/1999." http://spc.noaa.gov/cgi-bin-spc/getsevereplot.pl?Month=
04&Day=02&Year=1999 (November 5, 2007).

Storm Prediction Center, NOAA. "Severe Weather Report Archive—
06/03/1999." http://spc.noaa.gov/cgi-bin-spc/getsevereplot.pl?Month=
06&Day=03&Year=1999 (November 5, 2007).

Storm Prediction Center, NOAA. "SPC and its products." http://spc.noaa.gov/misc/
about.html (November 23, 2007).

Storm Prediction Center, NOAA. "SPC Annual Tornado Trends—Updated:
15-Mar-08." http://www.spc.noaa.gov/wcm/torgraph-big.png (March 16, 2008).

Storm Prediction Center, NOAA. "SPC Storm Reports for 000509."
http://spc.noaa.gov/climo/reports/000509_rpts.html (November 21, 2007).

Storm Prediction Center, NOAA. "SPC Storm Reports for 000510."
http://spc.noaa.gov/climo/reports/000510_rpts.html (November 21, 2007).

Storm Prediction Center, NOAA. "SPC Storm Reports for 000511."
http://spc.noaa.gov/climo/reports/000511_rpts.html (November 21, 2007).

Storm Prediction Center, NOAA. "SPC Storm Reports for 000512."
http://spc.noaa.gov/climo/reports/000512_rpts.html (November 21, 2007).

Storm Prediction Center, NOAA. "SPC Storm Reports for 000513."
http://spc.noaa.gov/climo/reports/000513_rpts.html (November 21, 2007).

Storm Prediction Center, NOAA. "SPC Storm Reports for 000514."
http://spc.noaa.gov/climo/reports/000514_rpts.html (November 21, 2007).

Storm Prediction Center, NOAA. "SPC Storm Reports for 000515."
http://spc.noaa.gov/climo/reports/000515_rpts.html (November 21, 2007).

Storm Prediction Center, NOAA. "SPC Storm Reports for 000516."
http://spc.noaa.gov/climo/reports/000516_rpts.html (November 21, 2007).

Storm Prediction Center, NOAA. "SPC Storm Reports for 000517."
http://spc.noaa.gov/climo/reports/000517_rpts.html (November 21, 2007).

Storm Prediction Center, NOAA. "SPC Storm Reports for 000518."
http://spc.noaa.gov/climo/reports/000518_rpts.html (November 21, 2007).

Storm Prediction Center, NOAA. "SPC Storm Reports for 20020622."
   http://spc.noaa.gov/climo/reports/020622_rpts.html (November 23, 2007).

Storm Prediction Center, NOAA. "SPC Storm Reports for 20020623."
   http://spc.noaa.gov/climo/reports/020623_rpts.html (November 23, 2007).

Storm Prediction Center, NOAA. "Tornado Watch 88."
   http://spc.noaa.gov/products/watch/ww0088.html (November 29, 2007).

Stormskies. "Saturday 22nd May 2004." http://www.stormskies.com/
   ChaseDiarySat22ndMay04.htm (November10, 2006).

Sumner County. "Sumner County Tornado History."
   http://www.co.sumner.ks.us/MV2Base.asp?VarCN=291 (November 18, 2007).

Tempest Tours. "Martin Lisius, President."
   http://www.tempesttours.com/martin_lisius.html (November 19, 2007).

Tempest Tours. "Our Team."
   http://www.tempesttours.com/tempest_tours_team.html (November 19, 2007).

Tiny Vital. "The Topeka Tornado of 1966."
   http://www.tinyvital.com/Weather/StormChase/topeka66.htm (May 16, 2005).

Topeka Capital-Journal. "29th and Gage Apartments Total Loss—June 1966."
   http://www.cjonline.com/indepth/66tornado/stories/com_aptsloss.shtml
   (May 16, 2005).

Topeka Capital-Journal. "City Officials Set Damage at $5 Million—June 1966."
   http://www.cjonline.com/indepth/66tornado/stories/com_damageestimate.
   shtml (May 16, 2005).

Topeka Capital-Journal. "The Day the Sky Fell."
   http://cjonline.com/stories/060103/our_tornado.shtml (May 16, 2005).

Topeka Capital-Journal. "Deaths Total At Least 13; Many Injured—6/9/66."
   http://www.cjonline.com/indepth/66tornado/stories/com_deathtoll.shtml
   (May 16, 2005).

Topeka Capital-Journal. "Destruction at WU in Millions—6/9/66."
   http://www.cjonline.com/indepth/66tornado/stories/com_wudestruction.
   shtml (May 16, 2005).

Topeka Capital-Journal. "Guardsmen, Police Patrol Downtown." http://www.
   cjonline.com/indepth/66tornado/stories/com_patrols.shtml (May16, 2005).

Topeka Capital-Journal. "Last Homes Standing." http://www.cjonline.com/
   stories/060703/loc_tornado.shtml (May 17, 2005).

Topeka Capital-Journal. "Legendary Mound is Vulnerable—June 1966."
   http://www.cjonline.com/indepth/66tornado/stories/com_burnettsmound.
   shtml (May 16, 2005).

Topeka Capital-Journal. "Survivors Bewildered—June 1966." http://www.cjonline.
   com/indepth/66tornado/stories/com_survivors.shtml (May 16, 2005).

Topeka Capital-Journal. "Twister Smashes East Topeka Area—June 1966." http://www.cjonline.com/indepth/66tornado/stories/com_easttopeka.shtml" (May 16, 2005).

Tornado Project. "The Fujita Scale of Tornado Intensity." http://www.tornadoproject.com/fscale/fscale.htm (November 21, 2007).

Tornado Project. "Top Ten Lists." http://www.tornadoproject.com/toptens/topten1. htm (May 16, 2005).

University Center for Atmospheric Research. "Hail Fact Sheet." http://www.ucar. edu/communications/factsheets/Hail.html (November 18, 2007).

Vortex Times. "Tornado Alley 2000." http://vortex-times.com/TornAlley2000 (November 21, 2007).

Vortex Times. "Tornado Alley 2003." http://vortex-times.com/TornAlley2003 (November 25, 2007).

Vortex Times. "Tornado Alley 2004." http://vortex-times.com /TornAlley2004 (November 26, 2007).

Vortex Times. "Tornado Alley 2005." http://vortex-times.com /TornAlley2005 (November 26, 2007).

Vortex Times. "Tornado Alley 2006." http://vortex-times.com /TornAlley2006 (November 28, 2007).

Vortex Times. "Tornado Alley 2007." http://vortex-times.com /TornAlley2007 (November 29, 2007).

Vortex Times. "Tornado Alley Index 1997-2006." http://vortex-times.com / TornAlleyIndex (November 23, 2007).

Wall Chamber of Commerce. "History of Wall/Badlands." http://www.wall-badlands.com/pages/history.html (March 17, 2008).

Wall Drug Store. "History of Wall Drug in Wall SD." http://www.walldrug.com/t-history.aspx (March 17, 2008).

Washburn University. "All was not lost after the tornado." http://www.washburn. edu/cas/art/cyoho/archive/essays/celebrate2.html (May 16, 2005).

Washburn University. "Our History." http://www.washburn.edu/crest/history.html (May 17, 2005).

Weather Channel, The. "Jim Cantore StormTracker." http://www.weather.com/ aboutus/television/ocms/cantore.html (November 18, 2007).

Wikipedia. "Betacam." http://en.wikipedia.org/wiki/Betacam (November 21, 2007).

Wikipedia. "Lightning—Properties of Lightning." http://en.wikipedia.org/wiki/ Lightning (March 20, 2008).

Wikipedia. "Timothy P. Marshall." http://en.wikipedia.org/wiki/Timothy_P._ Marshall (November 27, 2007).

Roger Hill has witnessed over 430 tornadoes as of the writing of *Hunting Nature's Fury*. He has also witnessed and documented nearly a dozen hurricanes and typhoons. He has chased storms from southern Texas to the Canadian Prairie provinces and has even flown to Taiwan in pursuit of a super typhoon. Hill has

been the subject of television programs such as National Geographic's *Twister Tours* and *Tornado Chasers*, The Weather Channel's *Storm Stories* and *Full Force Nature*, various Discovery Channel programs, NOVA's *Hunt for the Supertwister*, The Travel Channel's *Tornado Alley*, and many more. He has also captured video for every major television network in the country, and his photographs have appeared in various publications worldwide. Hill is co-owner of Silver Lining Tours, America's leading storm-chasing tour company. He lives in the high plains near Bennett, Colorado, where severe storms and tornadoes frequently occur, with his wife Caryn, her son Colton, and his favorite dog Radar.

Peter Bronski is an award-winning author whose interest in severe weather dates back to a childhood encounter with Hurricane Gloria in New York. In addition to co-authoring *Hunting Nature's Fury*, he is the author of *Powder Ghost Towns: Epic Backcountry Runs in Colorado's Lost Ski Resorts* (Wilderness Press) and *At the Mercy of the Mountains: True Stories of Survival and Tragedy in New York's Adirondacks* (The Lyons Press). His writing has appeared in more than 50 magazines, including *Men's Journal, 5280, Denver Magazine, Rock and Ice, Vermont*

Sports, and *Caribbean Travel & Life*. He is a recipient of a First Prize from the North American Travel Journalists Association's annual Awards Competition, and a Silver Award from the Solas Awards for Best Travel Writing. Bronski lives in Boulder, Colorado with his wife, Kelli, their daughter, Marin, and their dog, Altai. He can be reached at www.peterbronski.com.